The Right To National Self-Determination

The Faroe Islands and Greenland

NIJHOFF LAW SPECIALS

Volume 60

The titles published in this series are listed at the end of this volume.

The Right To National Self-Determination

The Faroe Islands and Greenland

Edited by Sjúrður Skaale

MARTINUS NIJHOFF PUBLISHERS

LEIDEN • BOSTON

A C.I.P. Catalogue record for this book is available from the Library of Congress.

Printed on acid-free paper.

ISBN 90 04 14207 x
© Copyright 2004 by Koninklijke Brill NV, Leiden, The Netherlands.
Koninklijke Brill NV incorporates the imprints Brill Academic Publishers, Martinus Nijhoff
Publishers and VSP.

http://www.brill.nl

Printed and bound in The Netherlands.

Table of Contents

Preface

Sjúrður Skaale[1]

Denmark – or "Denmark Proper" – is in itself a small state. It has a population of around 5.4 million people, and the total land and sea area of the country of Denmark is 149,000 square kilometres. Add to that, however, the northern dependencies which, together with Denmark Proper, form "All the Parts of the Danish Realm," and an altogether larger picture emerges.

The Faroes, or the Faroe Islands, encompass only 1,400 square kilometers of land that are populated by 48,000 people. But the total land and sea area of The Faroes is 268,900 square kilometres, almost twice the size of Denmark. In Greenland there are 57,000 people, but geographically Greenland dwarfs Denmark with its whopping 4,430,000 square kilometres of land and sea, thirty times the size of continental Denmark.[2]

Consequently, both Greenland and The Faroes contribute to making the State of Denmark a very large state in geographical terms. Through their size and strategic location, Greenland and The Faroes, both during the Second World War and throughout the Cold War, have lent enormous geopolitical importance to Denmark. By virtue of the combined size of those two territories, Denmark was able, first, to be counted as an Allied State, and then, to make significant contributions to the North Atlantic Treaty Organisation.

The State of Denmark, or the Realm of Denmark as the constitutional text refers to it, is thus a state where 97 per cent of the geographical mass lies outside the political centre. These waste areas make Denmark Proper appear as an enclave far away from its main geographical centre.

The Danish Constitution has an odd relationship with this reality. Originally written at a time when Denmark was a constitutional conglomerate with even more associated countries, the text can, and will by Danish nationalists, be interpreted as a constitution of a centralised and homogenous state without significant subdivisions.

---

1   Sjúrður Skaale, who works for the North Atlantic Group in the Danish Parliament, has been the Secretary of the Working Group that has written this report. He has a Master's Degree in Political Science from the University of Copenhagen, is a former editor and journalist, and former Advisor to the Faroese Government.

2   Numbers provided by the Danish land register institute, *Kort og Matrikelstyrelsen*.

Sjúrður Skaale (ed.), The Right To National Self-Determination, *vii-x.*
© *2004 Koninklijke Brill NV. Printed in the Netherlands.*

In reality, Denmark has features of a federal state because of the fact that the Home Rule Parliaments and Governments of Greenland and The Faroes in reality control most internal legislation and, furthermore, in some areas – e.g. fishery – in reality control their own international relations.

However, Denmark also has features of a colonial state because of the fact that neither Greenland nor The Faroes have joined the Realm by their own choice. These two countries and these two peoples have not been allowed to accept or reject the Danish Constitution as their own constitution through referenda.

Thus, this constitutional association consists of a small, but densely populated continental European country, and two sparsely inhabited territories, one a North Atlantic island group, and the other a vast North American territory. However, the arrangement begs a number of questions.

What is the status of The Faroes and Greenland, and the Faroese People and Greenland People, respectively? Are they Danish minorities? Are they indigenous peoples? Are they Peoples or Nations in their own rights? Do they enjoy any status under international law? Do The Faroes and Greenland have the right to national self-determination? And if so, what does this right include?

These are among the questions that have been discussed in Denmark, Greenland and The Faroes for a long while. They are of more than merely academic interest. The status and rights of The Faroes and Greenland under international law were discussed after the end of the Second World War when a Faroese referendum, showing a narrow majority in favor of independence, was overruled in 1946. They were discussed when the Home Rule Compact was implemented in The Faroes in 1948. They were also discussed when the Danish Constitution was officially promulgated in Greenland in 1953, and during the Danish-Greenland negotiations about Home Rule in the seventies. When during the eighties and early nineties there were negotiations about the rights to the Faroese underground, the Faroese argumentation was, largely, based on international law. When, in 2000, there were negotiations between Denmark and The Faroes about the establishment of a Faroese state, international law was, again, what the Faroese tried to base their claims upon.

The truth is, though, that neither the Greenland nor the Faroese authorities have always stood on solid ground when they have referred to international law in their negotiations with the Danish authorities. The Danish authorities have often rejected Faroese and Greenland international law based claims out of hand.

For this reason the North Atlantic Group in the Danish Parliament – established by the two Greenland and one of the two Faroese members of the Danish Parliament – in 2002 set up a Working Group in order to answer some of the above-mentioned questions and their further implications. Having pondered the different aspects of the issues, the Working Group decided to further investigate the following questions:

—   What is the constitutional history of The Faroes and Greenland?
—   Which are the consequences for Greenland of having the status of an "indigenous people"?

- What has Denmark stated and how has Denmark voted in other cases regarding self-determination – and what is the legal consequence of this?
- What is the legal significance to The Faroes and Greenland of the judgement of the Canadian Supreme Court on Quebec's claimed right to secede from Canada?
- How do the central organs of the UN look upon the issue of self-determination and other issues that are addressed in this report?
- How does the international profile and position of Greenland and The Faroes compare to that of other non-sovereign entities?
- How has Denmark reported to the UN about the status of Greenland and The Faroes?
- How do current developments in the EU influence the constitutional position of Greenland and The Faroes?

Each chapter of the report answers one of these questions.

In order to be able to give a reliable description of the constitutional history of the two countries, the Working Group undertook a comprehensive investigation into the Danish National Archive, where hundreds of hitherto unknown documents concerning the decisive historical moments were found. Some of these documents are used in this report. In the report named "*Kilder til Færøernes og Grønlands historie*" ("Sources of the History of The Faroes and Greenland") a summary of all the documents can be found in Danish.

The task of answering how the central organs of the UN look upon the issues addressed in this report made necessary a visit to the UN in New York. This visit took place in October 2003, when five members of the Working Group had eight meetings with relevant officials.

Now that the work is done, it is the hope of the North Atlantic Group in the Danish Parliament that the report will give decision-makers, scholars, journalists and the public a better understanding of the many and often complicated factors that are decisive for the status and rights of The Faroes and Greenland. As the situation of The Faroes and Greenland is in many aspects very similar to that of other stateless nations, it is our hope that the report will be of use elsewhere as well.

On behalf of the North Atlantic Group, I wish to offer my best thanks to the following members of the Working Group for their willingness to devote such a lot of time to, and put such a huge amount of effort into this work:

Gudmundur Alfredsson, Iceland, Doctor of Juridical Science, and Director/Professor at the Raoul Wallenberg Institute of Human Rights and Humanitarian Law in Lund;

Ole Espersen, Denmark, Professor of Law at the University of Copenhagen, former Danish Minister of Justice and former Commissioner on Democratic Institutions and Human Rights of the Council of the Baltic Sea States;

Lauri Hannikainen, Finland, Doctor of Juridical Science, Professor of International Law at the University of Turku;

Bogi Eliasen, The Faroes, Master of Political Science from the University of Aarhus, Denmark;

Mininnguaq Kleist, Greenland, Master of Political Philosophy from the University of Aarhus, Denmark;

Kári á Rógvi, The Faroes, Master of Law, Deputy Chairman of the Faroese Constitutional Committee, Editor of The Faroese Law Review;

Bjørn Kunoy, The Faroes, Master of International Law from the X-Nanterre University in Paris, France;

Hallbera Westh, The Faroes, Senior Student of Political Science from the University of Copenhagen, Denmark;

Maria Amalia Heinesen, The Faroes, Senior Student of History at the University of Aalborg, Denmark.

The above-mentioned people have written the chapters of the report in their own name, but the content has been discussed by the whole group. Only Mr. Bjørn Kunoy did not participate in any of the eleven meetings that were held.

1 – Summary and Main Conclusions

Ole Espersen

Introduction

As the preface makes clear, this volume is the work of a group of people who have written individual chapters for which the named authors are responsible. On the other hand, extensive discussions took place among the authors and our common goal is, of course, reflected in each chapter. This common goal is to be a source of information to the reader on the history, the constitutional developments, the general context within international law with regard to the notions of "people" and "self-determination", the relationships or possible relationships between the Faroe Islands and Greenland to international organizations and the (former) position within the United Nations system towards these two political entities.

The following summary and main conclusions represent in brief the outcome of some of the various chapters as well as the outcome of the discussions within the group. But I wish to stress that each chapter deserves to be read in full. This is especially true because summarizing is difficult, particularly as the authors have different backgrounds (lawyers, political scientists etc.). This fact we found to be quite natural, as hardly any international subject represents such a mixture of law and politics as does the subject of "peoples" and the subject of peoples and their right to self-determination.

Summary of Some Chapters of the Work

The Land of Maybe: A Survey of Faroese Constitutional History, by Kári á Rógvi

Kári á Rógvi has given his article the title, *The Land of Maybe,* because, in his view, this reflects the fact that the Faroese People are known to have had difficulties in agreeing on their own position with regard to independence. The Faroes is a "Land of Maybe", it is suggested, because the whim of the weather gives the Faroese People a pretext to be indecisive and frequently use "maybe", as you never know what the weather will be like tomorrow. And, according to the author, this way of thinking is also reflected in the discussions on independence or non-independence.

The author recommends that those who want to take a position on the constitutional or international position of The Faroes should pay great attention to the existence of three different paths, all three of which should be followed if you wish to understand the Faroese People: "First, the Faroese People have their own national tradition closely bound to the ancient land, the Faroe Islands. Second, the Faroese are also somehow to be found in the context of another people and its governing structure. Third, the Faroese People and The Faroes as a polity are part of the wider world with its common customs and relations."

The author then continues to briefly describe Faroese constitutional history from the very early days (year 800 or so): the dependency of The Faroes on Norway and Denmark, and its relationship to Danish legal history up till 1848, when the Danish King was forced to initiate a publicly approved constitution. And in this respect the author – having the Faroese people in mind – asks the very pertinent question: "For whom was this Constitution to be written?" He underlines the importance of the fact that the Danish authorities during the years preceding the Danish Constitution of 1849 decided not to convene the Law Thing (the Faroese Parliament), but instead of this, established an administrative governor to govern The Faroes as if it were a Danish province.

For whom then was the Constitution of 1848 written? The author concludes that the situation was fairly unclear. The Faroese did not, contrary to the Icelanders, show any great strength or political will at all to influence their situation. The official line was that the Faroese were an integral part of the Realm. The important historical events during the 1860s and the Danish internal fight on the King's power and the principal of parliamentarianism meant that not much interest was shown in the Faroese situation. Maybe not even from the Faroese themselves. The conclusion of the author is that the question of the Faroe Islands was "dormant until greater forces came around": the German invasion of Denmark in 1940.

"Fortunate Occupation"

While Denmark was occupied by Germany the British occupied The Faroes to prevent it from being taken by the Germans.

This division between the two parts of the Kingdom gave rise to strong national sentiments and strong demands that the Faroese should assume power and become independent. However, a compromise was reached as the Faroese Parliament and the British accepted an interim constitution.

The Faroese politicians did not manage to use the situation in any positive manner. The self-rule party split before the war and the unionists did not manage to gain enough strength to secure an orderly political discussion. After the war, the Danish Government proposed an offer according to which the interim constitution was recognized for the period of the war, but also proposed a future plan which accorded only limited powers to the Law Thing. The proposal was rejected by the Faroese, and then Denmark proposed and the Faroese agreed to hold a referendum on the continued Faroese association to Denmark.

The Faroese people were to choose between a Home Rule Act and full independence. A narrow majority of the votes favored independence, but the unionists interpreted the result as unclear due to the campaign before the referendum.

The Danish authorities ended up overruling the result, and arranged for an election to the Law Thing. These elections were won by the unionist forces after a campaign that has been strongly criticized by large parts of the Faroese people.

"Rule at Home"

After this, negotiations about a home rule system were taken up. They resulted in the 1948 Home Rule Act. It recognized Faroese national symbols, such as language and flag, and gave the Faroese authorities wide-ranging internal political competences.

The author of the chapter strongly criticizes the procedure before the adoption of the system and the various interpretations of the existing Danish Constitution and its background.

The conclusion of the author is that the constitutional system of The Faroes depends upon three different autonomous sets of law: firstly, the law of The Faroes themselves; secondly, the law of the country, Denmark, that claims jurisdiction over the islands; and, certainly, the law of those polities that recognize each other as sovereign.

"How to Get Out?"

The author finally discusses the possible procedural ways of obtaining self-determination or secession between Denmark and The Faroes. He first refers to the official position of the Danish Government and the Danish Parliament that if "there comes a wish from the Faroese side for sovereignty, they can have it".

The author notes that the Danish Constitution is not clear as to the way in which such a change in the relationship should take place.

In order to answer the question, "Who decides when and if and how it can be done?", he looks at the relationship between the Danish Government, the Danish Parliament and the Supreme Court of Denmark. He concludes that what the Government wishes and decides will usually be supported by a majority in Parliament, and the Supreme Court will not question such a decision. The author does not want to accept a common opinion according to which secession can take place according to Article 19 of the Danish Constitution. His conclusion is that: "Secession from the union with Denmark cannot be completed at will with reference to the Basic Law of the Danish Realm, *except by some action not provided for in the Instrument itself*".

A Phrase Loaded with Dynamite: Impressions from Walking the Corridors of the UN, by Sjúrður Skaale

The main purpose of this chapter is to inform the reader about the impressions which the Working Group obtained during a visit to the United Nations Headquarters in New York in October 2003, where the situation of The Faroes and Greenland was discussed with several leading UN officials.

However, this summary is preceded by some general comments on the very notion of self-determination. This section describes the first notions of this important concept as they were developed after the First World War. It describes the opinion of statesmen who saw great possibilities in establishing new states, but it also refers to serious concerns about the risk.

The United Nations self-determination system is described as a success so far. The question of who is the "self" and who has a right to "determination" is raised. One of the prerequisites is that the territory was put on the United Nations list of non-self-governing territories in 1946 or subsequently. The Faroes were never put on this list and "through clever Danish manoeuvring" Greenland was taken off the list in 1953. According to the author, it seems today to be generally accepted that a people has a right to establish its own state only in the following cases: if it is colonized and is on the United Nations list of non-self-governing territories; if it is under foreign military occupation; or if it is oppressed and its human rights are violated. The two Danish territories do not seem to fulfil these conditions.

After a legal and political consideration of the results of the meetings in New York, the conclusion of the author is that the UN, as an organization that is established and made up of states, is in itself unable to take any initiatives with regard to the sovereignty of areas such as Greenland and The Faroes as long as this subject is not put on the agenda by Denmark. Other Member States could also raise questions concerning The Faroes and Greenland, but this is not to be expected as Denmark is a very highly esteemed member of the United Nations and such questions would be considered to be a provocative interference in internal Danish affairs.

This negative result must, however, be accompanied by some factual/political considerations which, according to the author, would make the sovereignty of these territories a more "easy" and reasonable solution than is the case in many other non-sovereign countries:

— The national borders would be clear.
— There would be no big national minority in any of the territories – although a considerably bigger one in Greenland then in The Faroes.
— There is a stable political environment.
— Both countries seem to be at least as well or even better suited for statehood than many newly emancipating states.

It must be pointed out, though, that the situation in Greenland is more difficult in some respects than the situation in The Faroes.

Finally, the author discusses, *inter alia* by bringing Lichtenstein and Iceland into the picture, how The Faroes and Greenland would manage if they became members of the United Nations and how they would benefit from it.

The Quebec-Canada Case Compared to The Faroes and Greenland, by Lauri Hannikainen

This author analyzes the famous advisory opinion of the Canadian Supreme Court on Quebec's claimed right to secede from the Canadian Confederation of August 20, 1998. One of the questions examined was whether international law gives Quebec the right to effect the secession of Quebec from Canada unilaterally. The Court examined the "external side of the right to self-determination".

In its answers the Court stated that contemporary international law does not grant component parts of sovereign states the legal right to secede unilaterally from their "parent states". After discussing the situation of territories under the colonial domination of a state, the Court concluded that territories and their peoples within the sovereignty of democratic states do not have any right of external self-determination and secession in international law.

The Court also examined the question whether, in the event of a conflict between domestic and international law regarding the unilateral secession of Quebec from Canada, domestic or international law would take precedence in Canada. But in the Court's opinion there is no such conflict possible, because there is no unilateral right of secession.

It is interesting, however, that in the opinion of the Court the Constitution of Canada should not be seen as a straitjacket. According to the Court, the democratic institutions should accommodate a continuous process of discussion taking into account the constitutional right of each participant in the federation to initiate constitutional changes.

It is interesting that in the view of the Court a "clear majority vote ... on a clear question in favour of secession" ... would give legitimacy to such an initiative.

The condition of a "clear majority" should, I suppose, be seen in relation to the fact that the relations between Quebec and Canada are in many respects fundamentally different from the relations between The Faroes, Greenland and Denmark – not least due to the fact that The Faroes and Greenland are far away from Denmark, while Quebec geographically is an integral part of the territory of Canada.

The author stresses that the many statements by democratically responsible Danish politicians regarding what would happen if a majority (with no reference to a clear majority) of the Faroese or the Greenlandic people were to vote in favor of secession do not represent commitments under international law. They may, though, be seen as moral commitments, which might have an effect on deciding whether "the Faroese and Greenlandic people were ... offered fair conditions in a referendum to choose their status".

The Status of the Greenlandic Inuit: Are the Greenlandic Inuit a People, an Indigenous People, a Minority, or a Nation? A Practical, Philosophical and Conceptual Investigation, by Mininnguaq Kleist

These are the questions Mininnguaq Kleist wants to answer in what he calls "a practical, philosophical and conceptual investigation" of the matter.

In his introduction the author discusses the definitions of the various notions. Regarding the notion "indigenous people" he refers to the opinion that the colonial roots of that concept cannot be denied. He makes references to and uses ILO Convention No. 169 in his treatment of the subject. In this respect he refers to the definition in Article 1 of this Convention. The author notes how difficult it is to arrive at definitions. Throughout his chapter, he tends in general to subscribe to the opinion of Erica-Irene Daes who prefers to distinguish a number of factors which should be mentioned when an attempt is made develop an understanding of the concept of indigenous peoples:

    a.   priority in time, with respect to the occupation and use of a specific territory;

    b.   the voluntary perpetuation of cultural distinctiveness, which may include the aspects of language, social organization, religion and spiritual values, modes of production, laws and institutions;

    c.   self-identification, as well as recognition by other groups as a distinct collectivity; and an experience of subjugation, marginalization, dispossession, exclusion, or discrimination, whether or not these conditions persist.

With regard to the definitions of the terms "minorities" and "nation" one may agree with the author that these two notions are of no special relevance to the question of the possible independence of Greenland.

More interesting is of course the discussion of the term "peoples". According to the opinion of the author, the fact that a group of human beings is to be considered a "people" does not lead to any right of self-determination or secession. As he writes: "The metropolitan states exclusively decide whether or not the mentioned peoples should possess their own sovereign states. There is no existing international organ which can order (with any authority or muscle, so to speak) a metropolitan state to give or grant another people its own sovereign state."

After this examination of the problems of definitions, the author relates the result to the situation of Greenland. He makes reference to the fact that the Greenlandic Inuits are recognized as an indigenous people by themselves, by Denmark and by the international community. He is of the opinion, however, that to be recognized and base claims upon being an indigenous people may also cause difficulties. He has in mind the fact that ILO Convention No. 169 gives protection to indigenous peoples, but at the same time stresses that this in itself does not give them any rights as "peoples". He underlines this viewpoint in his conclusion where he states that the highlighting of the indigenous status should be done carefully in order not to impede a course towards full independence.

The author then goes on to mention the various reasons given for not granting the Greenlandic Inuit the status of full subjects under international law. He mentions border issues, the question of descendants of the original inhabitants and the culture. His conclusion is that such problems should not in any way restrict the right or the access to independence of Greenland.

In his conclusion, the author discusses a possible strategy for obtaining full independence. He mentions that "peoplesness" should be emphasized, possibly at the expense of being an indigenous people. He rightly underlines the possibility of achieving more and more competence in the international field instead of immediately trying to obtain full sovereignty. He also highlights the unsatisfying situation based upon the fact that the Danish Constitution does not necessarily prevent the unilateral repealing by Denmark of the Home Rule Act. This is of course seen as a situation which might at any time – if it were used – take away even the existing self-determination. This is mentioned as one example of the fact that Danes and Greenlanders are not on a legally and politically equal footing. He and his fellow countrymen want to keep a good relationship with Denmark. But they feel that they are left with the following alternatives:

> "You do not want to slam the door behind you, but the problem is, if you read between the lines of statements coming from Danish officials, that *if you want to secede, you will be slamming the door behind you. If you do not want to slam the door behind you when seceding, Denmark will do it for you.* You do not want this to happen. You can try to prevent this from happening if you work for a greater degree of autonomy within the Kingdom, or even secession, if you walk this path in a common agreement with Denmark."

The Faroes as a Non-Self-Governing Territory, by Bjørn Kunoy

The author examines the notions "self-determination" and "non-self-governing territory" in relation to the Faroe Islands. His thesis is that the UN Declaration on the Granting of Independence to Colonial Countries and Peoples (Resolution 1514 (XV)) inherently contains a right to self-determination of colonized people as a general principle of law. The condition is, however, that the territories have been listed by the UN under the obligations of Article 73 in the UN Charter.

The Danish Government did not – in contrast to Greenland – list The Faroes as such a territory under Chapter XI of the Charter.

The preliminary conclusion is that The Faroes do not constitute a subject in international law, because "*this territory is not subscribed under the obligations of Article 73 (e) of the UN Charter and the Faroese people are not in a situation of colonialism or subjection of peoples to alien subjugation, domination and exploitation*".

The author examines the legal character of Resolution 1541 and reaches the conclusion that, seen in relation with Resolution 1542, Resolution 1541 has been legally quali-

fied as international customary law. With regard especially to The Faroes he refers to the
principle according to which there *"prima facie is an obligation to transmit information in respect
of a territory which is geographically separate and is distinct ethnically / and or culturally from the
country administering"*. His final conclusion, therefore, is that Denmark "historically, morally
and in accordance with international law (is) bound to register the Faroe Islands as a non-
self-governing territory".

The failure to do so, according to this contribution, in no way denies The Faroes the
right as an international legal subject to demand total independence.

Non-Sovereign Polities and Their Access to the International Community, by Bogi Eliasen

The author analyzes what he would define as customary international law with regard to
the position of various non-sovereign polities all over the world. He investigates the practice of states and international organizations, statements by states and governments. His
main purpose is to define the present international profile of The Faroes and Greenland.

His investigation deals with many entities around the world. His research is *inter alia*
based upon questions to and answers from a big number of non-sovereign polities and metropolitan states.

His results are that certain countries are very liberal with regard to permitting non-
sovereign entities to be full or semi-full members of international organizations – of course
depending upon the will of the organization and its legal structure. Amongst the liberal
countries are, for instance, New Zealand, as exemplified by its relationship to the Cook
Islands.

Denmark is seen by the author as a rather conservative country in this respect.
According to the author, it would have been possible for Denmark to have The Faroes and
Greenland admitted to the Nordic Council as full members. His reasoning may possibly be
shortened as follows: if it is acceptable for The Faroes and Greenland not to be members
of the EU – and thereby not respecting the unity of the Danish Kingdom – why should it
be more difficult to see the territories as members of the Nordic Council, perhaps with a
change in the Nordic Council basic agreement (the Helsinki Treaty)?

The conclusions of the author are – briefly – as follows. The relationship between
non-sovereign polities and international organizations differ greatly, depending on the will
of the metropolitan states as well as on the possibilities of the organization in question. He
finds that there is a clear tendency in many states to give international room to the non-
sovereign polities, but with a less positive attitude in Denmark. Most of the international
organizations are open for non-sovereign polities within their specific areas, but of course
depending on the concrete legal situations. He finds that non-sovereign entities have, in
reality, in several respects, an effective status as subjects in international law, if the factual
interaction between these entities and international organizations is analyzed.

Main Conclusions and Viewpoints

History makes clear that the relationship between The Faroes and Greenland on the one hand and Denmark on the other has been characterized by strong feelings based upon solidarity and loyalty on the one side and a wish to obtain increased and perhaps total independence on the other side. Such mixed feelings are also found in today's Faroes and Greenland. However, positive and less positive feelings have always been accompanied by a realistic position and the desire to avoid open breaches – also in cases where the two peoples have justifiably felt disappointed or deceived by Danish positions.

In the preface of this book many important questions are posed – not all easy to answer, but all involving serious issues and sometimes strong feelings. However, the main issue is not so complicated to answer when the question is: do The Faroes and Greenland have the right to independence and full sovereignty if their peoples express a popular will to obtain this status?

The Working Group has dealt extensively with the past. Two chapters in this volume describe the constitutional history of The Faroes and Greenland, and in parallel with this volume, another report in Danish, *"Kilder til Færøernes og Grønlands historie"* ("Sources to the History of the Faroes and Greenland"), is being published.

The historical information provided certainly shows the attitudes of the Danish state, which are not always flattering or understandable. The methods which have sometimes been employed have given good reasons for feelings of manipulation and accordingly a critical attitude on behalf of The Faroes and Greenland.

With regard to The Faroes one example is the cancellation of the results of the referendum on independence in 1946. Another is the Danish plan of giving Faroese politicians the clear understanding that loyalty to the Danish state would bring with it money from Denmark, and thus twisting the Faroese debate away from the issue of national sovereignty, because The Faroes would be economically dependent upon Denmark. A third example is the deliberate political use of the Danish monarchy that has included frequent royal visits and decorations of leaders in Faroese society with the clear political purpose of creating loyalty towards Denmark.[1]

Although the Danish authorities have had a clear – and sometimes hidden – agenda, and although there has been a lack of respect for the Faroese people, the measures that have been used towards The Faroes have, at least for the most part, been within the framework of what might be called acceptable political manoeuvring.

When it comes to Greenland there is no doubt, however, that the Danish state has gone too far. When Greenland in 1952/53 was taken off the UN's list of non-self-governing territories and made an integrated part of Denmark, this was not done in a way that was acceptable according to democratic or legal principles. The UN was systematically misinformed and deceived, and the will of the Greenlandic people was clearly seen as a secondary factor in the process (see Chapter 3 of this volume, "Greenland under Chapter XI

---

1   See above, Sources to the History of the Faroes and Greenland.

of the United Nations Charter: A Continuing International Law Dispute", by Gudmundur Alfredsson). The circumstances surrounding the establishment of an American military base in Thule in Greenland, and the secret Danish permission to allow the US to keep nuclear weapons in Greenland are other examples of clear neglect of the rights of the Greenland people.

The establishment of the two home rule arrangements is commonly seen as a result of Danish respect towards the two peoples. To a certain degree – and not least compared to the way some other states have treated their overseas territories – this is indeed the case. But the arrangements can also been seen as steps that Denmark has thought it necessary to take in order to keep and reserve the sovereignty of the two areas for the Danish Realm. The historical material provided leaves no doubt that keeping the sovereignty of Greenland and The Faroes has been very important to Denmark. In order to do so, Danish authorities have sometimes set aside respect for the two peoples.

But this is not only a question of the past. Also in the present-day relationship the Faroese and the Greenland peoples sometimes feel the lack of political and human equality. Let me give an example – perhaps a trivial one, but illustrative nevertheless: during the review of the report of Denmark drawn up in accordance with the UN Convention on the Rights of the Child (May 2001), the Committee asked the 12-member delegation of Denmark, referring to the high rate of infant and maternal mortality in Greenland and the Faroe Islands, why representatives of Greenland and the Faroe Islands were not included in the delegation. According to the press release the answer of the Danish delegation was that "Greenland and the Faroe Islands were advised to come with information concerning the situation of children's rights in their territories, but no information was made available. Those territories were self-governing and it was up to the local authorities to supply the necessary information."

It follows from this answer that Denmark seems not to consider The Faroes and Greenland as important internationally although Danish international obligations of course extend also to those territories. One consequence of this is that wrong information supplied to the UN is not being corrected: it is, for instance, not true that the rate of infant and maternal mortality is high in the two countries: in The Faroes it is in fact extremely low.

During the same meeting in the Committee the Danish delegation denied the right of the Faroese and Greenland people living in geographical or "southern" Denmark to be seen as national minorities although this seems to be a violation of the European Convention on National Minorities. In other words: also in this millennium the peoples of The Faroes and Greenland have good reason to find that they are in a dependent and sometimes awkward situation, which might well be remedied by admitting stronger representation in international organs without necessarily changing international law or the Home Rule laws.

•   •   •

The contents of this book shows that independence is, in a way, both facilitated and made difficult by international law at the same time.

It is made difficult because the various notions – peoples, minorities, indigenous peoples, etc. – are unclear in the context and probably change from time to time. And so are the rights attached to these notions.

It is facilitated, however, because, as is affluently demonstrated in this book, The Faroes and Greenland must necessarily be seen as fulfilling all conditions to be considered:

— They meet all the criteria for being peoples in their own right.
— Their territory is clearly distinct from the territory of the motherland, by distance and, even, by an ocean. In themselves the territories are clearly distinguished because they are islands.
— They are polities with their own political and economic systems.
— Greenland was in the past a formal colony and the situation of The Faroes in many ways resembled that of a colony.
— They have never, by means of a referendum, accepted the Danish Constitution as their constitution.

So even if the peoples of The Faroes and Greenland are neither under foreign occupation, nor oppressed, nor on the UN's list of non-self-governing territories, and thus are not in the category of peoples with a clear right to self-determination, they do certainly have strong arguments for claiming the right. Various international resolutions and declarations, that have also been supported by Denmark, support this view.

On the other hand, even if this right clearly exists it is not, according to present-day international law, an enforceable right: the peoples of the two territories cannot apply to any international organ which can make decisions binding upon Denmark.

On the other hand, various Danish governments have repeatedly stated that The Faroes and Greenland will become independent as soon as they so decide by referenda.

This, however, is not the same as having or obtaining a right according to international law. If the "right" was only dependent on the attitude of the mother country, of course this mother country would be able also to list conditions according to which the right may be exercised.

It is therefore extremely important for the Working Group to underline that the "right" should not only be seen as a right based upon Danish law or Danish official attitude. It is a genuine international right, although there is no possibility of having it internationally enforced – which is the case with regard to many international law obligations.

This leads the Group to the conclusion that in order to be in accordance with general international practice as evolved after the Second World War with the creation of the United Nations, taking into account the independence obtained by most colonial areas, the right should be seen – not only as a right to immediate secession – but also as a right to a reasonable process to make this secession viable. What this means can only be assessed from case to case and time to time. A right, which does not involve the right to a reasonable process or procedure that leads to viable independence is in fact no right. The nation which deliberately created the dependence, economically or otherwise, should also be seen as responsible for a realistic road to viable independence.

It is important to underline that during the period of such a process many important steps could be taken, also without bearing any economic costs, to prepare for independence. I have in mind that a higher degree of acting on the international scene by the territories is possible and could be useful. Experiences from other states and their territories show that this could be materialized within many organizations – of course again with the cooperation of the Danish Parliament and Danish Government.

It seems that the Danish Government is cautiously opening up to such a stronger participation. The Working Group recommends that this process is accelerated in close cooperation between The Faroes, Greenland and Denmark as one of the roads preparing for a future viable independence – if this is the wish of the Greenland and/or Faroese people.

The argument against such a development has sometimes been that it would threaten the unitary state and thus be difficult to harmonize with the Danish Constitution. This argument is, however, hardly convincing, taking into account that Denmark (with the exception of The Faroes and Greenland) is becoming more and more involved in decision-making within the European Union. And this will even be accelerated if and when the Danish reservations regarding legal affairs and defence policy are lifted in the future. The Danish Government and the Danish Parliament have not seen this as at threat to the unitary state. Although it seems in a way more threatening than participation by The Faroes and Greenland in various typically non-decision-making organizations or allotment of independence internationally within certain specified areas.

2 – The Land of Maybe

A Survey of Faroese Constitutional History

Kári á Rógvi[1]

"Any understanding of the Faroese question must begin with a recognition from the Danish, without any reservations, that the Faroese are a People and that the Faroe People is a Nation with all the characteristics that are needed to be a Nation."

Robert Stærmose, Danish Politician

Maybe a Land

This survey takes its title from a British soldier's description of Faroe[2] – "*Føroyar*" in the Faroese language. To this outsider, everything that happened amongst the Faroese seemed to depend on the whim of the ever-changing weather. This had influenced the collective psyche of the entire nation, giving them the pretext to always hedge their plans with a "maybe – if the weather permits." In some way that pretty much sums it all up: in political and constitutional terms, too, the Faroe Islands seem to depend on shifting outside forces as well as an indecisive national character – a Land of Maybe.

---

1   LL.M, Deputy Chair of the Faroese Constitutional Committee. I would like to thank the North Atlantic Group in the Danish Parliament for the opportunity to write this piece and the other contributing authors for their suggestions and good company. I extend my gratitude especially to Ms. Hallbera West and Ms. Maria Heinesen for the extended research they did for this book project; their materials will prove invaluable for others who to ponder the Faroese question. Furthermore, I thank Mr. Bárður Larsen, Secretary to the Faroese Constitutional Committee and a very gifted jurist, for suggestions and comments. Much of what I say here is based on my earlier articles such as 12 Lov & Ret [2002, June] 22 "*Færøernes Retspleje frem fra glemslen*," 3 FLR (2003) "Except for some Action not proved for in the Instrument itself," and papers for the Faroese Constitutional Convention 2003 "Our Land Faroe," and "What is in a Document?"
2   Sydney Norgate: "*Kanska*" or The Land of Maybe (1943).

Sjúrður Skaale (ed.), The Right To National Self-Determination, 13-48.
© *2004 Koninklijke Brill NV. Printed in the Netherlands.*

In short, due to various historical, political and legal quirks, the Faroe Islands and the Faroese People are in a unique constitutional position. A distinct polity with no land-border disputes, a clearly defined legal jurisdiction with a very long history, a highly homogenous population with a rich cultural tradition, a developed economy, and almost all necessary government institutions of their own. This blissful land is politically associated to a much larger state, Denmark, which is at the same time also the principal in an association with Greenland, another polity with a relatively small population.

And yet, the collective soul of the Faroese has not been at ease for the last century or so, as the exact nature and possible future of The Faroes as a polity and the Faroese as a people has been in dispute or, at least, inadequately explained.

This position as a constitutional associate in a federation of sorts may seem marvellous to some (for instance, national minorities persecuted for insurrection), and inadequate to others (perhaps, those peoples that have travelled the high road to national sovereignty). For the Faroese themselves the inability to agree on their future direction, let alone their current position, causes feelings of both kinds, a national identity torn between feeling shamefully shackled and enviably enabled.

Focusing on certain selected periods in time, this survey will undertake to analyse the Faroese constitutional history and status from various angles, stating – if not the answers – at least the relevant questions that need to be addressed if one is to explain the Faroese constitutional position relative to other lands and realms.

A Fork in the Road

Going down the road to explain the Faroese constitutional question, you are bound to see the road split into three different paths. First, the Faroese people has its own national tradition closely bound to their ancient land, The Faroes. Second, the Faroese people finds itself entangled in the context of another people and its governing structure. Third, the Faroese people and The Faroes as a polity are part of the wider world with its customs and rules.

The constitutional situation of the Faroe Islands, therefore, depends on three different spheres of law at the same time. First – and foremost – the constitutional law of the Faroe Islands themselves. (Contrary to popular belief, and even at times scholarly writings, international law does not enable or establish polities and peoples. Rather, international law "happens" when nations and other entities, established on their own terms, interact in response to a perceived state of coexistence and need for co-operation). Secondly, there is the constitutional law of the Realm of Denmark that claims jurisdiction over the Faroe Islands. Finally, there is international law, the law created by those polities that recognise each other as sovereign. The other authors of this report will pursue the international law aspects, I will, therefore, concentrate most on National Faroese Law and Danish Federal Law.

Reaching a truly good understanding of the issues pertaining to the Faroese status in legal terms involves, of course, travelling all of these three paths. The problem with many attempts to analyse the Faroese situation is that the analyst in question only takes into account one of these sets of circumstances and fails to see, or on purpose neglects, that they all have their distinct impact and influence. I shall return to this point later. Suffice it to say, for now, that you are well advised to take all the three legs of the road in turn.

A Few Opening Remarks on How to Get Out[3]

Let us start with present day Danish constitutional law. As a diplomat once said to me in informal conversation, the questions on many outsiders' minds are: "What do you want, and what does Denmark have to say about that?"

The question is a variant of an age-old uncertainty. The Americans, for instance, declared themselves independent, but had to settle scores with Britain on the battlefield. Years later, the Americans themselves were faced with disintegration. President Abraham Lincoln declared on that same question in his first inaugural address: "I hold that in contemplation of universal law and of the Constitution, the Union of these States is perpetual. Perpetuity is implied… the Union will endure forever, it being impossible to destroy it except by some action not provided for in the instrument itself."

The words of Lincoln probably both reflect the instinctive view of a politician in charge of a given complex constitutional structure and the balance between laws and politics. Perpetuity is usually implied (legally) and any constitutional union will endure indefinitely unless broken (politically) by some force outside the scope of the agreed constitutional document.

To answer at least the second part of the question stated above, let us hear out the contemporary politicians. First, a question from the Faroese Nationalist side submitted by Mr. Tórbjørn Jacobsen, Member of the Danish Folk Thing[4] for the Faroese Republican Party:[5]

"Will the Prime Minister recognise the following indisputable facts:
a)   that the Faroese People in accordance with international law is a nation,
b)   that the Faroese people is a subject of international law, and
c)   that the Faroese people has the right to external self-determination in accordance with international law?"

Having refused this assurance, the Prime Minister, in his oral answer, summed up the Danish position, indicating that the Danish Folk Thing (Parliament) is likely to give its blessing, albeit not upfront and not with reference to international law:

---

3   These remarks are based extensively on the aforementioned article in 3 FLR (2003), "Except for some Action not proved for in the Instrument itself."

4   In this text, I use the words Folk Thing and Law Thing as directly translated terms for the Danish Parliament (*Folketinget*) and the Faroese Parliament (*Løgtingið*), respectively. Note, however, that the Danish Parliament before 1953 was bicameral with the Folk Thing being the larger lower house, the other house being the Land Thing, the upper house; collectively they were called *Rigsdagen* or "the Realm Day".

5   Question no. S 1737 – answered 17 April 2002 – Danish Parliament Session 2001 / 2002.

"To Mr. Tórbjørn Jacobsen I will say this in all tranquillity that Mr. Tórbjørn Jacobsen may freely suggest that the Faroe Islands and the Faroese Law Thing, the Faroese People, are above the Danish Basic Law, but it is and will remain a theoretical discussion, because it is of no practical importance for it has been indicated by a massive majority in the Danish Folk Thing and by successive Danish Executives that if there comes a wish from the Faroese side for sovereignty, they can have it."

The Danish position seems to be that the Danish Government accepts the political eventuality of the Faroe Islands leaving the Realm. It will not, however, state this as a legal right, nor indicate the legal source that such secession rights may be based upon, and, furthermore, the Danish Government reserves its formal response until the day that a formal request is put forth.

Further to this point, a proposal for a formal parliamentary resolution motioned by the Honourable Mr. Tórbjørn Jacobsen calling upon The Danish Executive to "...notify the United Nations that the Faroe Islands have unlimited right of self-determination in accordance with international law " was not adopted.[6]

The Faroese Law Thing (Parliament), for its part, has set up a timetable for achieving sovereignty – though, as always, with considerable dissent – based on language referring to legal rights:

"Recognising that the Faroese People is a Nation with inalienable and continuous right of self-determination, the Law Thing approves that a determined effort of achieving Sovereignty is undertaken. The Law Thing therefore approves that the Faroese Executive implements the following:
  – That the Faroese Government at the latest on January First 2012 assumes the full powers over all Policy Matters in accordance with the legal status of the Faroese people, except for those Matters that are directly connected to assuming sovereignty and, furthermore, that the Faroese Government in accordance herewith pays in full for these policy matters.
  – That [certain policy matters such as the State Church and family law] will be transferred to Faroese control on January 2002 at the latest.
  – That [certain policy matters such as the judicial system] will be transferred to Faroese control on January 2004 at the latest.
  – That [certain policy matters such as the police and currency] will be transferred to Faroese control on January 2006 at the latest.
  – That [certain policy matters such as emergency services] will be transferred to Faroese control on January 2008 at the latest.

---

6   Danish Parliament, Beslutningsforslag B. 107 Session 2001/2002.

– [To develop the Faroese Economy from subsidy based to self-sustained, and to reduce the block grant by 300-400 million DKK by January 1 2002 and then further until it is eventually abolished].
– [To establish a Faroese Economic Fund].
– That before the Faroe Islands are established as a Sovereign State, it shall be conditioned on the Faroese People deciding so in a referendum held in the Faroe Islands."

Faroese Law Thing Resolution (Bill no. 114/2000)

The Faroese Parliament passed the resolution with 18 votes in favour, 12 against, and 1 abstention (with one of the 32 members – an assumed nay-vote – absent). Furthermore, the timeframe for transferring policy matters has not been observed so far, but, and perhaps more important for the independence prospects, the reduction of the block grant has, indeed, happened.

The 2004 Faroese election gave the parties behind the resolution an increased share of the vote. However, a new parliamentary coalition was formed, less keen on the speed of transfer of policy matters, but apparently inclined to reaffirm the right of self-determination in a new Faroese Constitution.

Earlier, the Danish Folk Thing, responding to Faroese sovereignty overtures, articulated its position thus:

"The Folk Thing recognizes that it is the Faroese population that decides the future relationship between Denmark and the Faroe Islands.
The Folk Thing accepts the Prime Minister's account of the Danish Executive's position in the negotiations that have been initiated with the Faroese Executive.
The Folk Thing will elect a committee of 21 members to follow the negotiations and discuss questions regarding a regeneration of the relationship between Denmark and the Faroe Islands."

Danish Folk Thing Debate Resolution V 68 / 1999[7]

Although, as indicated by the Danish Prime Minister, the political event of a break-up is lurching into the Danish collective political psyche, the emphasis in the formal position is always on the "*future relationship* between Denmark and the Faroe Islands", however unorthodox this less than blissful cohabitation may prove to be.

More acutely, the question that always pops up in the mind of the Faroese is: Can The Faroes unilaterally withdraw from the present arrangement with Denmark and become a sovereign and independent state in its own right? Or does a successful transition from association to independence rely on Danish acceptance? If so, can the Danish Realm give its assurance that it will accept a Faroese wish to secede, or is it bound by certain consti-

---

7   Danish Parliament, Folketingsvedtagelse V 68 ved Forespørgselsdebat F 47, 6 April 2000, Session 1999/2000.

tutional procedures? Or is it perhaps impossible to get untangled from the Danish Realm because of some constitutional bar to secession? In other words: Who decides when, if, and how the Faroese can secede?

To some foreigners it might seem confusing that the Faroese become so agitated over this question, since the position of the Danish Executive and Parliament alike seems to be that the Faroese are free to go, even though the Danes evidently would prefer the Faroese to stay and will offer rewards aplenty to the remaining extremities.

In the Faroese debate, however, people attach enormous importance to the formal positions. Many people will view any sign of preconditions, mandatory procedures, or constitutional quirks as proof of "*ófrælsi*" (literally "un-freedom") and have taken these as a reason for leaving the Realm as an act of legal self-defence, thus protecting the right to self-determination.[8]

Indeed, in political rhetoric (external) self-determination seems expressed as synonymous to secession. The better view, in my opinion, is to regard self-determination as the right to choose between association and independence, and the numerous ways that both options can be realised, as well as – and this is very fundamental in our day and age – *the right to change one's mind* and opt again.

Now, this might seem controversial. Often, the analogy used is that of overseas colonies choosing either integration or independence at the time when they "wake up" politically. However, the better analogy, at least in the Faroese case, is that of the European tradition whereby the various polities have been able to associate with, disassociate from and re-associate themselves to one another. As will be touched upon later, Denmark has itself been an active part of this tradition.

For many, the question is, whether the Faroese right to choose depends on legally proving a status as "non-self-governing". It is my submission that The Faroes have had and have claimed a right to remain self-governing even in association and, in addition, claimed a right to renegotiate the terms of association without implicitly agreeing to a perpetual state of complete integration, thereby retaining the right to use the self-determination to secede when convenient.

The Basic Law of the Danish Realm is perhaps one of the most irrelevant constitutional documents in the western world. There are almost no cases of the courts annulling parliamentary acts or secondary legislation based on the Basic Law. Lawyers referring to constitutional provisions as a pleading of last resort are common laughingstock. Its real function is to be a national symbol of the rise of democracy. The Basic Law is featured in parliamentary debates, and certainly the text itself and its interpretation has significant

---

8   The Danes for their part could have been more flexible in recognising the Faroese potential. The former Prime Minister Poul Nyrup Rasmussen refused to accept international observers or mediators as part of the negotiations regarding a proposed treaty recognising The Faroes Islands as a sovereign state in free association with Denmark, this in possible violation of international law, see G. Alfredsson: 1 FLR (2001) 45.

political importance, but ultimately the parliamentary majority of the day decides its mean-ing – not the Supreme Court, as might in other jurisdictions be the case.

In 1999, to the great relief of those who have clung on to the legal relevance of the Basic Law, the Danish Supreme Court finally (almost) invalidated an Act of the Folk Thing.[9] However, there is no vengeance and furious anger in the opinion of the Court. It merely states "§ 7 of [the Act] is invalid in relation to the appellant the Free School of Veddinge Bakker." The Act was a blatant example of a Bill of Attainder (singular legislation) refusing grants to certain named private schools as a reprisal for alleged past misconduct. The Court struck one of its provisions down with reference to § 3 of the Basic Law that provides for the Separation of Powers. Note, however, that the Court did not annul the Act itself and made no general pronouncement, it only found one particular provision invalid in relation to one individual party in that specific case.

When it comes to matters of sovereignty and the like, the Supreme Court is even more expressly non-political and timid. On the question of EU membership being compat-ible with the Danish Constitution, the courts for a number of years held that Danish citi-zens did not even have legal standing to challenge its constitutionality.[10] When the question was finally admitted, the Court held, *inter alia*, that: "It must be seen as vested in the Folk Thing to decide if the Executive's participation in the EU-co-operation shall be subject to further democratic control."[11]

The power to guard democracy and presumably other fundamental principles of the Danish Constitution, therefore, is vested in the elected parliament. Furthermore, the apparent doctrine is that only unfairly picking on individuals – as opposed to determining the faith of a large plurality – will lead the Danish Supreme Court to strike down statues. This understanding leaves rather certain the assumption that of the Danish political bodies, it is the Folk Thing that ultimately decides the If and How of a secession in accordance with the Danish Basic Law or the wider Danish Constitution. The Parliament will do so upon the recommendation of the Executive, with which it is to a large extent intermingled, given the parliamentary system that has evolved. Most members of the Executive, the cabinet members, are also at the same time members of the Folk Thing. Their political parties will either hold the majority of the seats in the Parliament or, at least, govern with the consent of a majority in the Folk Thing. As the debate resolution above shows, there is a very strong tradition of striving for a national consensus in the Folk Thing on important issues. Even the opposition parties not supporting the administration of the day will often vote in favour of, and have influence on, so-called "*forlig*" – political concords.

This theory, that the Danish Supreme Court will allow gradual constitutional change, even contrary to the language of the Basic Law, seems to hold up in the only reported

---

9   See Den Selvejende Institution Friskolen i Veddinge Bakker *v.* Undervisningsministeriet, Ugeskrift for Retsvæsen U. 1999.841H.

10   See Helge Tegen *v.* Statsministeren, Ugeskrift for Retsvæsen U. 1973.694.Ø overruled in Hanne Norup Carlsen *et al* v. Statsminister Poul Nyrup Rasmussen U. 1996.1300H.

11   Hanne Norup Carlsen *et al v.* Statsminister Poul Nyrup Rasmussen U. 1998.800H.

case dealing with the separation of powers between the Danish Realm and the Faroese Government. The case dealt with taxation in the Faroe Islands, where a Danish physician did not get the same tax deductions as the native Faroese. Although the Basic Law § 43 expressly vests the Power of Taxation in the Folk Thing only, the Appeal Court implicitly accepted the taxation powers of the Law Thing. However, the Appeal Court ruled that § 10 (2) of the Home Rule Compact forbids discriminating between Faroese natives and other citizens of the Realm and ordered the tax authorities to resume the case on that basis.[12]

The Danish constitutional provisions pertaining to The Faroes and Greenland are obscure to say the least:

"§ 1. This Basic Law applies to all Parts of the Danish Realm"

It is, alas, difficult to discern just what this mentioning of the "parts" means. The provision seems to infer that the "Realm" (besides being Danish) includes more than the land of Denmark. The word used is *"rige"* in Danish (*"ríki"* in Faroese, *"rice"* in Old English, *"Reich"* in German). Historically, the King of Denmark has always been head of a number of entities outside of Denmark (see below) and the change in the wording to "all parts" was to signify incorporation of Greenland into the Danish Realm's constitutional sphere, whereas it previously had lingered outside the Basic Law in colonial limbo.

The provision signifies that there is a division between Denmark Proper and the Realm. Presumably, Denmark Proper is the core Part with Greenland and Faroe being the outer Parts. Unlike, for example, the Kingdom of the Netherlands or the British Monarch, the Danish Realm and the Danish Monarch have no Institutions of the Realm and no Privy Council encompassing representatives from the Parts per se. Unfortunately, the Danish Basic Law neither explains the difference between the parts, nor does it create any political bodies exclusively representing the parts or the whole. It says nothing, furthermore, on the possible dissolving of the Realm.

Other provisions contain short references to The Faroes and Greenland:

"§ 28. The Folk Thing is a unicameral house consisting of 179 members at the most, of which 2 members are elected on the Faroe Islands and 2 in Greenland."

"§ 32. (5) There can be enacted in statute special rules regarding the Faroese and Greenland parliamentary mandates and their commencement and termination."

"§ 42. (8) Particular rules on referendum, including to what extent a referendum shall be held in the Faroe Islands and Greenland, can be enacted by statute."

---

12   See Føroya Landsstýri *v.* Karsten Werner Larsen, Ugeskrift for Retsvæsen U.1983.986Ø. See also a recent case accepting a Greenland statute as "legislation" rather than "administrative regulation", *Perorsaasut Ilinniarsimasut Peqatigiiffiat som mandatar for A v. Paamiut Kommuniat,* U.2002.2591.Ø.

"§ 86. [Special rules can be enacted in statute on voters' age for municipalities and church councils in the Faroe Islands and Greenland]."

These provisions, mostly on elections and such trivia, cannot be said to reflect in any meaningful way on the relationship between the Parts and the Realm. But these provisions would surely stick out like sore thumbs if the relationship were terminated, especially if it happened without mutual agreement. Most acutely, a legitimate question is whether the provision on Faroese representation either precludes Faroese secession, or perhaps, allows die-hard unionists to continue returning MP's to the Danish Folk Thing, even after the Realm is actually dissolved. The same goes for the question of continuously claiming Danish citizenship. Of course, the Danish position after an agreed break-up or unilateral Faroese declaration of independence will be crucial in this respect – will the Folk Thing treat the provisions as obsolete or lapsed, or as a basis for clinging to its North Atlantic outpost?

Assuming implied perpetuity, one way of breaking up would be to amend the Danish Basic Law to allow secession. § 88 on the amendment procedure provides for a very cumbersome, but not impossible, way of amending the Basic Law: two consecutive Folk Things and a referendum carried by a majority consisting of a minimum of 40 per cent of all voters. The time involved, the unpredictability of the Danish voters, and traditional reluctance to amend the Basic Law all indicate that amendments are unlikely to pass in a time of "revolution". When the Faroese are ready to bolt the door, they are probably not going to await amendments of obscure Basic Law provisions.

Slightly more apt when painted into a constitutional corner is § 19. It is the provision that has been given most practical consideration. It appears to be the underlying belief of the Danish Government and the Faroese as well that this is the correct procedure to be used for dissolving the Realm:

"§ 19 (1) The King acts on behalf of the Realm in international matters. Without the approval of the Folk Thing, He cannot, however, undertake any action that increases or decreases the area of the Realm, or undertake any obligation when its fulfilment requires action by the Folk Thing, or otherwise is of greater importance. Neither can the King without approval by the Folk Thing cancel any international treaty, which has been ratified, without the consent of the Folk Thing.

(2)   [Armed conflicts]

(3) [The Foreign Affairs Committee]"

The Faroese Executive proposed in its White Paper on Faroese Sovereignty a Treaty of Free Association with Denmark. The two Parties would sign a Treaty between the Faroe Islands and Denmark that both Parliaments would ratify in Denmark by following the procedure in § 19.[13]

---

13   *Hvítabók* ("the White Book", Faroese Executive White Paper on Faroese Sovereignty and a Treaty of Free Association with Denmark) ISBN 99918-53-31-6.

With all due respect, this is utter crap. The Basic Law § 19 is not a procedure for dismembering the Realm. § 19 is a very traditional enabling provision giving the Executive (the King) the power to act in international relations. However, the Executive is not to act without parliamentary consent in certain situations (when treaties, internal legislation or borders are concerned), nor in any other matter of greater importance.

The Basic Law is quite clear when it comes to the separation of power between the Danish legislature and Executive. It may even suggest that the political bodies have the substantive power to amend borders or cede land to bordering states. The Basic Law is, however, completely silent on the prospect of a break-up of the Realm into its constituent parts. The "land-area" clause seems more minted on border changes than the complete withdrawal of associated lands. Neither the land-area clause nor § 19 as a whole give the political bodies substantive powers to authorise a break-up of the Realm. If such powers exist, they depend upon a proper construction of the Basic Law and the Constitution of the Realm in a wider sense.

The recently enacted Constitution of Finland states that: "The territory of Finland is indivisible. The national borders can not be altered without the consent of the Realm Day." The Finnish Constitution, thus, seems to distinguish between disintegration of the territory and border changes. The former is beyond the substantive powers of the political bodies, as "Finland is indivisible." The latter, altering the borders, is within the substantive powers of the Executive to negotiate and then for the Realm Day to ratify.

Had The Faroes remained aligned to Norway, as some have wished, the case for Faroese secession in accordance with the Constitution of the Realm would seem altogether more troublesome. The Basic Law of the Norwegian Realm states: "§ 1. The Kingdom of Norway is a free, independent and indivisible and in-transferable Realm…" What Lincoln assumed, the Norwegians spell out, and the same fundamentals apply: opting-out is an action not in the instrument itself. The words "free, independent and indivisible and in-transferable Realm" mirror the hopes and frustrations of the Norwegians, who have experienced their share of foreign domination, partition and transfer of allegiance. Thus, secession might be against the (basic) law, but it happens nonetheless, by political action not provided for by the legal instruments.

A very important question that I will leave for others to ponder is the question of how and by which procedures the Faroese themselves, in accordance with Faroese law and tradition, should decide to opt out. The options suggested include the following:

—   The Faroese ratify a Treaty with Denmark, with an optional referendum.[14]
—   The Faroese unilaterally withdraw from the Realm when the Law Thing so decides.[15]

---

14   The White Book (*supra* note 12) suggested this route. The idea is through the consent of Denmark to create a legal basis, valid in the Danish constitutional order, for Faroese sovereignty.

15   This might happen through a unilateral resolution of the Law Thing, possibly further sanctioned by the People in a referendum. In substantive terms, a unilateral withdrawal would be based on invoking the extra-legal phenomenon of popular sovereignty (the *pouvoir constituant*) as the source for this exercise of self-determination.

- The Faroese implement the 1946 referendum.[16]
- The Faroese secede by using the procedure for amending the Faroese Constitution.[17]
- The Faroese amend the Faroese Constitution to provide for a later secession procedure.[18]
- The Danish Constitution is amended to provide an opt-out clause.[19]
- The Faroe Islands claim to withdraw from the original Association of ca. 1270.[20]
- The Faroe Islands and Greenland collectively reveal themselves to be the lost Kingdom of Norway and formally end the Union of Bergen of 1450.[21]

Different people are suggesting all these different options. Although the Faroese are one of the most homogenous and distinct nationalities in Europe, they squabble loudly over this question. The current Faroese Constitution – the Faroese Act on Governing – is unclear as to the proper procedures that the Faroese are to use themselves.

Arguably, politics, and especially politics continued through the means of armed conflicts had a lot more to do with the expansions and contractions of the Danish Realm than had the intricacies of constitutional law. However, we must not dismiss constitutional or international law as made irrelevant by politics. Rather, we should accept that an interaction between the two will always exist.

The Danish Constitution – both written and traditional – gives no guarantees of secession, not even any particularly suitable procedure for leaving the Danish Realm. The Faroe Islands as well as Greenland will have to rely on a constitutional earthquake that leaves them on the right side of the fault line, should they wish to leave.

As we have seen several times, the Danish Realm is apt at and used to accepting loss of associated realms and lands. However, neither the Basic Law, nor the wider Constitution provide for clear rights for "associates" to leave or procedures for doing so. The Courts will probably accept anything ratified by the Parliament, and Parliament will follow the Executive and its recommendations.

Opting out of an Association is not under Danish law a legal right to be exercised at will. Under Faroese law and constitutional tradition it is a fundamental precondition for

---

16   As noted elsewhere, the referendum was highly controversial and much contested, but showed a majority favouring secession. Traditionally, the Nationalist side favoured using the 1946 referendum as the basis for secession.

17   This has been suggested by some in the Unionist camp, as it is the most cumbersome procedure in the book, and arguably therefore, the most appropriate procedure for fundamentally altering the constitutional status.

18   This has been suggested in the works of the Faroese Constitutional Committee.

19   This is the logical consequence of accepting that the Danish Constitution is a bar to Faroese secession, even by Danish parliamentary consent, thus creating a legalistic basis for self-determination.

20   This would be adopting the line that Iceland maintained in relation to that land's Treaty of 1262-64.

21   This is the view of Mr. Zakarias Wang and others, see, for instance, in 3 FLR (2003).

the consent of the governed. In relation to Danish tradition, leaving the Realm is a political action, a constitutional revolution that the Danish constitutional system has absorbed
and accepted with more or less ease time and time again. Secession from the association
with Denmark cannot be completed at will with reference to the Basic Law of the Danish
Realm, *except by some Action not provided for in the Instrument itself.*

Faroese Constitutional History – The Early Days

The Faroe Islands are an ancient constitutional entity with a fascinating history.[22] Around
the year 800, Norse people (Vikings, if you like) settled the Faroe Islands and established
a polity called, by themselves, a "land" with its own constitution that was, of course, free
of today's conceptual musts (a written constitutional legalistic text, fashionable separations
of power, bill of rights, etc.). Thus, the Faroese Parliament, the "Law Thing" (*Løgting*), has a
very good claim to being the oldest functioning parliament in the world.

In addition to local Chiefs and local Things in the six districts, the most notable institutions of the Faroese were the institutions of the Thing for all the Faroes, later named
the *Løgting* – the Law Thing. In Tinganes (the Thing Ness) in Tórshavn (Thor's Haven), the
islands' Capitol, the Norse population of the Faroe Islands held their parliament. By Norse
tradition, they divided the task of the Thing into deliberative functions and judicial functions.

Marked by ropes, the centre of the Tinganes was the venue for the elected representatives of the six districts to argue and decide questions of general importance. The debate
was an open-air affair, though; all free men could attend the assembly, albeit outside the
perimeter. Some accounts suggest that the representatives may have yielded to speakers
from the crowd. The term "All Thing" (the Thing for All) illustrates this part of the Thing
that all free men could attend. It may even refer back to an even earlier tradition before
the chiefs or elected representatives held the votes on the Thing. Today, All Thing (*Alþingi*)
is still the term used for the Icelandic Parliament.

The deliberative function of the Thing probably decided to accept the codes, or traditional bodies of laws, that seemed necessary to the settlers to provide a basis for law and
order in the islands. As most settlers came from the western parts of today's Norway, the
choice early on fell on the code of the Gula Thing. The Gula Thing was one of the four great
Things of what later came to be known as Norway.

The other main function of the Thing was the Law Right (*løgrættan*), a court with several divisions judging in disputes. The name reflects the Nordic notion of "righting the law",
probably a name fitting the functions of the Law Right as, first of all, an appeal court for

---

22   Another account of Faroese constitutional history (in Danish) appears in the Faroese Law
      Review, last issue of 2003. Written by Mr. Hans Andrias Sølvará, a Faroese historian, the
      article is well worth reading for a more detailed historical account. I have in part relied
      on that article. The most notable general account of Faroese history is Hans Jacob Debes:
      Føroya Søga, vol. 1-3. A collection of early Faroese legal and historical sources appear in
      Jacob Jacobsen: *Diplomatarium Færoense.*

the local courts and, secondly, an active court adapting and developing the codes and other sources of law to the particular Faroese circumstances. The judicial function of the Thing may have developed some of the principles that were later to be adopted in the Sheep Brief, the Faroese Code of 1298.

Much more is known about the deliberative function in Iceland, where the Thing adopted a succession of codes and law in the Free State period. However, from the scant records, we do know that the Faroese Thing, for instance, around 1400 adopted such general laws as rules of remuneration for the elected representatives and a regulation on the number of dogs allowed in each village. These laws of deliberation probably reflect a legislative activity to a great extent. The Thing probably kept its own Law Book and had a Law Man as its presiding officer, charged with the traditional Norse Thing function of reciting significant parts of the law every year when the Thing convened. The present Faroese Premier has retained the title Law Man (*Løgmaður*).

One very important example of this deliberative function was the reception of Christianity around the year 1000. Icelandic sagas have recorded that event, though probably in somewhat distorted form. However, the account probably gets the central point right: the Faroese debated and decided matters of great importance at the Thing. Politics will always be politics and those interested can read the Saga of the Faroese. It provides, if you like, a fictionalised documentary of the events that featured not only a feud of faiths, but had profound implications for the rivalling Faroese Chiefs, the growing powers of the rulers of Norway and, if the Icelandic scribes are to be believed, some sex and violence for good measure.

Norse settlers established settlements during the Viking period in many islands on the fringes of the British Isles, like Man, the Hebrides, Orkney, Shetland, and also Iceland and Greenland further west. Meanwhile, Norway at the time, was only loosely organised around four main "Things" but gradually competing strongmen replaced this decentralised structure and Norway was united as a kingdom.

Today, only The Faroes Islands and Iceland have fully retained that Norse identity, but the Isle of Man has retained much of the old constitutional tradition. The Isle of Man is another prime example of how a polity can survive through the ages relatively unscathed in constitutional terms.

The power of the Kings increased gradually in the Nordic lands from the 10th century A.D. to the end of the 13th century. The formation and strengthening of central powers led to the rolling back of the earlier Free State tradition and the Things and local Chiefs diminished in political importance. The power-hungry warlords spent most of a millennium establishing, consolidating, and fighting over what would eventually become three kingdoms of the Nordic region.

The king of Norway tried to extend his realm to the west. Lawyers and historians of a positivist tradition often point to the year 1035 as the year that Norway absorbed the Faroe Islands and the islands then became indistinguishable from any other tract of Norway Proper. That year the Norwegian King for the first time officially gave a Faroese Chief the Faroe Islands as fief in return for taxes. This was probably the same arrangement envisaged earlier when Christianity was proposed at the Thing; the King wanted to reign over all Norse lands as God's viceroy. In 1035, the vocabulary of civilised government was in place to explain the naked aggression in proper legal terms; and it has had its effect, most academic accounts revere this legal gibberish as great authority.

The better view, I submit, is to regard the writ of fiefdom as an attempt to legalise a conquest, no different from any other colonisations and invasions at that time or of later date. It was not, however, until the late 13th century that the lands of the west finally submitted on their own constitutional terms to Norwegian supremacy of some sort. This coincided with the height of power of the Kings back in Norway and a general economic decline out west.

We know the lands in the west individually concluded treaties with the King. In the case of Iceland, the forty-eight Chiefs that formed the deliberative part of the "All Thing" (the Icelandic Parliament) ratified a Treaty later referred to as "*Gamli Sáttmáli*" or "The Old Treaty". It took them two years from 1262 to 64 to ratify the Treaty, as the Icelandic constitutional tradition required unanimity among the voting chiefs.

The Faroese probably ratified their own Old Treaty around the year 1270. From approximately that year a preserved letter from the Norwegian King talks of the Land Code, a Norwegian Code to replace the different Codes of the Things, which is being promulgated to apply in the Faroese as well. The King then indirectly refers to an agreement made with the Faroese, promising amendments to the Code in line with what "Your own Law Book provided earlier."

In 1298, the Norwegian King sanctioned the amendments in what we could call a Faroese Code. As most of the laws peculiar to The Faroes concerned sheep farming and other aspects of agriculture, the Faroese have since referred to it as the Sheep Brief (*Seyðabrævið*). The Sheep Brief was the first in a very long line of statutes that recognised the Faroe Islands as a separate jurisdiction in a larger constitutional context.

The Faroe Islands enjoyed relative freedom in the times thereafter, maintaining their Thing and its functions. The church established its own bishop over the Faroes, and the bishop acquired a seat at the Norwegian Privy Council.

Through a Union of the Crowns, Denmark and Norway dynastically merged. In 1380, the young King Oluf became King of both Realms. This led to the formal Union of Bergen in 1450. The Danish Princess Margrethe, who was the mother of King Oluf and the effective ruler of both Denmark and Norway for a number of years, even managed to create the Kalmar Union with Sweden in 1397. Though Kalmar never stabilised and dissolved a few bloody wars later, the Norwegian-Danish Union lasted almost half a millennium. The main difference seems to have been the relative strength of the nobility in each of the countries that Denmark sought to dominate.

Many, many years later, in the late 18th century, in a time of relative tranquillity, the Danish King Christian VII promulgated a Basic Law on Natural Born Rights. In that law, we see the constitutional order of the time. The King is Prince of three Realms, Denmark, Norway, and Holstein, and various lands associated to them, ruling three peoples the Danes, the Norwegians, the Holsteins, and "those made equivalent to these."

Alas, the peaceful little association of Lilliputian lands was doomed. Larger forces were afoot and started nibbling at the fringes. The Danish King ceded Norway Proper to the Swedish King with the Treaty of Kiel 1814.[23] Again, the political events preceded the legal niceties. Denmark had joined the wrong side in the Napoleonic Wars, Copenhagen was strategically bombarded by the British and the new ruler of Sweden, Prince Bernadotte, though originally one of Napoleon's Marshals, managed to wrest Norway out of Danish hands. The Norwegians had already spontaneously enacted their own Constitution in 1814, but had to, for political and economic reasons, amend it in great haste and replace the Danish Prince (who later became Christian VIII of Denmark) whom they had elected as King with the erstwhile Marshal.

As is evident by this, constitutional law, limping along behind political action, has always acknowledged that political powers-that-be (states, kings, whatever) can surrender their lands and possessions by treaty or by grudging acceptance.[24] The King's Law of 1662 – the then written Constitution of Denmark – and its Norwegian counterpart of 1665 proclaimed absolute and eternal rule by the Danish Dynasty, but legal words are no match for military might.

Although they had just bombed Copenhagen, the British much preferred a weak Dane to a strong Swede in their own backyard. This probably induced the British to meddle with the Treaty of Kiel that allowed the King of Denmark to still retain his Norwegian dependencies, the remaining islands to the west, Faroe, Iceland and Greenland (he also acquired a bit of Swedish Pomerania, which he traded the Prussians for the small duchy of Lauenburg, just south of the King's duchy of Holstein).

For a long period preceding the Treaty of Kiel, the centre of this constitutional conglomerate, of which the King of Denmark was head, had consolidated the administration of all the different entities in Copenhagen. For the Faroes, the loss of Norway was, therefore, probably not very profound. The King was still there and laws, officials and trade still came from Copenhagen. Of importance, though, was the fact that the Danes, for reasons which are unclear, decided not to convene the Law Thing for a number of years and established an administrative Governor to govern The Faroes like a Danish province.

Some years later, absolutism fell and the King accepted elections for a constitutional convention that was to prepare a written Constitution for the Kingdom. Writing a constitution posed the question: for whom is the Constitution to be written?

---

23   Some very enjoyable reading, though a somewhat idiosyncratic analysis, of the Danish-Norwegian relationship can be found in the writings of Mr. Zakarias Wang, see *supra* note 20.

24   Until 1972, the Danish King claimed to be king of two lost peoples (*de Vender og Gother*), and Duke of several duchies, otherwise ceded to Prussia after the war of 1864 by the Vienna Treaty of 1864. The Danish King even had to be reminded by the Swedes that he was no longer eligible to the title of King of Norway under the Treaty of Kiel of 1814.

For Whom is the Basic Law Written?

Denmark A.D. 1848 experienced a popular rising. The rather dimwitted King gave way to popular demands for a written constitutional Basic Law, and in the end Denmark acquired a very liberal constitution by contemporary standards. All seemed well except for one crucial aspect. It did not square the circle of the constitutional associations Denmark had with other countries.

Sensibly, the Danes let the southern German duchies belonging to the King, Holstein, and Lauenburg, remain clearly outside the scope of the new Danish Basic Law. However, the problem came with the middle area, Schleswig (or Slesvig), a duchy of mixed Danish-German population and controversial status *vis-à-vis* the Danish Kingdom. At first, Schleswig was left out of the scope of the Constitution, but in 1863 it was extended not, as some had suggested, only to the Danish-minded northern half, but to the entire land. This led to the war of 1864 and Denmark's total humiliation whereby it lost all the duchies, including the entire territory of Schleswig (of which the northern part was handed back in 1920, following a referendum to determine local national allegiance).

Now, for our purposes the important thing here is, first, to note, yet again, how politics determine the scope of constitutions, Second, we have witnessed why the Danes lost the rather inclusive streak in their national character that we saw in the Basic Law on Natural Born Rights of Christian VII. The Danes were feeling beaten and ill-treated by the outside world and the defining motto after 1864 came to be "what is lost to the outside must be won on the inside" that lead to such silly notions as the claim that "Denmark is a unitary state". Regrettably, Denmark never got a "constitutional document" for the Realm and separate "constitutional documents" for the Parts. This has lead some, mistakenly in my view, to conclude that the original meaning of the Basic Law, or the meaning or intent of later revisions, was to pronounce a unitary state with no federal characteristics, no competing legislatures, and no sub-states.

Also left clearly outside the scope of the Basic Law were the genuine colonies, the present-day US Virgin Islands, two small trading posts in Africa and in India, respectively, and recently rediscovered Greenland. The Faroe Islands and Iceland were controversial. Iceland, due to its larger population and wealthier ruling class, and through retaining a written language of its own, enjoyed the blessing of a large number of people trained in law and language, producing not only the celebrated Icelandic sagas, but also legal and other documents that have proved very insightful for posterity. For its size, Iceland has an exceptionally large amount of constitutional and historical material that can be enjoyed by those so inclined.

For our purposes, it is sufficient to note that Iceland appears to have moved in parallel with the Faroes, only much further ahead. Comparing the two can prove useful to understanding the nature of the Faroese constitutional question. In the latter days of the absolute reign of the Danish monarchy, the Icelanders were much more self-conscious than the Faroese, better educated and all in all better prepared for the fall of the ancient regime. At the Convention that the King called to prepare the Basic Law, he gave Iceland five seats and a promise that they would have the final word on the status of Iceland. Just years before, in 1841, the King had agreed to reconvene the All Thing that, like the Law Thing, had not been summoned for a while after the loss of Norway.

To fully understand just how bookish and clever the Icelanders were, you must appreciate that the All Thing in 1843 (its second session since reconvention) voted to establish an Icelandic Law School, but the King vetoed this – 25 consecutive times.

These fellows were not joking when they turned up at the constitutional convention, declared that they invoked the Old Treaty, and refused to take part in preparing a Constitution for Denmark. The Danes ignored the eloquent Icelandic argument and sent a delegation to Iceland to promulgate the Basic Law of the Danish Realm at the All Thing. The Icelanders were prepared for this, lamented the illegal actions of the Danes, and protested passionately – in the name of the King. The meeting ended with the Danish envoys leaving fuming with rage and most all Icelanders at the meeting proclaiming: "We all protest" adding for good measure: "Long live our King Frederick the VII."

For years, the status of Iceland was in dispute. The result of this stand-off was that Iceland got a statute thrown at it in 1871 concerning its special status, and got a "constitutional document" in 1874 setting up its internal affairs. The two nations amended the status in 1903 giving Iceland something akin to the later Faroese Home Rule. Then, in 1918, Denmark recognised Iceland as a separate (and sovereign) Kingdom. Reading through the Danish Parliamentary debates, one gets a clear impression that the Icelanders had outsmarted the Danes again, as most Members seemed to think that this was a final settlement giving "them up north" enough "self-rule." However, with an implicit recognition of sovereignty and very explicit rules on termination of the Union between Iceland and Denmark and ending the Monarchy, the Icelanders had managed to legalise their secession.

Let us now go back to the years around 1850 and look a little closer at the status of the Faroe Islands.[25] Though the Faroese are said to have mourned the fall of the Law Thing,[26] they were not like the Icelanders very good at voicing their political wishes. The problem of communication is manifest throughout the Faroese-Danish relationship; Faroese politicians have never been very good at articulating their demands and reasoning in the most effective legalistic term mastered by the Icelanders.

Thus, the Faroe Islands did not seek or get a promise from the King to have their own say in the constitution-making process, nor did they protest against being included in the Danish Estate Parliament that proceeded the constitutional process. The King appointed the Governor of Faroe, Mr. Pløyen, member for the Faroe Islands in the partially elected Constitutional Convention. Pløyen was by all accounts a fabulous Governor, he took the islanders on excursions that improved their fishing techniques and otherwise totally

---

25   A very detailed account of the parliamentary debates is given in Dr. Jákup Thorsteinsson's doctoral thesis: *Et Færø som Færø*.

26   A rather good account is given by the only Faroese born Governor of the Icelands, Mr. Christian Bærentsen, who later became Appeal Court Judge in Denmark, reprinted in the anthology *Frælsmannamál*.

immersed himself in local life, even to the point of writing traditional Faroese poetry, notably *TheWhale Catchers' Song* that still retains ritual status in The Faroes. When discussing the coming election laws in the Faroes, he encouraged the Faroese to speak in their native tongue. However impressive Mr. Pløyen was, he was still loyal to the King and did not seek the same concessions sought by the Icelanders.

The Basic Law of the Danish Realm – the enacted written Constitution – was, as noted, rather indeterminate in scope. The Danes successfully promulgated the Basic Law in the Faroe Islands by the traditional method of reading it aloud in the six districts, probably without the Faroese taking all that much notice. However, the question remained, how exactly the Faroese were to be treated in relation to the concept of the Danish Realm. A great parliamentary debate ensued in 1850. Some have remarked that this debate was the high point in Danish political and legal deliberation on the Faroese Question. Indeed many very notable figures took part, like the philosopher and poet N. F. S. Grundtvig, the professor of law and former Premier A. S. Ørsted. The official line taken by the new Executive was that The Faroes were an integral part of the Realm. The different speakers elaborated greatly on the finer points of the Faroese situation and it seems likely that the Faroese could have greatly influenced the future governing of The Faroes had they been adequately represented. In the end, The Faroes got one member in each legislative house, and a few years later, they reconvened the Law Thing, although ostensibly as a provincial council. This rather puny version of the Thing of old was not as an inevitable result, as both the Icelandic case and the above-mentioned debate show, but as the consequence of inadequate representation and insufficient advocacy.

As Denmark lost its war over Schleswig, and amended the Basic Law in reactionary terms such as restricting suffrage, the time was lost to wrest concessions out of the Danes. Denmark was ruled by a minority of conservative, landed aristocracy until the year 1901; and the liberals, nationalists and then socialists fighting for power were not all that informed about and interested in the Faroese question for a while. Nor, for that matter, did the Faroese do much constructive work. In 1906, the Faroese divided themselves into a Unionist and a Self-Rule Party, with the Unionists for a long while enjoying electoral supremacy. A new Law Thing Act in 1923 reformed the Thing, but still placed the executive powers in the hands of the Governor. The Faroese Question, thus, lay dormant until greater forces came into play.

Fortunate Occupation

The Germans invaded Denmark on April 9, 1940 on their way to Norway. The Danish forces lost 9 men, most of whom were unaware of their Government's preemptive capitulation. The Norwegians gallantly fought for a month and both the king and the Government fled to Britain. Prompted by the invasion of Denmark and Norway, the British soon afterwards occupied the Faroe Islands to avoid them falling into the wrong hands. To the Faroese this seemed like the better option. The Faroese fully co-operated with the British and most of the Faroese fishing fleet supplied the British with fish throughout the war.

The freight of fish was a dangerous occupation and the use of the Danish flag meant that the Faroese vessels were doubly damned: they were British-allied vessels, but marked out as Axis-dependant nationals. The British, therefore, took the decision to recognise the clandestine Faroese Flag as the National Emblem of Faroe. What was probably not foremost in Mr. Churchill's mind at the time he notified the House of Commons on this, was that the Danes had fought most insistently against the recognition of the Faroese Flag for years.

The quite sensible step of recognising the Flag left the stranded Danish Governor in Faroe, Mr. Hilbert, fuming. Mr. Hilbert was the archetypal condescending Danish bureaucrat, not the fellow most likely to compose vernacular odes to whale catching. The Governor was in quite a spot at the beginning of the War, facing a Law Thing with increasingly nationalist sentiments; and the nationalists could smell political blood when cut off from Denmark.

Some Faroese voices suggested that the Faroese should assume power over all branches of Government and only recognise the Governor as a representative of the Danish Government. However, legalistic bluff on the part of the Governor and a British reluctance to accept a renegade regime resulted in compromise. The Parliament enacted, the Governor assented to, and the British accepted an Interim Constitution of the Faroe Islands.

The Interim Constitution had only a few basic provisions. Executive powers were to remain in the hands of the Governor with the Executive Committee of the Thing enjoying powers of advice and oversight. The Law Thing was to enact legislation, but the Governor could propose such legislation and had to assent to statutes before their official promulgation. Financial matters lay with the Governor, again with the Executive Committee and other Committees of the Thing enjoying powers of advice and oversight. The Judiciary needed an Appeal Tribunal, duly set up with lay people sitting alongside the lone Danish judge on appeal.

In constitutional terms, the wartime period was truly fascinating. In four years' time, the Faroe Islands went through much the same process as other countries took decades to complete. The Law Thing started to flex its constitutional muscles and politically arm-wrestle the Governor on a number of issues. Indeed, some of the Interim Statutes enacted in this period remain in force even today. Probably unwittingly, the good Governor Hilbert played the part of the retreating monarch and gave rice to a new parliamentary tradition.

You can view the wartime constitution of the Faroe Islands from several angles. Was the Governor assuming the powers and privileges of the Realm, acting, as it were, on behalf of the Danish Government? Was Britain, instead, acting as caretaker during Danish absence, and mediating a transitional arrangement? The best view, in my opinion, is to realise that these were extraordinary times, which constitutional law is simply inept at anticipating or explaining. The Faroese had acquiesced with foreign rule for so long and they failed again to agree amongst themselves on how to act. Comparing Faroe to Iceland is revealing, yet again. The Icelanders had a document, the 1918 Union Act, with which to dress up their national determination to secede from Denmark. To them, the war provided a very convenient time to gracefully end the Danish connection.

More in line with their own national character, the Faroese resorted to internal squabbling and bickering during the war. A great opportunity for a national consensus was missed.

The Self-Rule Party split just before the war. Their leader, the charismatic Mr. Jóannes Paturson was at the same time a poet and gifted orator and, in addition, the largest tenant of the King's land in The Faroes. His overconfident personality and his position on land reform (he opposed the distribution of the King's land to the poor) both contributed to his being ousted as leader of the nationalist Self-Rule Party. However, his popularity at large ensured that the Popular Party, consisting of his own followers and a small party, the Commercial Party, formed by trade interests, immediately gained a large following. At the elections, in 1943, the Popular Party gained 12 of the 25 seats in the Law Thing. In his day, Patursson had tried to argue along Icelandic lines for not recognising the Basic Law and its implicit incorporation of the Faroe Islands into the Danish Realm. Instead, he tried, when a member of the Danish Folk Thing, to negotiate a new constitutional arrangement with Denmark. Such a sophisticated point seems, however, utterly lost on the Faroese, who did not pursue it further.

Gradually, though, the lawyer and banker Mr. Thorstein Petersen from the commercial wing of the party replaced Paturson, whose wing of the party was lead by the bachelor lawyer Mr. Poul Petersen, a man completely lacking in the eloquence and charisma of Patursson. Mr. Thorstein Petersen was a man of action, but like Mr. Patursson, he was unable to unite the Faroese behind common cause. Mr. Petersen favoured independence, but could also be heard demanding two Faroese Members of the Folk Thing as part of a new arrangement.[27]

The Unionists, with their strangely submissive leader Mr. Andras Samuelsen, behaved as if they were true diehards in relation to the question of allegiance to Denmark. "I love Denmark" Mr. Samuelsen professed in a secret letter to the Danish Prime Minister immediately after the war, lamenting the fragile existence of the small-numbered Faroese. The Unionists voters were almost to a man the most dyed-in-the-wool, backwoods, down-to-earth Faroese old-timers you can imagine. To them the allegiance to the King and all things established were part of a conservative ideology. Even though a clear recognition of the Faroese right to self-determination with the Danish Realm would have served him better, Mr. Samuelsen fought tooth and nail to avoid any transfer of powers from Danish to Faroese authorities whatever their nature. Mr. Samuelsen was throughout the war in very close contact with the Danish Governor and gallantly fought a rearguard action for the Realm at the end of the War.

The Social Democrats and the rump Self-Rule Party joined the Unionists during the war, keeping the Popular Party away from power. Both these parties were very flexible and progressive in constitutional matters, but they lacked the nerve to take the ultimate steps. The Social Democrats even expelled the Member of the Law Thing, Mr. Jákup í Jákupsstovu, who sided with the Popular Party in calling for full independence at the end of the War.

---

27   The Danish Constitutional Committee, third meeting on 28 February 1946.

Once free of the Hun, the Danes could again turn to their possessions in the North. Iceland was lost, but Greenland and The Faroes were still salvageable. Danish officials duly formed a committee to negotiate with the Faroese. Encouraged by Governor Hilbert and Mr. Samuelsen, the Danes proposed what they referred to as the "Government's Offer". The Offer recognised the Interim Constitution and what had passed during the War, but proposed a future scheme with only limited powers to the Law Thing with the Governor attaining something akin to the Premiership of The Faroes.

Meanwhile the Unionist forces were hard-pressed in The Faroes. Mr. í Jákupsstovu and the Popular Party together held the majority of the Thing and were contemplating full secession from Denmark through a resolution of the Thing. The Unionists and their partners were, though, able to get the rebel member to sanction a referendum instead on the two basic options, Secession or the Offer.

Mr. Petersen, for his part, feared that the majority would favour the Offer. He, therefore, asked his followers who might not favour full independence to write "No" on the ballot to indicate that the choice was a false one. The Popular Party's hope was that the "Secession" and the "No" votes counted together would constitute a majority that could come in handy to press the Danes for concessions if full independence was unattainable.

Down in Denmark, a debate naturally arose concerning the future status of the dependencies. The debate this time around was much less expert than in 1850. The Danish Parliament was not as in 1850 at the height of its intellectual might. Back then, philosophers, professors and poets sought election to represent the people, believing that power was going to be in the hands of an elected assembly. However, real power remained with the bureaucracy and gradually academics and high-flyers stayed away from the rough and tumble of party politics.

The result for our purposes was a much less focused and informed debate. Still, it was with the Parliament that ultimate power rested in the Danish set-up. To get an impression of how far the Danes could have gone, let us listen to the words of the left-wing MF, Mr. Robert Stærmose, spoken in spring 1946, only months before the Septembr 14 referendum:

"Regarding the Greenland Question, we would like to see a Greenland Commission being established… [we must] avoid the lack of understanding that has earlier marked our relationship with the Icelandic people and the Faroese people…

Regarding the Faroe Islands, any understanding of the Faroese question must begin with a recognition from the Danish, without any reservations, that the Faroese are a People and that the Faroe People is a Nation with all the characteristics that are needed to be a Nation in that word's popular meaning…

[On a practical level, for future Arrangement of the Relations between The Faroes and Denmark, it would be beneficial] if we immediately recognise the Flag of The Faroes as a flag for the Faroese People. This can be done without prejudice to the future Constitutional Arrangement.

It is no longer than a decade ago that the Speaker of the [Danish Upper House] rang his bell and reprimanded as incorrect that the Faroese Representative used the expression 'the Faroese Nation'…

We have not always been so lucky with the civil servants [in The Faroes. They have] almost all been good servants of the Danish state, [but even a single one or a few appointments] have had profound implications for the national Danish-Faroese relationship, [we have] regarded The Faroes as a place of deportation for some people that could not be used elsewhere.

In a few months time a referendum will be held on the Faroes, [hopefully based on an understanding] that we have a strong and sincere will to respect all Faroese national demands, [including any future association] between The Faroes and Denmark, insuring that small Nordic Nation's continuing free development."[28]

Now, while this view definitely does not promote the naked self-interest of the Danish state, nevertheless no-one could have relied upon it as a guarantee that the Danes would have negotiated in good faith any settlement that the Faroese might want. Rather, it shows that legal concepts and constitutional texts are not likely to limit political will. Alas, the Faroese never really picked up on such signals.

Wartime Governor Mr. Hilbert was a civil servant quite possibly fitting the above description as an appointment creating profound disturbance in Faroese-Danish relations. As noted, he recommended that the Danish Government approve the Interim Constitution and the actions he had taken during the war.[29] Furthermore, he advised that it was imperative to find a way for the Law Thing to continue participating in legislation as it had during the War. He viewed legislative powers vested in the Law Thing as somewhat abominable to the Basic Law, but: "If Parliament accepts this, one can presume that the courts will not go against it." In any event, the Danish Parliament had to approve such submitted Faroese legislative initiatives.

The good Governor advised that in order to confront the Popular Party wish for independence, there should be a referendum on the continued Faroese association to Denmark. He gave several reasons:

1. There had been talks of a referendum in 1930, which the Danish Government had not rejected.
2. If a referendum was not out of the question in 1930, it should be so much more possible after five years of partial independence and before a general debate on the future arrangement.
3. A considerable minority of some 40 per cent of the electorate, holding 12 of the 25 seats, fought, using all means, for independence during the War.

---

28   General Debates of the Folk Thing 97th Session 1945-46, Volume A sp. 607-608, and sp. 7174-7175.

29   Governor Hilbert left several thorough reports, among them one dated 15 March 1945 in which he proposed a new Danish statute setting up the (local) government of Faroe.

4. There is a widespread superstition in Faroe that the islands should hold such mystical advantages for Denmark that Denmark will cling on to The Faroes at any cost.

5. Only a referendum can show whether the Faroese People take the same stand as the Popular Party. Only a referendum, after a clear statement saying that Denmark will respect its result, can dispel the notion that Denmark wants to continue the association against the wishes of the Faroese People. Only thus, can there be calm on the question for a considerable future.

Thus, a referendum took place. The majority of the votes favoured the option of Full Independence from Denmark, a minority voted for the Offer.

What happened next confirms every cynicism that critical legal studies can muster. Suddenly the Unionists relied on the no-votes, originally solicited by the Popular Party to bolster the independence vote and make it possible to demand further concessions. Now, the Unionist camp counted these votes as part of a "no to independence majority". Furthermore, the acting Governor, Mr. Vagn-Hansen, now stated that secession was illegal according the Basic Law and requested a Navy Patrol Boat to assist against any insurgency.

Remember that Mr. Petersen controlled a majority in Parliament counting the Popular Party and Mr. í Jákupsstovu. Looking back, the clever move probably would have been to negotiate some major concessions from the Danes, perhaps something akin to the Act of Union in 1918, or at least a significant increase in Faroese Powers combined with a formal recognition of future Faroese self-determination. However, Mr. Petersen set out to implement secession and ensuing events soon eclipsed his efforts.

For a while, the Danish system was stunned. The Prime Minister, Mr. Knud Kristensen, publicly announced that the Danes would respect the Faroese decision. Like Iceland, the Faroe Islands seemed to abandon Denmark in the aftermath of the wartime separation.

Following appeals from the Faroes, though, the Danish Government soon struck back. Prime Minister Kristensen somehow disappeared from the fray for a while and the Finance Minister Mr. Thorkild Kristensen took charge of the Executive's handling of the affair. The latter Kristensen stated that the referendum's questions as well as its result were unclear and sent a delegation of dignitaries to explore the situation. To further challenge the result, the King formally signed an Order according to the 1923 Law Thing Act, dissolving the Law Thing. The November 1946 election was a landslide victory for the Unionist forces. Soon afterwards, the negotiations started over again.

Rule at Home

Following the election, the Danes had to come up with another alternative. To further prepare a new deal, Mr. Niels Arup, a high-ranking official who had for some time worked on Faroese matters, went to The Faroes in August of 1947 to prepare a report.[30] Mr. Arup

---

30 "Faroese Problems" – an account from a tour of the Faroe Islands in August 1947 by Niels Arup.

provides a brutally honest insight into the mind of the condescending, yet well-intentioned Danish technocrat. Mr. Arup meticulously reports on fisheries, agriculture, infrastructure, financial sector, foreign exchange and trade, Faroese-Danish relations of both a political and cultural nature and other relevant issues. Mr. Arup is in no doubt that it is in the Danish national interest to preserve Danish rule of the islands; at the same time he is equally convinced that it is in the Faroese interest to benefit from Danish intervention. Included in his recommendations were a new financial institution to finance the fishing industry and improvements of the interim airport built by the British, all undoubtedly economically beneficial to the Faroese. However, the political benefits for the Danish state were always foremost in Mr. Arup's mind:

> "[Even the bank led by] Member of the Folk Thing Thorstein Petersen has problems providing working capital… [In my opinion it will only strengthen the Faroes' interest in holding on to Denmark if Danish capital to a greater extent was invested in Faroese industry]… and as the captains of industry in The Faroes to a very great extent are members of the Popular Party, there would be created a dependence on Denmark (in a wider sense)…"

The diligent agent goes on to recommend, using the honours system to decorate Faroese civil servants and politicians, again especially those at the political centre, who may be swayed either way. Mr. Arup notes that the British have skillfully used this method in their dependencies. Furthermore, Danish popular magazines and improving the paper "*Dimmalætting*" (supportive of the Unionists) will benefit the cause, as will increased hospitality by the Danish Governor, and needless to say: "Should the Royal Couple, after the implementation of the new constitutional arrangement, visit the Faroes, such a visit would undoubtedly serve as splendid propaganda for Denmark." All of Mr. Arup's recommendations seem to have been implemented in one way or another.

On the Faroese side, there was much confusion. The Unionist side had continuously been in direct contact with the Danes, but it was itself fractured between those wanting as little change as possible and those favouring some progression in terms of increased powers to the Faroese. The self-rule camp was wavering between pursuing the referendum result and getting a good deal out of the Danes.

After a very thorough debate in 1947, however, the Law Thing agreed on some points in a resolution laying out the mandate for the negotiations. The Faroese Parliament unanimously voted to give the Faroese negotiating delegation a mandate, stating among other points:

–   "The Law Thing has unrestricted legislative power"
–   "The Law Thing elects a Faroese Delegation to negotiate with the Danish State Authorities concerning the constitutional status of the Faroe Islands"
–   "The compact that the delegation concludes with the Danish Authorities is to be submitted to the Law Thing and implemented by law".

At least the Faroese, thus, could phrase what is probably the unanimous view of all Faroese. They all consent to the powers of the Law Thing to the extent that the Thing itself defines them. Furthermore, the relationship with Denmark is contractual; through negotiations the two create a compact, make a deal, which they affirm using the appropriate legal instruments.

The problem as always was that the Faroese were not very good at stating long-term unity and common principles. Instead of appearing as a true national delegation, the Faroese mission was fraught with differing short-term goals of the various political parties and party leaders. The Faroese mission at the negotiations resembled a forum for debate more than a diplomatic task force. In the end, the Danish side offered a text that became the Home Rule Compact.

Already before the Home Rule provisions could be ratified, the Danish Parliament showed its willingness to bend the Basic Law any which way. The Popular Party leader, Mr. Petersen, had in the Danish Constitutional Committee, set up immediately after the War, demanded that the Faroese got two members instead of one the Folk Thing (lower house of parliament), in addition to the one seat they held in the Land Thing (upper house). To sweeten the up-coming deal, the Danes by statute increased the Faroese representation effective in the first election held in The Faroes after the War. This representation out of proportion to the population shows once again the ability and authority of the Danish elected assembly to define the broad-sense constitution of the Danish Realm. The two members for Faroe and, likewise, two for Greenland were reaffirmed by the 1953 Basic Law.

The Law Thing sanctioned the Compact as previously agreed "by law." The Law Thing enacted the Compact and the Governor promulgated it in accordance with the Interim Constitution as two parallel texts, in Faroese and in Danish. The Faroese version used in its preamble the Faroese word for "Nation" concerning the Faroese, whereas the Danish text as previously prepared by the Danish used a Danish word better translated as "Community of People."

The text was otherwise not very rich in symbolism, the language was dry and legalistic, giving the impression of a delegation of powers from the Danish Parliament rather than, as we know, being the 11th hour deal that prevented the Faroese taking the high road as the Icelanders had a few years earlier. The basic scheme of the text was also to provide a procedure for transferring powers successively in the future rather than recognising immediately the powers of the Law Thing.

For such reasons the Popular Party voted against the Home Rule Compact, which consequently was enacted 12 to 8 by the Unionist Party, the Social Democratic Party and the Self-Rule Party. The Danish Parliament soon after enacted the Danish version of the text with slightly differing words.

Though dry and less than engaging, the text and the circumstances of the Home Rule Compact are extraordinary. The Compact borrows from the structure and method of the earlier Icelandic constitutional acts, using a preamble, otherwise not practised since the advent of the Basic Law, and being enacted as a statute by both parliaments. The Danes use the word "*lov*" meaning statute and usually translated as "act" to describe it. Personally, I find the circumstances, content and parallels more properly support using the word "compact", noting the joint enactment by two political bodies. For obvious reasons the Unionist majority avoided a referendum this time around.

The enactment of the Home Rule Compact was in itself a great accomplishment. It struck the deal, it provided the procedures for future expansion of the Faroese self-government, and effectively recognised that the Faroese could get what they wanted, if only they could agree amongst themselves. However, both the Danes and the Unionists failed to state this in the appropriate symbolic and constitutional terms.

The performance of Mr. Poul Niclasen, the Unionist Faroese Member of the Land Thing, in the Danish Parliamentary debate on the home rule compact is very symptomatic. Instead of stressing the obviously relevant national, legal, symbolic and other points pertaining to such a manifestly significant constitutional document, he went on and on about Faroese culture through the ages, bragging about the "80,000 verses of ballad songs" and other accomplishments of the Faroese People. Though magnificent in themselves, the Faroese songs were hardly to the point at the time, and the Danish legislators seemed just to be puzzled and overbearing with this simple creature from an obviously less developed political culture. This rambling did not inspire them to go the extra constitutional mile to fully satisfy all the Faroese and explicitly recognise future Faroese self-determination even to the point of secession as they had done in the case of Iceland thirty years prior to the Home Rule arrangement.

Nonetheless, the Home Rule Compact has been the constitutional link between Denmark and Faroe ever since. The legislative powers of the Law Thing were recognized, the Flag and Faroese as an official language likewise, a number of listed policy areas could be "taken over" by the Faroese, the Faroese Executive was established, replacing the Governor, who in turn was reduced to a Representative of the Realm, and the Faroese effectively gained control over aspects of foreign affairs, notably fishing rights so close to political hearts. The Home Rule Compact slashed through a number of the privileges of the Danish Parliament and Executive, granting legislative, tax levying, executive and other powers to the Faroese Government. The above-mentioned preamble acknowledges that the Faroe Islands have a unique cultural, historical and geographical placing within the Danish Kingdom.

Danes, both officials and scholars, have tried their best to paddle back up the stream of self-determination. For instance, during the preparations for the Greenland Home Rule, an official statement opined that "when a part of Denmark achieves Home Rule this means that the part in question stays an integrated part of the Danish Kingdom, and that the sovereignty is totally in the hands of the authorities of the Kingdom. A Home Rule system within the framework of 'the Danish State-Community' rules out the option that the area in question achieves the status of a sovereign state, be it through a total break away or through a union, a union state or a federal state."

They wish!

A hugely important event following the enactment of the Home Rule Compact was the enactment of a Faroese (Internal) Constitution of 1948, replacing the Interim Constitution, but also emphasising the constitutional tradition of the Faroe Islands. The Faroese have never regarded the Home Rule Compact as the Constitution of Faroe, as seems to be the case in Greenland. In 1994, a new Faroese Constitution replaced the 1948 Constitution.

From the enactment in 1948 and until the 1970's, not much happened in constitutional terms. The Unionists were in the governing coalition most of the time, and though not in principle against taking over powers, they did not seem to find the time quite right just yet. For a brief period in the sixties, the new National Party, the Popular Party, the Self-Rule Party and the one-man Progressive Party tried to reinvigorate the independence mood, but with no significant results.

During the 1970's and 1980's a number of policy areas were taken over, some only pursuant to the "lesser" procedure, whereby the Faroese gained political control, but the Danes provided the finance. This created a Faroese administration, though, admittedly, administrate is not what we do best. Notably also, this led to the annual Danish Block Grant, which at its peak provided the Faroese Government with around a billion Danish Crowns, at times around a third of its total revenue.

The Faroese economy grew and diversified in this period, the population doubled and The Faroe Islands more and more developed the character of an independent country with its own infrastructure, culture, governmental and non-governmental structures in all areas. The 1972 decision to remain outside the EC, later the European Union, ensured that the Law Thing in effect today has legislative powers over more policy areas than the Folk Thing has. This circumstance coupled with the hands-off approach by the Danes through most of the period has meant that the Faroe Islands are in real terms more independent than most comparable polities, sovereign or otherwise.

There was still a craving for further and formal recognition, and the instinct manifest in most nations for self-reliance and, if you like, freedom. Following the economic depression of the early 1990's and the Danish Government's handling of the collapse of the Faroese banks, a very strong mood arose demanding a new arrangement with the Danes.

The 1998 elections led to a huge majority of the Law Thing (19 against 13) deciding to establish a sovereign Faroese state. After two years of preparations, negotiations with Denmark were initiated in March 2000. The Faroese proposal was to use the Icelandic Union Act of 1918 as a model for recognising Faroese sovereignty, though for the time being in close federation with Denmark.

The Faroese side spoke very much in legal terms, claiming to represent a People that had never decided to become an integrated part of the Danish Kingdom. Therefore, they claimed that the Faroe Islands have the right to self-determination, being a subject of international law, enjoying the right to negotiate the issue of Faroese sovereignty in a context of international law as an entity separate from Denmark.

The Danish Government, probably for political and tactical reasons, would have none of it. It refused to recognise the Faroese as a People separate from the Danes, refused to recognise the Faroese as a subject of international law, and refused to recognise any Faroese right to self-determination. The Danish Government claimed that negotiations between Denmark and the Faroe Islands could never be anything but a domestic Danish matter. Based on this they also refused to let any external observer follow the negotiations, and declined the Faroese wish to agree upon the minutes from the meetings. The Danish Government also refused to be drawn into negotiations on a gradual reduction of the Block Grant, facilitating a soft landing for the independent Faroese state.

Frustrated by the way the negotiations went, the Faroese Government even took to communicating directly with the UN. The Faroese complained that "the Kingdom of Denmark has not yet shown sincere readiness to conclude a treaty with the Faroe Islands", and asking the UN to give information regarding "all relevant procedures applicable when the United Nations and/or its agencies participate as a third party at international negotiations." Not surprisingly perhaps, the UN answered that the organisation could only participate as a third party at such negotiations at the request of a Member State. Soon afterwards, the Faroese-Danish negotiations collapsed.

However, a new strategy was undertaken, resulting in the Block Grant being reduced by a third and a number of policy areas taken over, including the to a seafaring nation important policy matter of Safety at Sea. The Faroese Government in that context expressed its strong desire to become an Associate Member of the International Maritime Organisation, the IMO. The Faroe Islands, thus, in 2002 became an Associate Member of IMO, following the deposit with the United Nations of notification to this effect by Denmark. This was the first time that the Faroe Islands achieved such membership of a UN organization. Arguably, this shows that the Faroe Islands are a potential state, a polity of a higher order.

The current government coalition, consisting of the Popular Party, the Unionists and the Social Democrats, has agreed to pursue the traditional path of widening the list of policy areas to be taken over by the Faroese. In addition, the coalition proposes a new Faroese Constitution, building on the work initiated by the previous and sovereignty-minded coalition. Especially if the Nationalist Party and the smaller opposition parties agree on the Faroese Constitution, this may infer that the parties have finally achieved Faroese unity with an adequately symbolic Constitutional Document with references to nation status, self-determination and procedures for further development, including the potential secession from the Realm.

A Note on Other Theories

"Hereby, a constitutional structure was created with two tiers: as the upper tier a common constitution for all the parts of the Monarchy; on the tier below a Basic Law geographically limited to the Kingdom and materially to its special policy areas, as there were special constitutional arrangements in the duchies... In other words, a constitutional structure that had shared characteristics with the structure of a federal state, namely the division of powers between the whole and the individual part."
Professor Max Sørensen on the Danish constitution after enactment of the Basic Law[31]

---

31   Max Sørensen: *Statsforfatningsret* 2nd edition 1973, page 41.

The author quoted above admitted, though perhaps reluctantly, that Denmark was federated to other higher-order constitutional entities when the Basic Law – the Danish Written Constitution – was enacted. Indeed, Professor Sørensen is one of the few Danish constitutional experts to refer to the Constitutional Acts of 1855 and 1863 regarding Schleswig, the Constitutional Act of 1871 regarding Iceland and the Act of Union between Iceland and Denmark of 1918.

These are statutes that show how the political actors disregarded – or at least bend the written Constitution as the ultimate source of law and legitimacy. The political realities were such that Parliament had to disregard the wishes of some Danish nationalists to pretend that Denmark was a unitary state.

Conventional legal wisdom has been unable to reconcile the differing perceptions of where the Faroe Islands are in legal terms, complicating the decision-making on where to go and how to get there.

One of the biggest problems is the misconception of the origins of the Faroese claim to self-determination. The Faroese relationship with Denmark is not colonial but dynastic. The powers and legitimacy of the Faroese Parliament and other political institutions is not delegation from Denmark, but rather, the continuous consent of the Faroese People that pre-existed the treaties (or treaty-like deals) formed for reasons of *realpolitik* by the Faroese Parliament with the outside powers of the day.

The most common error committed by Danish educated lawyers (including a great many Faroese) when describing the legal status of the Faroe Islands is using some point in history when Danish or Norwegian authorities issued some writ or other as the ultimate starting point for the legal existence of the Faroe Islands.

You will hear some of them mention 1035 as the date when the Faroese came under Norwegian rule. Others will use the year 1948 as their "big bang" – at that point in time the Faroese gained Home Rule from Denmark through the promulgation of the Home Rule Act. Such approaches are not only very simple and of too little use; they are plainly wrong.

Equally misguided are those who only look to international law as the source for the existence of a Faroese nation, a Faroese claim to self-determination and its potential uses. To them, the enactment of this or that treaty forms the basis of the Faroese claim to self-determination. Both camps, the "Danish/Norwegian Constitutional Law Camp" and the "International Law Camp" are, in my opinion, wrong in their basic approach.

First, they both seek the status of The Faroes externally – either outside The Faroes or outside the Danish Realm (Kingdom), thereby ignoring the "internal" nature of the sources and claims of Faroese self-determination and the internal dynamics needed to make use of any external opportunities.

Secondly, they ignore the political reality shaping before their eyes. The autonomous development of Faroese law and practise and the "contractual" or "treaty" nature of all dealings between the Kingdom's Government and the Faroese Government clearly indicate something different from a mere province lapping up its dish of devolution and, also, more than a mere colony waiting in a state of exploitation for freedom from its vicious oppressor.

Thirdly, the two theoretical camps appear to lack a proper understanding of history, their use of history is usually confined to memorising a few important dates or names rather than interpreting the historical events and development in a legal context.

The most entertaining theory is that of the celebrated Mr. Zakarias Wang, who considers the Faroe Islands together with Greenland to be the remnants of the Norwegian Kingdom. According to this theory, the Faroe Islands were completely integrated into Norway before its union with Denmark. As Denmark conveniently ceded Norway to Sweden in 1814, the Faroe Islands and Greenland constitute the rump of the Norwegian Kingdom (never mind how Iceland got out).[32]

Going all the way on the other extreme was a late professor of Danish Constitutional Law who famously said in his constitutional text book that the Home Rule Status of The Faroes was only delegation of powers, which could have been given to Amager or Taasinge, two Danish islands that are not even municipalities in their own right. Such views are plainly wrong as regards Danish constitutional history. Such views are, also, plainly absurd and obnoxious to anyone remotely familiar with political realities.

My basic premise is that the constitutional situation of the Faroe Islands depends on three different autonomous sets of law at the same time: Faroese, Danish and international. The inadequacy of many papers written on the Faroese question results from the inability to comprehend that these three tiers interact and in their legal and political intermingling, Faroe exists.

The Land of Maybe

The Faroes are constitutionally a Land of Maybe.

International Law, as treated in the other chapters of this book, may grant the Faroese as a people certain rights with more or, notably, less effective remedies to pursue.

Danish Constitutional Law has a very long and consistent tradition of federation. The Danish State will act in its own perceived self-interest, but it is constitutionally capable of bending over backwards to make any arrangement fit; history shows that the Danish Constitution is evolving very similar to the British tradition, not really bound by any single legal text. Under Danish constitutional law, The Faroes and the Faroese people can become a sovereign state and an independent nation. The Danish political bodies, as demonstrated, have got much room to manoeuvre. This includes, for political reasons, the ability to frustrate the Faroese with terms and conditions for secession or other arrangements. Regrettably, however, Danish conceptualistic jurisprudence may obscure available options.

Faroese Constitutional Law is very ancient, arguably even older than the Danish tradition. The Faroese tradition also shares characteristics with constitutional traditions of common law countries, with ever-developing conventions governed by important events and documents, though no one single document or precedent rules supreme.

---

32   *Supra* note 21.

In the end, it all boils down to the question the diplomat posed: "What do you want, and what does Denmark have to say about that?" Adding, perhaps: "And what do other states say?"

These questions will have changing answers from time to time in the Land of Maybe.

Appendix

A Concise Legal History of The Faroes

Ca. 600 AD	Celtic monks visit The Faroes, possibly some settlements.
Ca. 800 (probably earlier)	Norse settlers inhabit The Faroes. The settlers establish courts of law around the islands and a traditional parliament, a Thing, with legislative and judicial functions.
Ca. 1000	The Faroese assembly, the Thing, receives Christianity as the official religion.
1035	The King of Norway claims supremacy over the Faroes, assigning them as a fief to a local strongman.
Ca. 1270	The Faroese accept Norwegian overrule. Earlier that century the other Norse settlements out west did the same, among them Iceland, Greenland, Shetland, Orkney and Man. The Norwegian King promises to respect local autonomy, maintain trading links, and grants representatives from western lands seats at his Council.
1298	The Sheep Brief, a codification of Faroese law differing from general Norwegian law, gains the King's assent.
1380	The Danish and Norwegian crowns are united through marriage.
Ca. 1400	The Law Thing enacts laws on compensation to members of the Thing and on the keeping of dogs, examples of ongoing legislative activity.
1450	The Treaty of Bergen formalises the Union between Norway and Denmark.
1469	Orkney and Shetland, to which the Faroese were very close, are ceded to Scotland by the King as collateral for his daughter's dowry, never to be successfully redeemed. Control over other Norse lands, like the Hebrides and Isle of Man, was lost earlier.
1538	The Reformation, change of allegiance from the Catholic Church to the Evangelical Lutheran Church, implemented on the King's orders. The Crown gains the Church estates, half the land in The Faroes. The independent See of Faroe is abolished.

1814	In the Treaty of Kiel, The Danish-Norwegian King relinquishes his title to Norway to the King of Sweden, following the Danish defeat in the Napoleonic Wars. The Danish King retains The Faroes, Greenland, and Iceland.
1816	The Faroese Parliament, the Law Thing, is dissolved and a Danish Governor installed, the same goes for the All Thing of Iceland.
1841	The All Thing in Iceland is reconvened.
1848	Following war and unrest, the King reluctantly calls a Constitutional Convention, elected to draft a Constitution for Denmark. A former Governor, appointed by the King, represents The Faroes. The five elected representatives of Iceland demand their own constitution.
1849	The Basic Law, the written Constitution of Denmark, is enacted. The Basic Law is not promulgated in the duchies south of Denmark, where the Danish King reigns as sovereign Duke, even though the duchy of Schleswig is partly inhabited by Danes.
1850	Without consultation, the Danes promulgate the Basic Law in Faroe. The Faroese lack a political body to respond to this unilateral act.
1851	The Icelandic at a general convention reject the Basic Law as applicable to Iceland. A long constitutional stand-off ensues.
1852	The Law Thing is reconvened as a provincial council with limited powers.
1863	The Basic Law is extended to Schleswig, ethnic Germans revolt, helped by Prussia and Austria. King of Denmark looses all the duchies, including Danish-speaking parts.
1871 and 1874	The Danish King and his Government recognise the special status of Iceland and promulgate a special constitution for Iceland.
1918	Iceland is recognised as a sovereign Kingdom, with the Danish King also made King of Iceland, in a Union with Denmark. Iceland has formal right to secession after 25 years.

1923   A new Law Thing Act provides a new internal constitution for The
               Faroes, increasing the powers of the Law Thing. The Governor remains
               speaker, though he loses his vote.

1928   The Executive Committee of the Law Thing is created to assume execu-
               tive powers from the Governor.

1933   The Permanent Court of International Justice in a controversy between
               Norway and Denmark deems Eastern Greenland rightly to be part of
               the Danish Realm. The Court, however, states that before the Treaty of
               Kiel, Greenland, Faroe, and Iceland were part of Norway.

1940   Nazi-Germany occupies Denmark without struggle. Shortly after,
               British forces occupy The Faroes. Allied forces also occupy Iceland and
               Greenland.

1940   With British assent, the Law Thing and the Danish Governor agree on
               an Interim Constitution for Faroe. The legislative powers of the Faroese
               Parliament are increased, as is the Executive Committee's part in the
               executive powers. An Appeal Court is established. The Faroese language
               gains official status. During the War, the Faroese deal directly with the
               British.

1941   The British Government recognises the Faroese Flag.

1945   After the end of the Second World War, the Danish Government recog-
               nises the Faroese Interim Constitution and Faroese right of self-deter-
               mination.

1946   A referendum is called to choose between a new arrangement of limited
               autonomy and full independence from Denmark. A majority favours
               independence. Much turmoil ensues; unionist point to a number dis-
               carded "no-votes"; Danes call secession "illegal". The King dissolves the
               Law Thing and calls for newer election to the Law Thing; the result is
               victory for the Unionist side.

1947   The Law Thing authorizes negotiations with the Danish Government on
               a new constitutional arrangement, stressing that this is an agreement to
               be made between the two parties.

1948   The Law Thing and the Danish Folk Thing enact The Home Rule
               Compact. This enactment of both Parliaments provides for the constitu-

tional arrangement between Faroe and Denmark, allowing the Faroese to assume legislative and administrative powers over most policy areas.

1972   The Law Thing unanimously votes to remain outside the EEC, later EU.

1974   A new Governing Coalition without the Unionist Party sets out to transfer control over many policy areas from the Danish Government in accordance with the Home Rule Compact.

1977   Faroese Exclusive Economic Zone is extended to 200 nautical miles. This marks a high point in Faroese pursuit of control over fishing resources. Other accomplishments include control over the negotiations of international fisheries agreements.

1988   The system of ad hoc subsidies from the Danish Government is replaced by an annual block grant, marking the end of Danish day-to-day participation in governing The Faroes.

1992   Legislative powers over the sub-soil resources are transferred to the Faroese Government, making possible oil revenues subject to Faroese control.

1992   The biggest economic depression in The Faroes since the 1950's takes hold, caused by failing fish stocks and economic mismanagement, the down-turn leads to fall in population, widespread commercial collapse, including the bankruptcies of both major banks. As Danish Government refuses to bail out the banks, Faroese Government becomes heavily indebted.

1994   A new Faroese Constitution, the Faroese Act on Governing, creates a new framework for the Faroese Government, which has expanded significantly during the Home Rule period.

1998   Following much resentment over constitutional and economic arrangements, a vast majority of returned members of the Law Thing promise changes. A governing coalition with a large majority sets out to establish The Faroes as a sovereign state based on the model used by Denmark and Iceland in 1918.

2000   The Danish Government refuses to accept the Faroese Government position, claiming a right to self-determination as a people under international law, including a right to a transition period in which the block grant was to be reduced, and a right to third party monitoring of the negotiations. Instead, the Danes offer a four-year reduction in the event of secession and refuse an arrangement of free association.

2000   The Faroese Government appeals directly to the UN, which refers to Denmark's position. After a few rounds the negotiations break down.

2002   The Faroes are admitted as an Associate Member of IMO. This follows further transfers of powers to Faroese control. This marks the first time The Faroes achieve membership of a UN organization.

2002   The independence minded governing coalition retains its majority at the polls but soon falls apart due to internal strife.

2004   The election strengthens the independence wing, but a new coalition is formed, seeking continued development of self-government within the association to Denmark.

3 – Greenland under ·Chapter XI of the United Nations Charter

A Continuing International Law Dispute

Gudmundur Alfredsson[1]

Introduction

When a subordinated colony is incorporated by a metropolitan State and when that State seeks to obtain approval from the United Nations while overlooking substantive and procedural UN guarantees of Chapter XI of the UN Charter and of fair play, there is good reason to call for caution. A former colony, which has been incorporated by an administering power, must have a continuing right to opt for modification or even fundamental change in its international status under these same UN rules, concerning full information about the choices and full participation in the determination process, unless and until they have been scrupulously observed.

---

[1] This article draws in part on the author's doctoral dissertation entitled *Greenland and the Right to External Self-Determination* (for the S.J.D.-degree, Harvard Law School, 1982) and his contribution to the International Law and Constitutional Law Working Group of Greenland's Self-Governance Commission, established by the Home Rule Government, under the chairmanship of Johan Lund Olsen, in Working Paper on Basic Choices under International Law of 2002 which is reproduced on the Commission's website at "www.namminersorneq.gl". See also the author's articles entitled "Greenland and the Law of Political Decolonization" in *German Yearbook of International Law*, vol. 25, 1982, pp. 290-308; "Greenland" in *Encyclopedia of Public International Law*, edited by Rudolf Bernhardt, Amsterdam: North Holland, published with the Max Planck Institute, vol. 2, 1995, pp. 623-625; "The Faroese People as a Subject of Public International Law" in the Faroese Law Review, vol. 1, no. 1, 2001, pp. 45-57; and "The Greenlanders and their Human Rights Choices" in *Human Rights and Criminal Justice for the Downtrodden, Essays in Honour of Asbjörn Eide*, edited by Morten Bergsmo, Martinus Nijhoff Publishers, 2003, pp. 453-459. The author is an Icelandic lawyer, now Director of the Raoul Wallenberg Institute of Human Rights and Humanitarian Law and Professor at the Law Faculty of Lund University in Sweden.

Sjúrður Skaale (ed.), The Right To National Self-Determination, 49-93.
© 2004 Koninklijke Brill NV. Printed in the Netherlands.

By Resolution 849 (IX) of 22 November 1954, the UN General Assembly approved the removal of Greenland from the list of non-self-governing territories and its incorporation into Denmark. Integration along with independence and free association was, and is, an accepted option when peoples exercise the right of self-determination in an external sense (see below). This chapter is concerned with the decolonization process as it affected the legal status of Greenland. It is examined, with reference to international law of that time and the facts as they were known and presented by the contemporaries, whether the integration was lawfully brought about and which options the Greenlanders still possess.

In 1953-54, the case of Greenland was one of the first integration acts with which the United Nations dealt in the decolonization process. Over a hundred former colonies have exercised the right of self-determination in modern times, practically all of them by opting for statehood and independence. On a few occasions, at least for the time being, the United Nations has succumbed to unilateral withdrawal of colonies from the list of non-self-governing territories by administering powers, following acts of supposed integration.[2]

Events Preceding Integration[3]

Developments in Denmark and Greenland

With Denmark under German occupation and with United States presence in Greenland during much of World War Two, new winds started blowing which led to Greenlandic requests for self-government. These were directed to and discussed in the Standing Committee on Greenland in the Danish Parliament. Already in its 1946 deliberations with a Greenlandic delegation, the Committee endorsed the request for admission of regular Greenlandic members, albeit with the reservation that their participation was only necessary when special needs or occasions would arise and not worth annual journeys to Denmark. A proposal for increased equality was favorably received, albeit somewhat half-heartedly, after the Committee had come to this enlightening conclusion:

> "The delegation's request for increased equality between Danes and Greenlanders in
> Greenland is not an expression of a wish for the introduction of Danish legislation

---

2   Comparative reference can be made to diverse, past and/or current decolonization practices by France, Italy, the Netherlands, Portugal, Spain, the United Kingdom and the United States. See also James Crawford, The Creation of States in International Law, Oxford: Clarendon, 1979, pp. 431-434.

3   For additional research and sources of information, some of those referring to parallel or similar developments in the Faroe Islands, see other presentations and the book that is published simultaneously in Danish, "*Kilder til Færøernes og Grønlands historie*" ("Sources to the History of the Faroe Islands and Greenland") with sources collected by Maria Amalia Heinesen and Hallbera West.

for the Greenlandic population – everybody recognizes that this would not generally correspond to Greenlandic interests – but an expression of the opinion that the
Danes, in a series of different practical domains, have privileges which cannot be
considered fair from a Greenlandic point of view."[4]

The Danish Prime Minister, Hans Hedtoft, with the purpose of strengthening the ties
between the two countries, suggested in 1948 that Danish private capital should be
employed in the development of the Greenlandic economy. During a subsequent visit to
Greenland, in an address to the provincial councils, he asserted a Danish desire to retain
the sovereignty over Greenland and asked whether the Greenlanders wanted to send a representative to Parliament. The councils replied that the time was not ripe for such a decision and repeated the wish for representation in the Standing Parliamentary Committee.
In 1949, the provincial councils agreed to keep open the possibility of later negotiations
concerning Greenlandic representation in Parliament.[5]

Accordingly, the special commission observed in its 1950 report that "the question of
parliamentary representation was not yet actual", but it nevertheless recommended that it
would be:

> "... very desirable if the constitutional commission would study the inclusion in its
> proposal of a paragraph which grants the general legislature competence to regulate
> the constitutional status of Greenland. This is all the more desirable because on the
> whole it seems correct that the constitution mentions Greenland and provides the
> fundamental basis for the status of this country within the State."[6]

Apparently more far-reaching than the 1948 and 1949 resolutions of the provincial councils, this conclusion was signed by representatives of both sides. Extensive legislation about
Greenlandic affairs, enacted around 1950 in continuation of the special commission's work,
accommodated some of the earlier Greenlandic requests and paved the road for the integration steps which followed.[7]

---

4   *Betaenkning afgivet den 12. juni 1946 af Rigsdagens Grönlandsudvalg i Forening med en af de grön-
     landske Landsraad valgt Delegation og Representanter for Grönlands Styrelse*, Copenhagen: J.H.
     Schultz, 1946. The quotation is from p. 18. As an example of the privileges, to which there
     is a reference, was access to merchandise, including alcoholic beverages.

5   Axel Kjaer Sörensen, *"Ophaevelsen af Grönlands kolonistatus – et gršnlandsk krav"* in Jyske
     Samlinger – Ny Raekke, vol. XII, no. 1-2, 1977, pp. 166-174; and *De forenede grönlandske
     landsraads Forhandlinger*, Copenhagen, 1948, pp. 76-79.

6   *Grönlandskommissionens Betaenkning, vol. II (politiske og administrative forhold, retsplejen)*,
     Copenhagen, 1950, p. 36.

7   Legislative acts of this period saw the separation of administration from trade and judicial
     functions, the removal of church authority over the education system, the abolition of
     quarantine, and the loosening of the trade monopoly.

In a speech in the Provincial Council in 1951, a newly elected member, Auge Lynge, expressed in strong terms the desire to achieve equal status with other Danish citizens and to obtain representation in Parliament. The Council did not adopt a resolution on the issue, and it does not appear to what degree other Council members supported his suggestion. In meetings of the Standing Parliamentary Committee, held in February and March 1952, Lynge reiterated these wishes, but the formal step taken by the two-member Greenlandic delegation was more non-committal: they inquired about the eventual status of Greenland in the new Constitution and about representation in Parliament. The two questions were placed and treated separately since termination of the colonial status was not considered an automatic consequence of parliamentary representation.[8]

It was thus on the basis of inquiries made by Greenlandic delegates, seemingly reflecting their personal views concerning Greenland's constitutional future, that the Standing Parliamentary Committee submitted the matter to the Prime Minister. Even though the Minister still seemed to have doubts about Greenland's support, he asked the constitutional commission to draft exact proposals for Greenland's integration, including parliamentary representation, even though no extensive debates had been held or formal requests made to that effect by the Greenlandic political bodies.[9]

A sub-committee of the constitutional commission submitted in June 1952 proposals on Greenland's constitutional status, prepared by Professors Poul Andersen and Alf Ross.[10] These were forwarded to the Provincial Council by the Prime Minister on 13 August 1952 and read, as far as integration was concerned:

> "The provisions of this Constitution apply to all parts of the Danish State. Greenland shall in the future, as a consequence hereof, be represented in Parliament."[11]

This draft proposal was on the agenda of the Provincial Council during its 1952 autumn meeting. The Danish Governor, chairing the Council, introduced the item late in the afternoon of 8 September and urged a quick conclusion:

> "(I) call attention to the fact that, as it is desired to accelerate the work of the constitutional commission as much as possible, the Prime Minister has informed me on behalf of the Danish Government that he would appreciate an indication of the atti-

---

8   Sörensen, *supra* note 5, pp. 179-185.

9   *Betaenkning afgivet af forfatningskommissionen af 1946*, Copenhagen: J.H. Schultz, 1953, pp. 84-86.

10   Poul Andersen and Alf Ross, »*Responsum vedrørende Grönlands og Faeröernes statsretlige stilling*" in Betaenkning, *supra* note 9, pp. 84-85. The opinion was dated 17 June 1952, but printed "with later additions".

11   Letter, dated 13 August 1952, from the Prime Minister to the Chairman of the Provincial Council in Betaenkning, *supra* note 9, pp. 89-90.

tude of the Provincial Council to the proposal submitted by the Danish Government at the Council's earliest convenience."[12]

Following introductory speeches by the Governor and Auge Lynge and a brief debate, the Council, on the Chairman's recommendation, went into a closed session. The reply was delivered early in the afternoon of 9 September 1952:

> "(T)he Provincial Council of Greenland has unanimously accepted the proposal sub-
> mitted for a new constitutional provision according to which the Constitution of the
> State of Denmark will comprise Greenland and according to which Greenland will
> be represented in Denmark's Parliament…. The Provincial Council is aware that
> the changing governments and Parliament have up to this time always taken special
> Greenlandic circumstances into consideration and counts on that this practice will
> also be continued in the future passing of statutes and decrees."[13]

It was, however, not until 29 January 1953 that the constitutional commission, which had no Greenlandic members, submitted its final draft for a new Constitution.[14] Neither changes in the wording of provisions applicable to Greenland nor the new Constitution as a whole were discussed in the Provincial Council. A referendum about the new Constitution, held in Denmark in May 1953 in accordance with the 1915 Constitution, was not extended to Greenland.

The new Constitution entered into force on 5 June 1953. Its Article 1 reads: "This Constitution applies to all parts of the Danish State," thus omitting a direct reference to Greenland. Article 28 provided for two Greenlandic members of Parliament, out of a maximum of 179.[15] The first parliamentary elections in Greenland took place in August 1953.

The 1953 changes in Greenland's status, as far as Danish constitutional law was concerned, were nothing less than fundamental. The Greenlanders were from then on to enjoy the same rights and assume the same duties as citizens of metropolitan Denmark. The colonial status was terminated, integration was accompanied by representation in Parliament, separation of powers was instituted, and constitutional protection of civil rights established.[16]

---

12 Betaenkning, *supra* note 9, p. 93. For an English translation provided by the Danish Government, see UN document A/AC.35/L.155, Annex III, p. 2.

13 Betaenkning, *supra* note 8, p. 95. For an English translation provided by the Danish Government, see UN document A/AC.35/L.155, Annex III, p. 5.

14 Betaenkning, *supra* note 9, p. 13.

15 For an English translation provided by the Danish Government of the relevant constitutional provisions, see UN document A/AC.35/L.155, Annex II, pp. 1-5.

16 Paul Andersen, *Dansk Statsforfatningsret*, Copenhagen: Gyldendal, 1954, pp. 93-94; and Max Sörensen, *Statsforfatningsret*, Copenhagen: Juristforbundets Forlag, 1969, pp. 44-45.

Participants in the process and later observers have confirmed that the integration of Greenland was brought about as a result of a Danish initiative and advocacy. In its 1948 report on Greenland as a non-self-governing territory, the Danish Government informed the United Nations that:

> "(I)t is the intention of the Danish Government to inquire during 1948-1949 into the question of establishing Greenland as a part of Denmark on an equal footing with the rest of the Kingdom."[17]

A 1948 interview with Eske Brun, a high-ranking Danish official in the Greenland administration, reported that the aim of Danish involvement in Greenland was to make the island a Danish province.[18] It was, however, the Prime Minister himself who made the inquiry about Greenland's desire to be represented in the Danish Parliament in his address to the provincial councils in August 1948. In a speech later that same year, Hans Hedtoft made an emotional appeal, very demonstrative for the motivations and attitudes involved, for continued Danish sovereignty:

> "Denmark is a small country and we have had problems in holding firmly onto the possessions which we have had in the course of history. But one, Greenland, we still have left. I believe we can without shame look back to the work our countrymen have till today carried out in our northern possession. From Hans Egede through Knud Rasmussen to modern Pearyland expeditions, Denmark has exercised an influence characterized by love for the country, for the population, and for the magnificent nature. Understanding officials and colonizers have functioned with honour and common sense. First and foremost, we have not based our work on exploitation, but we have considered it as our moral duty to protect, defend and elevate the primitive people whose development was entrusted to us. It will be difficult for Denmark to defend this large possession militarily, but all of us have a moral commitment to show the other nations of the world through our example how we in a humane manner know how to lead the Greenlanders from the more primitive stand up to the level on which we find ourselves. This is vis-a-vis the world our title to possess Greenland. The connection between the past, present and future shall not be broken. Greenland has made Denmark larger, has been the playground for Danish daring and initiatives, and has internationalized Danish science. Denmark on her side has explored the past of the country, given the Greenlanders their present and provided the right framework for their long term future as we have colonized, christianized and civilized the people."

---

17   Non-Self-Governing Territories. Summaries and analyses of information transmitted to the Secretary-General during 1948 (Lake Success: United Nations, 1949, p. 50.

18   Sörensen , *supra* note 5, p. 172.

After emphasizing "Danish-Greenlandic cooperation", the Prime Minister continued:

> "We Danes have reason to expect that the Greenlanders wish to form their future together with us under the Danish flag and we have a duty to exercise our influence so that the future can become as bright and happy as possible."[19]

This was in 1948. In 1952 or four years later, the same Prime Minister, Hans Hedtoft, was still hammering away at the Danish desire for integration:

> "We ought to aim at unmistakable determining in our new Constitution that Greenland is an inseparable part of the Danish State. It will be of interest for us in the parliamentary committee and for the members of the constitutional commission to know whether this is also the wish of the Greenlandic representatives. I will consider it as an important step if we, with Greenland's support, can have permission to establish this. I believe that all Danes would be happy about such a decision and it is my impression that the Greenlandic people share this wish, but this we would like to have confirmed. We have now realized, concerning Greenland's wish for representation in the parliamentary rule, the Greenlanders' own wish for representatives in the parliamentary committee, but I now understand that the members of the Provincial Council entertain a wish to have a position established which resembles the status of the Faroe Islands, with direct representation in Parliament. I believe that we will all follow the wish which the Provincial Council would have. Personally, I like to see Greenlandic representatives in Parliament. It gives, as it were, a stronger anchorage for Greenland in the Danish State. It will be of tremendous value if Denmark can say to the surrounding world that the Greenlandic people has representatives who can participate in the parliamentary work on completely equal footing with the representatives of the population in Denmark."[20]

These remarks confirmed that the Greenlanders had not yet approved the planned constitutional changes.

While Greenlandic requests for increased self-government in the years after World War Two may have prompted talks about revising the colonial administration, the appearance and speedy implementation of the integration idea was undoubtedly caused by a desire to have Greenland removed from the UN list of non-self-governing territories.[21] Hermod Lannung, a long-time and influential member of the Danish delegation to the General

---

19 Hans Hedtoft, *Grönlands fremtid*, Copenhagen: Det Grönlandske Selskabs Aarsskrift, 1949, pp. 39-40.

20 Sörensen, *supra* note 5, p. 184-185.

21 Worries about the further expansion of American interests in Greenland were another possible reason for the integration drive, see Sörensen, *supra* note 5, pp. 169-170, 173 and 189.

Assembly, said in a 1947 interview that his work at the United Nations had strengthened his conviction that the Greenlanders, as soon as circumstances allowed, should achieve parliamentary representation "so that Greenland can be lifted up from its position as a colony to that of an equal part of the Danish State". In a 1948 speech, Lannung argued that the political situation in the United Nations threatened Danish sovereignty over Greenland.[22]

In a post-integration article, Lannung described how he had reported to the United Nations that:

> "we Danes had considered it a responsibility, and also a privilege, to lead the people of Greenland forward to full equality and participation in the government of the common fatherland."[23]

The verb "lead" deserves underlining; the lack of other constitutional alternatives is worth remembering.

Max Sörensen and Niels Haagerup have pointed out that "it was considered as somewhat degrading to have to account for the administration to others" and that unforeseeable changes in UN policies on decolonization constituted "an additional consideration" for the Danish move.[24]

In a study on the Greenland case in the United Nations, Finn Petersen has clearly shown that UN supervision played a major role in shaping Danish policy concerning Greenland's status and that plans for seeking later integration had surfaced within the administration as early as 1946. In addition to early preparations for integration, Petersen has described a session in the Foreign Ministry where the Danish UN delegation received direct instructions to start preparing for the debates about Greenland's incorporation. This meeting took place on 27 August 1952, before the Provincial Council had approved the proposal from the constitutional commission. Despite Petersen's disclosure of the origin and purpose of the integration act, he nevertheless contended that:

> "the equal status was a natural step in the development of the Greenlandic society. This shows that in my opinion there was no sign of the Danish Government manipulating the Greenlandic Provincial Council to an unanimous acceptance and thus avoiding a referendum.... ."[25]

---

22   Sörensen , *supra* note 5, pp. 170-172.

23   Hermod Lannung, "Grønlandssagen in FN" in Grønland 1955, p. 146. See also UN document A/C.4/SR.427, p. 204.

24   Max Sörensen and Niels J. Haagerup, *Denmark and the United Nations*, New York: Manhattan Publishing Company, prepared for the Carnegie Endowment for International Peace as part of the series of National Studies on International Organizations, 1956, p. 113.

25   Finn Petersen, *Grönlandssagens behandling i FN 1946-54*, Odense: Odense Universitetsforlag, 1975, pp. 14-18, 24-28 and 93, note 1. The quotation is from p. 8.

The chronological order and nature of events and the above-listed comments serve to show that integration would not have taken place at this time if it had not been proposed and pushed through by Danish authorities. Max Sörensen and Haagerup called it:

> "an interesting case in which United Nations supervision of the administration of colonial territories has accelerated a political development that might have occurred anyhow, but that would quite certainly have been delayed if the question had remained a purely Danish concern."[26]

These developments would, indeed, constitute quite an interesting case of adverse effects of anti-colonial efforts at the United Nations if a premature but supposedly final integration act, anchored in the decolonization process, were to lead to a subsequent denial of the right to self-determination.

Contemporary Danish positions on colonial issues at the United Nations may further explain the actions taken at home. Denmark regularly sided with the administering powers in the various UN fora. Max Sörensen acknowledged that this was due to Danish interests in Greenland:

> "Denmark's obligation under the Charter in connection with the administration of Greenland … has considerably influenced the Danish attitude toward the innumerable questions that have arisen concerning United Nations supervision of non-self-governing territories. Together with other colonial powers, Denmark has tried to counteract the prevailing tendency to extend the General Assembly's authority in this field."[27]

Denmark repeatedly opposed proposals to establish a special body to examine information from the administering powers of the non-self-governing territories, to include human rights information in Article 73e reports, to institute visiting missions, and to allow territory representatives to participate in meetings of a supervisory committee. During debates in the General Assembly on the lists of factors, Denmark placed great emphasis on the option of integration with an administering power, particularly with a unitary State, as one of the possible results of political decolonization. In taking this position, according to Max Sörensen and Haagerup, there was "no doubt that the Danish delegation had Greenland in mind, and that self-interest was therefore its leading motive."[28]

On the other hand, Denmark played a certain balancing act on decolonization issues, perhaps in order not to alienate the anti-colonial bloc in the United Nations. While uphold-

---

26   Max Sörensen and Haagerup, *supra* note 24, p. 113.

27   Max Sörensen and Haagerup, *supra* note 24, p. 111.

28   Max Sörensen and Haagerup, *supra* note 24, p. 111-113 and 232. The quotation is from p. 113. See also S. Hasan Ahmad, *The United Nations and the Colonies, Bombay*: Asia Publishing House, 1975, pp. 55-56 and 77-78; Petersen, *supra* note 25, pp. 12-13 and 16-18; and UN documents A/C.4/L.127, pp. 1-4 and A/AC.35/SR.103, p. 13.

ing a restrictive view on the competence of the General Assembly, it complied with resolutions passed, for example by including constitutional information in the annual reports.[29] Denmark also participated actively in debates and voting, for example on the termination of Greenland's non-self-governing status, even if the information submitted was sometimes misleading or incomplete and even when it considered the issues concerned to fall outside the scope of UN competence.

International Developments

In a letter of 3 September 1953, the Danish Government informed the UN Secretary General about the termination of Greenland's status as a non-self-governing territory and unilaterally announced the cessation of transmission of information as required by Article 73e of the Charter:

> "(O)n 5 June 1953, a constitutional amendment was adopted, according to which Greenland has now become an integral part of the Danish realm with rights corresponding to those of other parts of Denmark. Its population has obtained in Parliament an equal footing with the rest of the Danish population. In the light of this change in the constitutional position and status of Greenland and its inhabitants, the Danish Government regard their responsibilities according to Chapter XI of the Charter as terminated and have therefore decided to bring the submission of information pursuant to Article 73e to an end."[30]

Attached to the letter in three annexes were an explanatory memorandum, excerpts from the new Constitution, and excerpts from the 1952 minutes of the Provincial Council.[31] Furthermore, during the General Assembly session in 1954, the Danish delegation distributed three publications to members of the Fourth Committee: "Report on Greenland 1954" from the Prime Minister's Greenland Department; "Greenland" from the Ministry of Foreign Affairs; and "A booklet in Danish and Eskimo on the objectives and activities of the United Nations which was being used in study circles and discussion groups in Greenland."[32] Denmark also submitted in 1954 the annual report on Greenland as a non-self-governing territory for the year 1953.[33]

---

29 Denmark took credit for the transmission of constitutional information, see Lannung's remarks in the Fourth Committee of the General Assembly, in UN document A/C.4/SR. 324, p. 45.

30 UN document A/AC.35/L.155, p. 3.

31 UN document A/AC.35/L. 155, Annexes I-III.

32 UN document A/AC.4/SR.423, p. 182.

33 Non-Self-Governing Territories. Summaries and analyses of information transmitted to the Secretary-General during 1954 (New York: United Nations, 1955, pp. 268-277.

The aim of this documentation, according to Finn Petersen and apparent enough in the Danish communication and other official explanations to the UN, was to demonstrate as clearly as possible that the steps taken had Greenlandic approval, that Denmark had never really treated Greenland as a colony and certainly never financially exploited the territory but rather reinvested profits for the benefit of the local population, and that Denmark had acted in accordance with her obligations under the UN Charter. Among the concerns expressed in official Danish circles during the drafting process were the lack of a referendum, the absence of the inhabitants of North and East Greenland from full partnership in the new constitutional status, and the presence of American military bases in the territory. An effort was made to keep these latter issues out of the UN debate.[34]

Denmark's communication formally maintained the unilateral right of an administering power to remove a colony from the list of non-self-governing territories. This attitude was in line with the traditional view of the colonial powers at the time; only the constitutional relationship between the parties counted and the United Nations was simply to take notice of such internal political developments. Denmark had made her position clear on this issue of UN competence on several earlier occasions. Hermod Lannung re-stated it in a 1953 Fourth Committee meeting:

> "(The Danish delegation) considered that the State responsible for the administration of a territory had the right to determine the constitutional status of the territory placed under its sovereignty. None of the provisions of Chapter XI could be interpreted as modifying that principle in any way whatever. Denmark had always been ready to transmit to the United Nations information concerning not only the economic, social and educational situation in the territory it administered, but also the political situation and the development of the constitutional status in the territory. Nevertheless it had never considered that the United Nations was thereby empowered to review or revise any action which had been taken by the constitutional bodies of Denmark."[35]

This view was reiterated during the 1954 debates at the United Nations about the communication. A Danish representative declared in the Committee of Information that his delegation "took exception to implications that the Committee was competent to examine information of political nature."[36] Despite the objections, Denmark nevertheless actively cooperated in the UN discussion of its communication and cast its vote in all instances. It was apparently willing to take advantage of a positive UN vote on its unilateral termination of Greenland's non-self-governing status, but at the same time ready to ignore a negative conclusion.

---

34   Petersen, *supra* note 25, pp. 31-38.
35   UN document A/AC.4/SR.324, pp. 45-46.
36   UN document A/AC.35/SR.104, p. 7.

The So-called Integration

General Assembly Resolution 849 (IX)

The Danish communication about ending the listing of Greenland as a non-self-governing territory was discussed and approved by three UN bodies: the Committee on Information from Non-Self-Governing Territories, the Fourth Committee and a plenary meeting of the General Assembly. Two Greenlandic representatives, appointed by the Provincial Council, were attached to the Danish delegation and addressed both the Committee on Information[37] and the Fourth Committee.[38]

Several questions were directed towards the Danish delegation during the debates, mainly by non-European States. The inquiries concerned the extent to which the Danish Government had taken into account the lists of factors or decolonization guidelines as adopted by the General Assembly, how the Greenlanders had expressed their free will, the constitutional powers of the Provincial Council before and after 1953, the freedom of option, the non-representation of North and East Greenland, the Greenlanders' right to later modify their status, the economic situation, cheap and rapid communications, ethnic and cultural differences, and higher education opportunities for the Greenlanders.[39] Either the questioners were not very insistent or Danish replies were satisfactory on most or all points because, in the end, the General Assembly approved the Danish action. The Danish Government also received much praise from both fellow administering countries and traditional anti-colonial States.

A resolution of the Committee on Information, reacting favorably to the Danish communication, was endorsed unanimously.[40] The final resolution, approved in the Fourth Committee by 34 votes to 4, with 12 abstentions,[41] was adopted by a plenary meeting of the General Assembly on 22 November 1954. The vote was 45 to 1, with 11 abstentions.[42]

A controversial part of the resolution was the last paragraph of the preamble, an amendment proposed by Uruguay in the Fourth Committee. This change, relating to the question of UN competence rather than the immediate issue at hand, was the source of most of the dissenting votes and abstentions.[43]

---

37   UN document A/AC.35/SR.103, pp. 10-11.

38   UN document A/AC.4/SR.429, pp. 213-214.

39   Also summarized by Ahmad, *supra* note 28, p. 307.

40   UN document A/AC.35/SR.104, p. 5.

41   UN documents A/AC.4/SR.432, p. 229 and A/2795, p. 5.

42   UN document A/PV.499, pp. 306-307. Three countries were absent: Haiti, Iceland and Nicaragua.

43   For the results of voting on specific paragraphs and explanations of vote, see UN documents A/PV.498-499.

General Assembly Resolution 849 (IX) reads:

"The General Assembly,

Recalling that by resolution 222(III) of 3 November 1948, the General Assembly, while welcoming any development of self-government in Non-Self-Governing Territories, considers it essential that the United Nations be informed of any change in the constitutional status of any such Territory as a result of which the responsible Government concerned thinks it unnecessary to transmit information in respect of that Territory under Article 73 e of the Charter,

Having received from the Government of Denmark a communication dated 3 September 1953 informing the Secretary-General that, as a result of the constitutional amendment adopted on 5 June 1953, Greenland has become an integral part of the Danish Realm with a constitutional status equal to that of other parts of Denmark and that, as a consequence of this constitutional change, the Danish Government regarded its responsibilities under Chapter XI of the Charter in respect of Greenland as terminated and had, therefore, decided to bring to an end the transmission of information under Article 73 e of the Charter,

Considering that resolution 742 (VIII) adopted by the General Assembly on 27 November 1953 instructs the Committee on Information from Non-Self-Governing Territories to study any documentation transmitted under resolution 222 (III) in the light of the list of factors approved by resolution 742 (VIII) and other relevant considerations that may arise from each concrete case.

Having studied the report prepared by the Committee on Information from Non-Self-Governing Territories during its session of 1954 on the question of the cessation of the transmission of information on Greenland and presented to the General Assembly in conformity with paragraph 2 of resolution 448 (V) of 12 December 1950,

Having examined the communication of the Government of Denmark in the light of the basic principles and objectives embodied in Chapter XI of the Charter, the criteria established by the list of factors, and of all the other elements of judgement pertinent to the issue,

Bearing in mind the competence of the General Assembly to decide whether a Non-Self-Governing Territory has or has not attained a full measure of self-government as referred to in Chapter XI of the Charter,

1. Takes note of the conclusions set forth by the Committee Information from Non-Self-Governing Territories in its resolution;

2. Takes note of the opinion of the Government of Denmark that due to the new constitutional status of Greenland the Government of Denmark regards its "responsibilities according to Chapter XI of the Charter as terminated" and that consequently the transmission of information under Article 73 e of the Charter in respect of Greenland should be brought to an end;

3. Commends the action of the Member State concerned in including in its delegation to the General Assembly representatives elected by the National Council of Greenland or the purpose of furnishing information on constitutional changes in Greenland;

4. Takes note that when deciding on their new constitutional status, through duly elected representatives the people of Greenland have freely exercised their right to self-determination;

5. Expresses the opinion that, from the documentation and the explanations provided, Greenland freely decided on its integration within the Kingdom of Denmark on an equal constitutional and administrative basis with the other parts of Denmark;

6. Notes with satisfaction the achievement of self-government by the people of Greenland;

7. Considers that due to these circumstances the Declaration regarding Non-Self-Governing Territories with the provisions established under it in Chapter XI of the Charter can no longer be applied to Greenland;

8. Considers it appropriate that the transmission of information in respect to Greenland under Article 73e of the Charter should now cease."

The Legal Effect of General Assembly Resolution 849 (IX)

Charter provisions about the competence of the General Assembly are centred around the word "recommend". As a rule, such recommendations "lack sanction in the juridical sense". With respect to decisions concerning the administration and execution of mainly internal UN affairs, for example budget matters and the activities of certain subsidiary organs, the binding character of recommendations is now generally accepted.[44]

---

44   Jorge Castaneda, *Legal Effects of United Nations Resolutions*, New York: Columbia University Press, 1969, pp. 11 and 19-21.

Due to the evolutionary and often repetitive character of GA resolutions, questions concerning GA decision-making competences continue to arise. One such question relates to the removal of colonies from the UN list of non-self-governing territories. More specifically, a crucial question given the broad and definitive language of GA Resolution 849 (IX), especially operative paragraphs 4 and 5, does the General Assembly have the authority to dispose of particular, concrete cases? Did Resolution 849 (IX) effectively seal Denmark's incorporation of Greenland? Is it binding upon the Greenlanders? Does such a GA resolution, settling a potential or an actual dispute between contending parties, have any *res judicata* effects?

In the Northern Cameroons Case, both parties admitted and the International Court of Justice (ICJ) confirmed, that GA Resolution 1608 (XV) had effectively terminated a trusteeship agreement. The Court, however, pointed out that it had not been necessary "to consider whether the Court has authority to revise or reverse conclusions" of the General Assembly because the applicant had not asked for it.[45] Michael Reisman has correctly called attention to the fact that the Court had not surrendered "a current or future competence to review General Assembly resolutions", even though he found that the case "in terms of operational effects" represented a "step towards finalizing … General Assembly decisions, assuming" that the Assembly was acting within its competence.[46]

The Charter, in Article 85, expressly grants the General Assembly a greater role with respect to trust territories than non-self-governing territories. In this context it is also important to keep in mind, as spelled out by the ICJ in the South West Africa Case, that mandates and trusteeships are based on "an international agreement having the character of a treaty or convention."[47]

In the 1971 Namibia Opinion, the ICJ found that the General Assembly, as a party to such an agreement, had lawfully invoked its unilateral right, as provided for in customary law and later codified in Article 60 of the Vienna Convention on the Law of Treaties, to repudiate the treaty relationship on account of a material breach by South Africa. For this reason, the Court was "unable to appreciate the view that the General Assembly" had "acted unilaterally as party and judge in its own cause." Rather, the Court chose to consider the GA action as an example of those "specific cases" in which the GA could adopt "resolutions which make determinations or have operative design."[48] The Court did thus not share the view of Judge Spender, expressed in his separate opinion in the Northern Cameroons Case, that "all UN functions with regard to trusteeship agreements, including the determination of when the objectives of a trust had been achieved, were vested exclusively in the General Assembly."[49]

---

45   ICJ Reports 1963, pp. 24 and 32-34.

46   W. Michael Reisman, *Nullity and Revision: The Review and Enforcement of International Judgements and Awards*, New Haven: Yale University Press, 1971, pp. 345-346.

47   ICJ reports 1962, p. 330. Reiterated in the Namibia Advisory Opinion, ICJ Reports 1971, p. 47.

48   ICJ Reports 1971, pp. 47-50.

49   ICJ Reports 1963, pp. 76-78.

In another separate opinion in the Northern Cameroons Case, Judge Fitzmaurice argued that the termination of a trust was "inherent in the declared aim" and part of the UN conduct of the trust.[50] Disputable as this argument may be and despite the absence of special non-self-governing agreements, it can likewise be maintained that GA capacity to remove a non-self-governing territory from the UN list of such territories is implied in the supervisory role of the General Assembly and in its competence to determine when a situation of this kind arises. Accordingly, Resolution 849 (IX) could be considered a legally valid termination of Denmark's obligation to submit information and of Greenland's non-self-governing status with the United Nations. The question remains, however, whether the resolution has binding effect beyond the withdrawal of direct UN involvement. Is GA termination of non-self-governing status to be equated with the extinction of an international personality?

General Assembly Resolution 849 (IX), or any other resolution of the same sort, is clearly distinguishable from GA resolutions calling in general for political decolonization and external self-determination and from processing annual reports in a supervisory capacity. It is also markedly different from GA resolutions dealing with the UN regulatory or standard-setting role in matters concerning non-self-governing territories, for example the passing of rules and guidelines about substance and procedure to be followed by the administrative powers.

Instead, a resolution like 849 (IX) really amounts to a quasi-judicial application of Charter provisions and of the rules and guidelines laid down by the General Assembly itself. Be it the termination of a territory's international status, or the settlement of a territorial claim or a border dispute, a GA decision in a concrete case is of a different nature than regulatory resolutions, needing not only knowledge and ascertaining of the law, but a careful and objective examination of the facts and of the presentation of these under rules guaranteeing due process. Is the General Assembly the proper forum for such a determination? And if it nevertheless takes such decisions, is it properly a final instance? Can the decision be challenged and on which grounds?

The General Assembly is a political body, the rough equivalent of national legislatures, or more accurately their little, big brother with much reduced powers. In the late forties, it took a treaty between the victorious superpowers and Italy to grant the Assembly authority, still binding only on the State Parties, to dispose of self-determination claims made by the Italian colonies.[51] As noted before, Denmark favored a similar understanding in 1954 inasmuch as it was not willing to recognize an unfavourable outcome of the GA debate on Greenland's integration.

It is admittedly not always an easy task to determine whether a GA resolution is of a judicial or legislative character. The Charter, however, in situations concerning non-self-

---

50   ICJ Reports 1963, pp. 117-118.

51   Louis B. Sohn, "The Second Year of United Nations Legislation" in American Bar Association Journal, vol. 34, 1948, p. 315; and A. Rigo Sureda, *The Evolution of the Right of Self-Determination*, Leiden: A.W. Sijthoff, 1973, pp. 93-94.

governing territories, places two parties opposite each other, as Articles 73 and 74 distinguish between a metropolitan administering State and a non-self-governing territory. The Charter, reinforced by numerous GA resolutions and subsequent practices of the United Nations and by States, establishes general and specific obligations of administering States towards their colonies with emphasis on the need for protection of the weaker party. For the sake of this protection, the United Nations and in particular the General Assembly have become, not a guardian for juveniles or invalids, but an overseer entrusted with the task of providing a forum for the lawful exercise of the right to external self-determination.

According to Article 92 of the Charter, the ICJ is "the principal judicial organ" of the United Nations. As noted by Reisman, the Court has not surrendered its jurisdiction to review GA decisions on trust and non-self-governing territories.[52] In the Western Sahara Opinion, the Court thus granted that the Assembly has a "measure of discretion with respect to the forms and procedures" by which the right of colonies to self-determination is to be realized, even in certain instances to the point of dispensing "with the requirement of consulting the inhabitants of a given territory", but the Court took upon itself the examination of the basic decolonization principles and of the resolutions bearing specifically on the decolonization of Western Sahara.[53]

After rejecting the conclusions of Judges Fitzmaurice and Spender about "the complete exclusion of the judicial safeguard in cases in which the General Assembly decided upon the fate of trust territories", Judge Bustamente in a dissenting opinion in the Northern Cameroons Case observed that "(t)he judicial guarantee … means the primacy of law over other factors: interests, negligence, abuse or force."[54] Two or three of these factors were present, as will be shown below, and they were probably influential in the GA treatment and resolution of 1954.

The presence of these Bustamente factors and the very structure of the UN system underline the political background and nature of GA Resolution 849 (IX). Therefore, it is difficult to accept that such decisions can have legally binding effect on the parties. It would have been appropriate if the General Assembly in cases involving disputed Charter interpretations – in 1954 there was for example no accepted definition of the expression "full measure of self-government" in Article 73 of the Charter – had asked the International Court for an advisory opinion before passing a supposedly determinative resolution. As the Court advised in the Western Sahara Case:

> "(A)n opinion given by the Court in the present proceedings will furnish the General
> Assembly with elements of a legal character relevant to its further treatment of the
> decolonization of Western Sahara."[55]

---

52   Reisman, *supra* note 46, p. 345.

53   ICJ Reports 1975, p. 36.

54   ICJ Reports 1963, p. 179.

55   ICJ Reports 1975, p. 37.

This role of the Court, as analyzed by Judge Bustamente, relates to the two phases of preventing a "deviation in the application of the law" and correcting a deviation when it occurs.[56]

Scholarly writings reflect the uncertainty caused by the political character of the General Assembly and the evolutionary nature of its resolutions. Inis Claude thus remarked that:

> "the evolution of constitutional relationships within the United Nations system has tended to make the General Assembly the unrivaled principal organ of the entire system."[57]

Louis Sohn observed that:

> "a decision of the General Assembly which applies a principle of the Charter to a particular case is binding because the Charter is binding and the General Assembly 'resolution merely gives effect to, and interprets, the Charter in a specific case,' thus creating a legal obligation."[58]

For another view in evaluating the legal value of a GA resolution in the present context, one can look at Castaneda's statement:

> "(R)esolutions that are not the expression of an agreement among the parties concerned, but that represent rather the will of a majority in a political organ, are inadequate instruments today for settling territorial problems or even for adjusting particular situations. Almost always, these problems entail and reflect a plurality of interests, relatively consolidated, that often give rise to genuine but conflicting rights."

In Castaneda's opinion, determinative resolutions must not:

> "restrict the pre-existing rights of the states or entities to which the resolutions are directed, nor, in the last resort, bring about a change in territorial status, even de facto or provisional, without the consent of the parties concerned."[59]

---

56   ICJ Reports 1963, p. 180.

57   Inis L. Claude, *Swords into Plowshares. The Problems and Progress of International Organization*, New York: Random House, 1971, 4th ed., p. 181.

58   Louis B. Sohn, "The Shaping of International Law" in Georgia Journal of International and Comparative Law, vol. 8, 1978, p. 23.

59   Castaneda, *supra* note 44, pp. 131-133.

This qualification has generally been applied to traditional territorial disputes affecting non-self-governing territories, with the General Assembly calling for negotiations between the parties. Given the international status conferred upon non-self-governing territories, partly through efforts of the same Assembly, an obvious discrepancy arises, if not a contradiction to the very essence of self-determination, if the Assembly could render decisions on the future of colonies but not on territories in dispute between States. Indeed, Castaneda stated that in situations where:

> "there still remain some traces of sovereignty vested in the parties ... the adequate instrument for a solution can only be a resolution that reflects an agreement among the parties and states principally concerned."[60]

Crawford, on the basis of Chapter XI of the UN Charter and GA Resolution 1541 (XV), saw "no termination functions" granted to UN organs. Rather, he found that "non-self-governing status ceases automatically upon the achievement of full self-government". If the administering power and the General Assembly could not agree on what constituted such an achievement, "the situation becomes one for political negotiation."[61]

Another element of disagreement in the scholarly literature relates to an equation between a GA determination as to when a non-self-governing situation arises and when it has been or can be brought to an end. According to Rigo Sureda, GA competence has stretched out to cover "the question whether or not a territory has exercised self-determination or whether or not a territory should exercise it."[62] The Assembly has claimed such competence, for example in Resolution 849 (IX), and passed resolutions adding or dropping territories from the list of non-self-governing territories, but the results of the two types of resolutions can be dramatically different.

The competence to add non-self-governing territories to the list is a necessary prerequisite for carrying out GA functions under Chapter XI. In addition, such resolutions do not render a final determination about the future status of the entities concerned but rather make a series of alternatives available, including the option to integrate with the administering power.

The latter type of GA resolutions about removing territories from the list of non-self-governing territories, unless the parties have agreed to their contents, border on or overlap functions which are of a judicial character. They may carry the implicit and sometimes explicit endorsements of a new constitutional status of the affected entities. In the case of integration with an independent State, this may mean the elimination of future alternatives. Again, without the freely expressed and informed consent of an already advanced non-self-governing territory and its people, case-specific GA resolutions can hardly have any legal effect beyond the termination of UN involvement.

---

60   Castaneda, *supra* note 44, p. 133.
61   Crawford, *supra* note 2, pp. 368-369.
62   Rigo Sureda, *supra* note 51, p. 65.

Challenging General Assembly Resolution 849 (IX)

Even if the General Assembly were to have competence to deliver binding decisions on particular issues, there are ample reasons for doubting the validity of those parts of GA Resolution 849 (IX) which purport to settle matters between Greenland and Denmark. It is generally recognized that an arbitral award, in whole or in part, may under certain conditions be null. A classical author has written that, if an award is deemed null, it "is considered to be wholly lacking in legal effect and existence and to have no effect upon the status of the parties."[63] Article 35 of the Model Rules on Arbitral Procedure, prepared by the International Law Commission, lists excess of powers, corruption among the arbitrators, failure to state the reasons for the award, a serious departure from a fundamental rule of procedure, and the nullity of the compromise as grounds for challenging the validity of an award.[64]

A rehearing of the case, leading to a revision of the decision, is one possible avenue of redress. Article 61 of the Statute of the International Court of Justice spells out the conditions for such an application, and so does Article 38 of the Model Rules:

> "(T)he discovery of some fact of such a nature as to constitute a decisive factor, provided that when the award was rendered that fact was unknown to the tribunal and to the party requesting revision, and that such ignorance was not due to the negligence of the party requesting revision."

The underlying reason for this rule is well explained by a saying traced to Lincoln: "Nothing is settled until it is settled right."[65] It could thus be argued that the arbitrator, in this instance the General Assembly, was unfit to decide the case without knowing all the facts. The "new fact" can involve either "sufficient new evidence or sufficient evidence of fraud to warrant" a reopening.[66]

Under the Charter, the Statute of the International Court of Justice and the Model Rules, the Court would be a proper forum for seeking an annulment or a revision. Greenland's general lack of access to the Court and temporal arguments could, however, constitute barriers on this road. A rehearing could also be sought from the General Assembly, in terms of submitting an application to the tribunal which rendered the award.[67]

---

63   Kenneth S. Carlston, *The Process of International Arbitration*, New York: Columbia University Press, 1946, pp. 221-222.

64   *Yearbook of the International Law Commission*, vol. II, 1958, p. 86.

65   Carlston, *supra* note 63, p. 234.

66   Special Rapporteur Georges Scelle, "Draft Convention on Arbitral Procedure adopted by the Commission at its Fifth Session" in *Yearbook of the International Law Commission*, vol. II, 1958, p. 11; and Durward v. Sandifer, Evidence before International Tribunals, Chicago: The Foundation Press, 1939, p. 284, quoted by Carlston, *supra* note 63, p. 232.

67   Scelle, *supra* note 66, p. 11.

An absolute time limit may not apply to the General Assembly. A still existing tribunal entrusted with a series of cases, according to Sandifer, quoted with approval by Carlston,

> "has jurisdiction to grant a rehearing upon the basis of newly discovered evidence of a decisive character at any time before its final adjournment."[68]

Choosing the General Assembly as a forum would fall in line with its acquired competence to determine when a-non-self-governing situation arises. The Assembly could reverse its earlier decision either by re-listing the territory concerned as non-self-governing or by admitting the territory as a new Member State if, unilaterally or not, independence has been declared. The Assembly may indeed, in the Greenland case, have left the possibility of review open by referring, in operative paragraph 5 of Resolution 849 (IX), to "the documentation and the explanations provided" as the basis for its opinion on integration with Denmark. In addition to the fora mentioned, the parties could agree on a new tribunal.[69]

A number of grounds could justify an annulment or revision of the award contained in GA Resolution 849 (IX), as examined below. Interestingly enough, and this may already illustrate the inherent weaknesses of the resolution, a long list of traditional grounds, based in contemporary law, can be raised in the instant case and some with considerable force, such as fraudulent evidence and essential error.

1. Invalid Compromise

The compromise in this case being Chapter XI of the UN Charter, the Greenlandic people could possibly challenge the validity of Chapter XI and especially the alleged quasi-judicial powers of the General Assembly since the Greenlanders had no part in the Charter's creation or in subsequent practice leading to interpretations of the Charter. The part of this argument relating to the validity of Chapter XI is admittedly a non-starter because the Charter is generally recognized as the highest law of the international community, but the part concerning a challenge to Assembly authority and to its competence with regard to Charter interpretations may indeed have merits.

2. Excess of Jurisdiction

Conflicting views about the legal effect of GA resolutions disposing of particular, concrete issues have already been described. On the one hand, there are plausible arguments against *res judicata* effects of resolutions passed by a political body without a clear mandate. On the other hand, it can be maintained that the General Assembly has passed other such resolutions and that these have apparently been accepted by the international community. The question is certainly intriguing enough to give rise to serious doubts about the validity of those parts of Resolution 849 (IX) which go beyond merely dropping Greenland from the

---

68 Sandifer, *supra* note 66, p. 299; quoted with approval by Carlston, *supra* note 63, p. 225.

69 Carlston, *supra* note 63, p. 223.

list of non-self-governing territories and which affect the future international legal status of Greenland and its people.

3.   Corruption

The rule later embodied in Article 35, paragraph 2, of the above-mentioned Model Rules, was so outlined by Carlston:

> "The parties have a right to a decision of a tribunal free from corruption and manifest and willful partiality. The tribunal should conduct itself in a judicial manner and should not in bad faith violate the principle of impartiality."[70]

While corruption may not be the suitable expression, it is inherent in the decision-making process of a political body like the General Assembly that the factors mentioned by Bustamante may outweigh impartial, judicial considerations. The "arbitrators" are diplomats acting under direct orders from their governments many of which, especially back in 1954 during the very early stages of political decolonization and still with very limited UN membership, had obvious self-interests in frustrating or slowing down the anti-colonial drive for independence.

The Danish integration move in the General Assembly was preceded by a thoroughly planned diplomatic effort which was conceived in the Danish Foreign Ministry at least as early as 1948. Lannung, the leading Danish diplomat on this case, has in addition described the distinctly un-judicial, but typically diplomatic and political conversations and considerations which took place in the conference rooms and behind the scenes during the 1954 GA debate about Greenland's integration.[71]

4.   Minimum Procedural Standards

If the competence of the General Assembly to dispose of particular issues concerning the fate of non-self-governing territories is recognized, that is a competence bordering on a judicial or quasi-judicial function, especially in the context of terminating colonial status with incorporation into the administering power, it must be seen as a minimum requirement that the Assembly adhere to certain basic procedural standards for ensuring a proper and just treatment of the cases. This is not merely a matter of form, but a precondition for trustworthiness and reliability, expected and required in both national and international judicial and arbitral proceedings. Self-determination without consulting the people is not credible.

Louis Sohn referred to this requirement, in the very context of UN decisions, as "the basic principle of all well-balanced legal systems – due process of law."[72] In a situation

---

70   Carlston, *supra* note 63, p. 53.

71   Lannung, *supra* note 23, pp. 142-146.

72   Louis B. Sohn, "Due Process in the United Nations" in American Journal of International Law, vol. 69, 1975, p. 621.

affecting a specific non-self-governing territory, this duty of the General Assembly and the participation and consultation rights of the territory and people concerned are contained by implication in Chapter XI of the Charter where special protection is afforded to one of the parties, that is the weaker party.

5. Representation

One of the fundamental rules of procedure or "one of the most elementary procedural rights is the right of a party to be heard, to present its arguments and proofs."[73] This right was not taken seriously, neither during the earlier reviews of the annual reports nor during the 1954 proceedings. It is, of course, of particular importance for the legal value and validity of Resolution 849 (IX) to the degree it amounted to a judicial or rather quasi-judicial determination.

The bulk of the information about Greenland, which was available to the General Assembly, came through Danish channels. Denmark had steadfastly opposed the direct representation of non-self-governing peoples in UN organs dealing with their legal and political status. The two Greenlandic members of the Danish 1954 delegation to the General Assembly were the newly elected members of the Danish Parliament who were also members of the Provincial Council and, as teacher and manager, employees of the Danish Government. They were accompanied to New York by the Danish Governor of Greenland.[74] Both briefly addressed the Committee on Information and the Fourth Committee where they, in general terms, strongly recommended the integration act. Questions of other delegates were, however, directed to and answered by Danish diplomats.

The timing of the appearance by the two Greenlanders, according to Lannung, was determined by the Danish delegation:

> "At the rather late moment we found appropriate, we arranged that the two good Greenlandic representatives, Frederik and Auge Lynge, whose presence was of great importance in relation to the most anticolonial countries, got the floor. They testified in warmhearted words to the Greenlanders' full satisfaction with the integration."[75]

The expressed choices of the Greenlandic delegates must also be seen and evaluated in light of Charter stipulations about the political advancement and aspirations of non-self-governing peoples and about their free political institutions.

Two high-ranking UN officials, Assistant Secretary-General Hoo and Secretary of the Committee on Information Benson, who visited Greenland in 1950 were handpicked and

---

73   Carlston, *supra* note 63, p. 40.

74   *Beretninger vedrörende Grönland*, Copenhagen, 1952, no. 5, p. 44; and UN document A/AC.35/SR.101, p.4.

75   Lannung, *supra* note 23, p. 145.

invited by the Danish Government. The stated purpose of the visit, according to the Danish delegation, was "to create a useful contact and exchange of experience" between the UN Secretariat and Government officials; furthermore, the delegation noted with pleasure that Danish officials had thus gotten in touch with UN officials. The two UN staff members did not submit a public report about their journey, and they did not participate in the 1954 UN debates. In general, Denmark opposed the idea of visiting missions in decolonization settings and denied that her invitation was a precedent for such undertakings.[76]

6.   Fraudulent Evidence

Another fundamental rule of procedure for evaluating GA resolution 849 (IX) is the "right to proceedings free from fraud."[77] Fourteen concrete examples from Danish texts will now be presented for showing that the reports submitted and statements made by Denmark to the United Nations intentionally constituted a distorted overall picture and a gross misrepresentation of particular facts pertinent to the situation in Greenland. It is argued that, had the full truth been known, the General Assembly would have come to a different conclusion. This is not a case of merely partial information submitted by counsel and leading to "a false impression,"[78] but something going to the roots of the issues at stake.

Example I:

> "From the time of its discovery in the tenth century, when it had been settled by Scandinavian immigrants, it had always been connected with one of the Nordic realms. It had come under the Danish-Norwegian Crown, remaining with Denmark when the two countries had separated in 1814. Though the Norsemen had died out after five centuries and their place had been taken by Eskimos migrating from Canada, the Danish Kings had always considered themselves Kings of Denmark."[79]

The Norsemen did not discover Greenland except for themselves and Europeans; the Inuit had already inhabited the island for thousands of years. This was a known fact in the 1950s. Furthermore, even though the Norse discovery and settlements are only relevant to a historic title of the colonial type, the statement did not get the historical origins of Danish rule straight. The Norse settlements in Greenland were not always formally connected with one of the Nordic States; for much of the next three centuries or so they constituted an independent entity.

---

76   Lannung, *supra* note 23, p. 145; Petersen, *supra* note 25, p. 15; and UN document A/C.4/L.127, pp. 1-3.

77   Carlston, *supra* note 63, p. 57.

78   Carlston, *supra* note 63, p. 58.

79   UN document A/C.35/SR.101, p. 5.

As to the argument that the Kings of Greenland resided in Copenhagen from the time the Norsemen perished in the 15th century, one can maintain that this was true in the sense of distant colonial rulers, but in reality it was on paper only and the Danish authorities rarely had contacts with and certainly no control over the island until it was recolonized in the 18th century.

Example 2:

> "In the early 18th century the missionary Hans Egede had established the principle which had since been the basis for Danish work in Greenland that the Greenlanders should enjoy the same fundamental rights as all other peoples. Denmark itself had at that time been governed by an absolute monarchy and there had therefore been no question of Greenland's becoming autonomous. In 1849 the Danish people had acquired the free constitution under which they were still living. The provisions of that constitution had not been extended to Greenland, for a very good reason. The Eskimo people had become thoroughly adapted to the rigorous conditions in which they lived; their economy, indeed their lives, depended entirely on the seal, which gave them food, fuel, clothes and material for building their boats and houses. The Greenlanders were a hardy, independent, self-supporting and undoubtedly happy people. It was that condition that the Danish Government had endeavoured to maintain for two hundred years after Hans Egede's arrival there; it had given the people schools aid a health service but had sheltered them from the outside influence which would have disrupted their economy and way of life. It had therefore excluded Greenland from the 1849 Constitution."[80]

After stating the basic principle of the "same fundamental rights", the Danish delegate proceeded immediately to a self-contradiction, namely to a description of how the Danish and Greenlandic peoples were treated differently under the name of paternalistic protection which inevitably implied one side being superior to the other both in terms of culture and power. If the Greenlanders were so happy, why not leave them alone? Comparing the different treatments, does it mean that dependent and unhappy Danes, hitherto suffering under absolute monarchical powers, needed the constitutional guarantees of 1849 whereas the hardy, self-supporting and happy Greenlanders did not? To carry the reasoning to a logical conclusion, can one not conclude from this Danish statement that the Greenlanders, after more than 200 years of foreign rule, had now sunk to a level where they were ready for integration, that is for the enjoyment of the same constitutional guarantees as accorded to the Danish people?

---

80   UN document A/C.35/SR.102, pp. 5-6.

Example 3:

> "The Greenlanders ... enjoy priority as regards appointments under the Administration of Greenland, provided they possess the necessary professional qualifications."[81]

This sounds nice, but it conveniently overlooked the fact that most high and medium level positions in the political, administrative and economic power structures throughout the colonial period had been and were still held by Danes. Part of the trick was the qualification requirement, as Greenlanders were not given, if not excluded from, opportunities for training and education in the relevant professions.

Example 4:

> "All trading and industrial activities in Greenland are being carried on by the Danish Government which, according to existing law, is bound to apply all working profits accruing from such activities to the benefit of the Greenlanders. For the past century, the Kingdom of Denmark has derived no economic advantages from Greenland. Trade within the country and free trading activities are in the hands of the Greenland population."[82]

The State-run Royal Trading Company, through a legalized monopoly which lasted until 1950, dominated the economic life in Greenland, including internal trade. The introduction in 1950 of limited free trade meant in effect the promotion of private Danish commercial interests rather than the introduction and support of Greenlandic enterprise. The often repeated assertion that Greenland had never "been an object of exploitation"[83] remains disputable and certainly controversial. The figures quoted have been insufficient in so far as they have not revealed funds flowing back to Denmark in the form of taxes, salaries and commercial profits nor disclosed the indirect political and economic benefits which Denmark has derived from its northern possession.

Example 5:

> "(F)ishing had replaced seal hunting as the principal occupation of the Greenlanders and the new industry had resulted in the introduction of a money economy into Greenland, forcing the Greenlander to adapt a cooperative rather than an individualist way of life."[84]

---

81   Non-Self-Governing Territories, Summaries and analysis of information transmitted to the Secretary-General during 1947, Lake Success: United Nations, 1948, p. 57.

82   Non-Self-Governing Territories, *supra* note 81, p. 57.

83   UN document A/C.35/SR.102, p. 7.

84   UN document A/C.35/SR.102, p. 6.

While climatic changes may have partly caused the occupational shift, other reasons not mentioned must have played an important role. Inuit concentration around Danish missionary and commercial stations, new material needs resulting from the Danish presence, and a policy of creating, in the Danish view, a more viable and profit-making industry to sustain the population inevitably brought about the introduction of new ways of life.

The comment about a cooperative society replacing individualist ways of life was doubly misleading. First, it ignored basic indigenous characteristics of Inuit customs of community sharing and cooperation. Second, the State-run monopoly, so dominating in Greenland and based on Danish supremacy, signified everything but the working together of the two peoples concerned.

Example 6:

> "(L)ocal self-government had been instituted in the 1850's and had since been extended again and again."[85]

Given the purpose, functions and composition of the boards of guardians established around 1860, it was a mockery of the United Nations and of the political decolonization efforts to call the boards self-governmental. The boards and subsequent local institutions were restricted to mainly advisory functions and only entrusted with decision-making power, albeit subject to Danish administrative control and possible reversal, in matters relating to social affairs.

Examples 7 and 8:

> "It was interesting to note that the leader of the Greenlanders, in his opening speech to the National Council of Greenland which had convened only a few days previously, had expressed the desire for the representation of Greenland in the Danish Parliament. He (Mr. Lannung) was sure that such representation would be welcomed in Denmark and would be accorded in due time, when among other things, it had become possible to make the appropriate amendments in the Danish constitution."[86]

> "The revolutionary change in Greenland's economic life and the maturity gained by the Greenlanders through education and through participation in political life had necessarily led to a change of Greenland's political status within the Danish realm."[87]

---

85   UN document A/C.35/SR.102, p. 6.
86   UN document A/C.35/SR.34, p. 5.
87   UN document A/C.35/SR.102, p. 6.

While Auge Lynge was undoubtedly an important Greenlandic politician, he was not "the leader of the Greenlanders" but rather a newly elected member of the Provincial Council. He got the floor as the second speaker of the Council session from its chairman, the Danish Governor, who gave the opening speech. What practically all the Danish statements to the United Nations on this point left out, self-incriminating as the information would have been, was the Danish initiative, motivation and timing behind the integration move.

While "the maturity gained by the Greenlanders" was sufficient to warrant integration from a Danish point of view, it was at the same time insufficient for allowing any substantial increase in local autonomy, as was done, for example, when home rule was granted to the Faroe Islands in 1948 or to Greenland in 1979. Although minimal authority had been delegated to the Provincial Council of Greenland in the early 1950s, the question can be raised whether it was properly considered competent by the Danish Government to take the far-reaching, supposedly final decision on the island's future constitutional and international status.

Example 9:

> "With regard to the factor of cultural considerations, it was a fact that Greenland and Denmark had a long history of common traditions."[88]

This piece of information is hardly worth a comment. The traditions referred to were obviously Danish impositions in the fields of religion, language and media which were pressed forward by the clergy and the administration at the cost of Inuit customs, with very limited and often no consultations. On the other side of the ocean, in Denmark, the only influence of Greenlandic traditions could be found in the written works of anthropologists and explorers and in museum possessions.

Examples 10, 11 and 12:

> "There had never, incidentally, been any racial discrimination as was illustrated by the fact that the population of Greenland was of mixed Scandinavian-Eskimo origin."[89]

> "Since the re-establishment of regular communications between Scandinavia and Greenland in the eighteenth century, there had been countless marriages between the indigenous population and Scandinavians so that the present population was Eskimo-Scandinavian. Mr. Lannung mentioned in passing that the word "Eskimo" was never used in Greenland."[90]

---

88   UN document A/C.35/SR.103, p. 12.
89   UN document A/C.35/SR.102, p. 6.
90   UN document A/C.35/SR.427, p. 202.

"Since the beginning of the eighteenth century the majority of the population has mixed mainly with those of Scandinavian blood to such an extent that it can no longer be said to be of the Eskimo race."[91]

These statements were intentionally and grossly misleading on a point of paramount importance to the United Nations, even at that time. In the same breath as denying racial discrimination, the diplomat referred to the protective shelter and isolation and the maturity gained through Danish education, guidance and presumably marriage. Similar attitudes were echoed in other Danish explanations of the period and were clearly based on the assumption that the race, culture and political wisdom of the Danes were superior to that of 'the primitive natives' who needed enlightenment, albeit only at a pace convenient to Danish interests.

The statement about the disappearance of "the Eskimo race" was dubious at best or just plainly wrong. It stood in contradiction to official population statistics as submitted by Denmark to the United Nations, for example for the years 1944 and 1952, when there were listed, respectively, 20, 574 and 23,360 "natives" and 494 and 1408 "non-natives", indicating at least two distinct population groups.[92] One may also ask how these "ethnic connexions" arose given the proclaimed Government shelter from "outside influence."[93] Finally, while the word "Eskimo" found frequent application in the Danish language, it was presumably not much used in Greenland because it was not part of the Inuit language and not because of a lack of a separate identity.

Example 13:

"Greenland's geographical position had acquired a new significance as modern means of communication developed; Greenland was in fact near the focus of great economic activity and many of the shortest air routes between the great centres of population passed over the territory."[94]

This statement as justification for integration was somewhat diminished by a later explanation:

"With regard to the question raised by some representatives concerning the distance between Greenland and. Denmark, the two countries were within six hours' flight

---

91	Non-Self-Governing Territories, *supra* note 33, p. 268.

92	Non-Self-Governing Territories, *supra* note 81, p. 57; and Non-Self-Governing Territories, *supra* note 33, p. 268.

93	UN document A/C.35/SR.103, p. 12.

94	UN document A/C.35/SR.102, p. 6.

from each other and were linked by a fortnightly service by sea. The Scandinavian people regarded the sea as a connecting link."[95]

The statement was, however, devastated when it came down to specifics. One of the Greenlandic representatives, followed by a Danish endorsement, told the Committee on Information that:

> "(T)he fact that the northern and eastern provinces (of Greenland) were not yet represented in the Danish Parliament was admittedly a shortcoming, which was, however, due to natural difficulties. Those provinces were so difficult of access at present that, even if they were represented in the Danish Parliament, their deputies would not be able to keep in touch with their constituents, so that such representation would be meaningless in practice."[96]

The diplomats omitted mentioning that refuelling stops in Greenland on transatlantic and polar air routes did not improve Greenlandic communications with the rest of the world; there was no connection or other interaction with the Inuit. Their statements also left out reference to the fact that the airports in Greenland were built by the United States for military purposes and that Denmark had in 1951 ratified a bilateral defense agreement with the United States entitling the latter to operate military bases in Greenland.[97]

Example 14:

> "Greenland's history as a Non-Self-Governing Territory had been somewhat different from that of other Territories, in that it had never been a colony in the classical sense of the word."[98]

In fact, the relationship between Greenland and Denmark bore all the traditional characteristics of colonial control. The Danish UN strategy, however, as summed up in this statement, proved to be successful salesmanship in a political body susceptible to diplomatic manoeuvering. Many States bought the Danish explanations without question as they coincided with their own self-interests. Denmark unhesitatingly made use of its political influence, and benefited from its image as a fair and just, democratic Scandinavian State.

In connection with fraudulent evidence in a decolonization setting, one can also refer to additional instances when evidence was either wholly or partially suppressed. The reports were incomplete in so far as they did not reveal the extent to which the Danish lan-

---

95   UN document A/C.35/SR.103, p. 11.

96   UN document A/C.35/SR.103, p. 11.

97   2 UST, Part 2, 1951, Washington: United States Government Printing Office, 1952, pp. 1485-1498; and Lovtidende C, 1951, pp. 314-324.

98   UN document A/C.35/SR.102, p. 5.

guage was used in schools and administration; the lack of university and technical school education and training among the Greenlanders; the social problems which resulted from the replacement of old customs by the enforced introduction of Danish culture and a foreign way of living; the disproportionate role of church and trading officials in education and administration; and major differences in the legal, administrative, political and economic systems of Greenland and Denmark.

7.   Reasoned Judgement

Again quoting Carlston, the statement of reasons which should accompany a decision:

> "need not be in meticulous detail; a statement indicating in a general way the legal reasons upon which the award is based will be valid and binding."[99]

GA Resolution 849 (IX) is brief and vague on everything except its conclusions, although further reasoning is contained in the deliberations of the "arbitrators" in published debates of the Committee on Information, the Fourth Committee and plenary meetings of the General Assembly. More interesting is perhaps the purpose of the right to a reasoned judgement, "that is the guarantee that the decision shall be in accordance with law and pursuant to the compromise."[100]

8.   Essential Error

Vague as the concept of essential error or denial of justice may be, many jurists agree that a decision which is evidently unjust and unreasonable, constituting "a mistake of fact or law", should be considered null. This is especially true for an award which fails to apply a "rule of law stipulated in the compromis", a nullity ground which borders on excess of jurisdiction. Greenland's case is anyway not a case where the prejudiced entity has to suffer from the incapacity of an arbitrator whom the party itself has selected.[101] Needless to repeat, Greenland did not choose the forum.

In 1953 and 1954, the rules of law applicable to the relationship between Greenland and Denmark were to be found in the UN Charter, in resolutions passed by the General Assembly, and in slowly emerging international customary law. The lists of factors annexed to GA resolutions 567 (VI) and 648 (VII) were explicitly provisional, that is indicative guidelines to "be taken into account" in the consideration of "each concrete case". In addition to this somewhat hesitant approach, the resolutions were not without ambiguities:

> "(T)he factors, while serving as a guide in determining whether the obligations as set forth in Article 73 e of the Charter still exist, should in no way be interpreted as

---

99   Carlston, *supra* note 63, p. 53.

100   Carlston, *supra* note 63, p. 50.

101   Carlston, *supra* note 63, pp. 185-192.

a hindrance to the attainment of a full measure of self-government by the Non-Self-Governing Territories."[102]

Resolutions 567 (VI) and 648 (VII) were passed by voting, the latter with more opposition. Resolution 849 (IX) on Greenland also referred to the list of factors annexed to Resolution 742 (VIII) which the General Assembly approved on 27 November 1953, that is after the supposed integration of Greenland but before the termination of Greenland's non-self-governing status. Dissenting votes represented States arguing both that the General Assembly did not have competence to pass rules of this kind and that the Assembly did not have competence to consider political information from the non-self-governing territories.

The factors will now be considered one by one; in addition, the cumulative effect of various alleged errors should be taken into account. The contemporary facts to which references are made here have been drawn from official Danish sources, perhaps not all of them available to the General Assembly, and from Danish explanations and statements to the United Nations prior to and during the 1954 debate.

9.   Political Advancement

Article 73a of the UN Charter obliges the administering powers to ensure political advancement of non-self governing peoples. Article 73b similarly refers to "the political aspirations of the peoples" and "the progressive development of their free political institutions", according to "their varying stages of advancement". Operative paragraph 6 of GA Resolution 567 (VI) interpreted these requirements to mean that political advancement was one of two "essential factors to be taken into account in deciding whether a Non-Self-Governing Territory has attained a full measure of self-government" and defined this in the following manner: "Political advancement of the population sufficient to enable them to decide upon the future destiny of the territory with due knowledge."

All three lists of factors contained clauses on political advancement of territories heading for free association and integration. The Danish delegate in the Committee on Information stated, after pointing out that the list of factors annexed to Resolution 742 (VIII) "had been adopted six months after the Danish Constitution", that "the conditions laid down in the list had been fulfilled."[103]

Revealing evidence about the political advancement of Greenland in the years immediately preceding integration can be found in official Danish reports. The parliamentary committee concluded in 1946 that it was not worthwhile for Greenlandic representatives to participate regularly in the committee's work concerning "the orientation about Greenlandic affairs"; it was only "purposeful with a few years in between". The committee also acquiesced in a request of the Greenlandic delegation to continue the trade monopoly and the country's isolation "because the Greenlanders cannot yet be deemed to have

---

102   Operative paragraph 3 of GA Resolution 648 (VII).

103   UN document A/C.35/SR.103, p. 11.

reached so far in intellectual and material development as to justify an opening of the country now or in the nearest future."[104]

In response to Greenlandic requests for administrative changes, the 1950 special commission listed as an argument in favour of reform:

> "the pure psychological feature that it must be considered natural for a people, which like the Greenlandic one has gradually achieved a certain political and cultural maturity, that its affairs be administered to the extent possible from the country inhabited by the people."[105]

Danish belief in Greenlandic maturity did not, however, reach very deep as demonstrated by the limited scope of functions delegated to Greenlandic organs by the legislative changes of 1950 and 1951. The 1950 report of the special commission emphasized that the functions of the Greenlandic organs would necessarily be more limited than those of Danish municipalities because the Danish State would have to remain in charge of activities, such as schools, libraries, hospitals and harbours, for which Greenlandic financing was insufficient.[106] In a 1952 expert opinion to the constitutional commission, Andersen stated in the context of a constitutional provision about self-government:

> "The question about such a self-government is supposedly not an actual one and a provision without self-government could lead to unfortunate results. Besides, both the economic and general state of affairs in Greenland make the introduction of a Greenlandic self-government highly difficult, if it is to go beyond the right of municipalities to manage their own affairs as prescribed in Art. 89 of the Constitution."[107]

These examples from internal Danish reports show an official attitude to the effect that, while the Greenlanders were making progress under beneficial Danish coaching, they still had a long way to go before they reached the more advanced Danish levels. Lannung admitted as much in a 1954 Fourth Committee meeting. Talking about the political aspects of integration, he "realized that there were still shortcomings, and Denmark's efforts would continue without remission."[108]

An examination of the internal political scene in Greenland in the early fifties leaves the same impression about the stage of political development. Denmark informed the United Nations in 1948 that "(n)o political societies have been formed" in Greenland.[109] There were no organized political movements, neither for liberation nor unification, not

---

104　Betaenkning, *supra* note 9, p. 13.
105　Betaenkning, *supra* note 6, p. 19.
106　Betaenkning, *supra* note 6, pp. 30-31.
107　Betaenkning, *supra* note 9, p. 87.
108　UN document A/C.4/SR.427, p. 204.
109　Non-Self-Governing Territories, *supra* note 81, p. 62.

even labour unions "in the accepted sense of the word."[110] Members of the Provincial Council were elected on a personal basis, a system fundamentally different from the organized and diverse party structure in Denmark. Submission to Danish rule was widespread; one of the Greenlandic members of the 1954 Danish GA delegation, Frederik Lynge, bragged to the Committee on Information that:

> "(m)embers of the Danish Government and Parliament had visited Greenland on several occasions and the Territory had even been honoured by royal visits in 1921 and 1952."[111]

The Greenlanders' conception of the outside world, including UN activities, was amply demonstrated by Auge Lynge whom a Danish diplomat had designated as the "leading Greenlander" in his remarks in the 1952 Provincial Council debate about integration:

> "Out in the world the United Nations work persistently to obtain even for underdeveloped countries representation in the national assemblies of their mother countries."[112]

These circumstances prompted Robert Petersen, himself a respected Greenlander, to remark at a 1976 conference:

> "The various Greenlandic politicians expressed enthusiasm for the new arrangement so consistently that today one is tempted to ask if they understood the extent to which the colonial regime remained unchanged."[113]

The booklet about the objectives and activities of the United Nations, which Denmark distributed in the Fourth Committee, was not published until February 1954 and was therefore not available in Greenland before or at the time of the constitutional integration.[114] Despite these shortcomings in the political development in Greenland and despite the fact that most of the information was available to the General Assembly, Resolution 849 (IX) in operative paragraph 6 noted with "satisfaction the achievement of self-government by the

---

110 Non-Self-Governing Territories, *supra* note 33, p. 274.

111 UN document A/C.35/SR.103, p. 10.

112 UN document A/C.35/L.155, Annex III, p. 4.

113 Robert Petersen, "Continuity and Discontinuity in the Political Development of Modern Greenland" in *Continuity and Discontinuity in the Inuit Culture of Greenland*, Danish-Netherlands Symposium on Developments in Greenlandic Arctic Culture, Arctic Centre, University of Groningen, 1977, p. 5.

114 P.P. Sveistrup, *De forenede Nationer, Godthaab: Grönlands folkeoplysningsforening*, 1954, 207 pages. Hermod Lannung wrote the foreword. 1500 copies were printed.

people of Greenland", a finding which amounted to a serious misreading of either the facts or the law or both.

10. Free Political Institutions

The Charter requirement for the progressive development of free political institutions was hardly met in Greenland. The 1952 Provincial Council had been remodelled in 1950 by a Danish statute and it was elected in 1951 for the first time on an almost island-wide basis (excluding northern and eastern Greenland). The Council possessed consultative functions, with restricted decision-making powers on mainly social affairs. Initiatives, advice and decisions of the Council could be overruled or circumvented by the central Government. It was chaired by the Danish Governor who played an active role in its deliberations, and Danes who had resided in the country for at least six months had the right to vote.

Under Danish law, the Council did not have the authority to take constitutional decisions. In addition, this upcoming constitutional question had not been an issue in the 1951 election campaign for seats on the Provincial Council. Still, it was this Council, in which the Danish Government had so little confidence, which was entrusted, and relied upon by the very same Government, with the fundamental and supposedly final decision concerning Greenland's constitutional integration and the termination of its international status.

For the reasons now listed, it cannot be seriously maintained that the Council members had a mandate from their constituents to take a supposedly final decision on the integration act. This was certainly not a constitutional assembly; the basis for the 1951 elections was a Danish statute which foresaw a narrow role for the Council and fell below the Greenlanders' expectations for the new body.

With no Greenlandic lawyers contributing to the debate on the constitutional process, there is no information to the effect that the Provincial Council had the counsel of Danish or other foreign legal experts. These could have pointed out consequences of and alternatives to integration, for example concerning the rights of non-self-governing territories, the expected finality of the act, and the early but clear trends of political decolonization worldwide. Contributing further to the inequality between the parties was the constant use of the Danish language in discussions and formulations pertinent to the Greenlandic-Danish relationship.

GA Resolution 849 (IX) failed to recognize the restricted scope and non-progressive development of the Provincial Council as well as the inequality of the parties when it, in operative paragraph 4, took note that the people of Greenland, "through duly elected representatives," had freely exercised its right to self-determination. Resolution 849 (IX) also overlooked the factor, contained in the lists annexed to Resolutions 567 (VI), 648 (VII) and 742 (VIII), which called for consideration whether there were "powers in certain matters constitutionally reserved to the Territory".

11. Democratic processes

The other "essential factor" in determining whether a non-self-governing territory has achieved self-government was so defined in GA Resolution 567 (V), operative paragraph 6:

> "The opinion or the population of the Territory, freely expressed by informed and democratic processes, as to the status or change in status which they desire."

All three lists of factors included identical provisions about the opinion of the population in territories heading for free association or integration. This stipulation is of particular importance for the integration alternative because of the intended finality of such a step. The requirement to respect the will of the people is underlined by the Charter principle of self-determination and it is closely linked to the obligations set forth in Article 73 of the Charter. The calls for "political advancement", "political aspirations" and "free political institutions" would be meaningless if they did not encompass respect for the freely expressed will of the people.

A referendum on the constitutional integration was not held in Greenland. In anticipation: of the upcoming debate in the General Assembly, there had been official Danish awareness of and worries about the lack of popular approval.[115] But when asked in the Committee on Information about the lack of a referendum, a Danish delegate reference to the unanimous decision of the elected members of the Provincial Council and stated:

> "For that reason the Danish Government had felt that to hold a referendum ... would do nothing more than cast doubt upon the sincerity of the desire which had been freely expressed by those representatives.... The population of Greenland had freely chosen its new status, and it would feel offended if it was asked whether it really wished to be integrated into Denmark."[116]

As described above, integration had not been at issue in the 1951 election campaigns for the Provincial Council so that the population was in fact never directly consulted on this fundamental question. The absence of any dissenting views on the issue in Greenland, which Lannung pointed out in the Fourth Committee,[117] is actually more suspicious than convincing.[118] It must be seen as an illustration of a serious lack of political advancement and awareness rather than any absolute agreement.

The Greenlanders did not participate in parliamentary elections held in Denmark in connection with the constitutional amendments or in a State-wide referendum on the same amendments held in winter and spring of 1953, as prescribed by Article 94 of the 1915

---

115   Finn Petersen, *supra* note 25, pp. 35-36.

116   UN document A/C.35/SR.103, pp. 12-13.

117   UN documents A/C.4/SR.427, p. 204 and A/C.4/SR.430, p. 217.

118   Robert Petersen, *supra* note 113, p. 156.

Constitution. The Greenlanders were not entitled to vote because of their colonial status, or as the Danish delegate explained it to the Committee on Information:

> "(A)t the time of the last referendum the Danish Constitution had not applied to Greenland, so the population of Greenland had not been consulted on that occasion."[119]

This was an obvious inconsistency. In Denmark, with democratic traditions and old institutions, a few constitutional amendments were subject to approval in a referendum and repeatedly in Parliament which, at that time, had no Greenlandic members. In Greenland, however, with colonial traditions and a newly established, more or less powerless assembly, the adoption of the Danish Constitution as a whole, rather than just the amendments, was entrusted to the Provincial Council. It was the whole Danish Constitution which the Greenlanders were asked to subscribe to. The only questions, however, submitted to the Provincial Council in 1952, related to Greenland's new status. The rest of the constitutional system had to be bought as a package and unseen to the degree the constitutional commission did not submit its proposals until January 1953.

Another relevant element in this context was the short period of time which the Danish Government afforded to the Greenlanders for this important decision. As elaborated above, the concrete integration proposals were prepared by the constitutional commission in spring and summer of 1952 and sent to the Provincial Council in August of that year. Under Danish chairmanship, the Council spent two days, 8 and 9 September 1952, discussing the item, much of that time in closed session. This time frame practically excluded the possibility of a serious public debate.

Even though integration ideas in general had been discussed among the Council members for a few years, the lack of adequate time for a thorough examination of the integration proposals and their full consequences undermines the validity of the Council's decision. Greenlandic wishes in the late forties had been directed towards increased self-government and equality with metropolitan Danes and towards improved economic and social conditions, all of which could have been accomplished without submission to Danish sovereignty.

The time allocated for the study of the particular proposals of the constitutional commission, was probably designed to suit Danish convenience. The next meeting of the Provincial Council, because of weather conditions, was not scheduled until late summer in 1953 while the new Constitution entered into force in June 1953.

Irrespective of these flaws, and in the face of available evidence to the contrary, GA Resolution 849 (IX) went ahead to determine, in operative paragraphs 4 and 5, that the people of Greenland had freely, decided on integration and thereby exercised its right to self-determination.

---

119 UN document A/C.35/SR.103, p. 12.

12. Full Geographic Representation

With respect to the requirements of "free political institutions" and "the opinion of the population", it is to be noted that the inhabitants of East and North Greenland were not represented in the 1952 Provincial Council. Nor did the Danish Government submit the integration proposals to their local councils for advice or approval. A conscious effort was made to minimize this lack of representation in Danish reports to the United Nations. In an explanation given to the Committee on Information, it was stated that the lack was:

> "due to natural difficulties. Those provinces were so difficult of access at present that, even if they were represented in the Danish Parliament, their deputies would not be able to keep in touch with their constituents, so that such representation would be meaningless in practice".[120]

A part of the Greenlandic people, albeit only a small minority of the population, was thus incorporated into Denmark without ever being asked for an opinion. GA Resolution 849 (IX) failed altogether to mention this missing consultation and to provide for any sort of guarantees concerning future approval.

13. Freedom of Choice

The headings in the lists of factors, annexed to Resolutions 567 (VI) and 648 (VII), established three alternatives open to non-self-governing territories upon the termination of that status. These were independence, other separate systems of self-government, or integration. These options are further underlined by the Charter's principle of self-determination and the requirements of Chapter XI. With reference to the right to self-determination of peoples, GA Resolution 742 (VIII) identified freedom of choice as a component.[121]

Under the heading "factors indicative of the free association of a territory on equal basis with the metropolitan or other country as an integral part of that country or in any other form," freedom of choice was defined differently:

> "The freedom of the population of a Non-Self-Governing Territory which has associated itself with the metropolitan country as an integral part of that country or in any other form to modify this status through the expression of their will by democratic means."[122]

In this regard, a Danish delegate stated unambiguously in the UN Committee on Information, in response to inquiries by several delegates, that:

---

120 UN document A/C.35/SR.103, p. 11.

121 In Second part, A, paragraph 2 of Resolution 742 (VIII).

122 In Third part, A, paragraph 2 of Resolution 742 (VIII).

"(t)he Danish Constitution contained no provision for the possibility of secession by any part of the country."[123]

What is important in this context, however, is not the later right to modify but the duty to allow for options and alternatives prior to and during the decolonization process. It is hardly compatible with the Charter or the early GA resolutions that decolonization results could be chosen and unilaterally promoted by the administering power. Such an interpretation could have made a mockery out of these instruments, particularly their references to political aspirations and free political institutions.

This question of alternatives came up in the GA debate on Greenland. A Danish delegate remarked, or blundered, in the Committee on Information that:

"(n)o referendum had been held and even if one had been held the only choice would have been between incorporation or remaining as a Non-Self-Governing Territory."[124]

This comment was corrected in the Fourth Committee. Lannung

"felt that, taken out of its context, the remark … was misleading. What was meant was that at no time had the people of Greenland manifested any desire other than integration in the Danish realm. If they had done so, they would have been given a correspondingly wider choice. The remark was therefore a statement of a factual and not of a legal nature – a description of a purely factual situation."[125]

The attempt to separate the factual and legal nature of the first statement is hardly convincing. The fact remains that Denmark initiated and promoted integration while never offering or explaining the available options of independence and free association. GA Resolution 849 (IX) failed, despite abundant evidence, to pay any attention to this lack of alternatives and, consequently, did not make any reservations about the Greenlanders' later right to modify their status.

14.   Economic and Social Advancement

Article 73a of the Charter established the obligation of administering powers to promote the well-being of the inhabitants and to ensure the economic and social advancement of non-self-governing peoples. Furthermore, Article 74 expressed the agreement of UN Member States among themselves:

---

123   UN document A/C.35/SR.103, p. 11.
124   UN document A/2729, p. 7.
125   UN document A/C.4/SR.429, p. 211.

"that their policy in respect of the territories to which this Chapter applies, no less
than in respect of their metropolitan areas, must be based on the general principle of
good neighborliness ... in social, economic, and commercial matters."

GA Resolutions 567 (VI) and 648 (VII) listed "economic and social jurisdiction" as among
the factors to be considered in connection with "other separate systems of self-government". Resolution 742 (VIII) included the item "economic, social and cultural jurisdiction"
as one of the factors indicative of integration with the metropolitan country:

"Degree of autonomy in respect of economic, social and cultural affairs, as illus-
trated by the degree of freedom from economic pressure as exercised, for example,
by a foreign minority group which, by virtue of the help of a foreign Power, has
acquired a privileged economic status prejudicial to the general economic interest
of the people of the Territory; and by the degree of freedom and lack of discrimination against the indigenous population of the Territory in social legislation and social
developments."[126]

Danish reports to the United Nations admitted readily that economic and social conditions in Greenland did not equal those in Denmark. In the last annual report on Greenland
as a non-self-governing territory, the economic policy of the Danish Government was
described as follows:

"The current view is that Greenland is a less prosperous part of the Realm and must
be aided by the rest of the country. The main object is to raise the living standards
materially and to create such conditions as would increase productivity."[127]

The report acknowledged, despite the abolition of the trade monopoly and isolation, that
"(m)ost of the commercial and productive activities ... are still operated by the government" and that the Government was "virtually the sole employer."[128]
    As far as social conditions are concerned, the report also stated that:

"(s)ocial problems affecting the relationship between Greenlanders and Danes consist chiefly of questions of equality of treatment in legal and economic matters....
In the economic field, wage policies aim to achieve conditions in which Greenland
wage earners shall, as far as possible, attain a standard of living equal to that of their
counterparts in Denmark."[129]

---

126   In Third part, C, paragraph 5, of Resolution 742 (VIII).
127   Non-Self-Governing Territories, *supra* note 33, p. 269.
128   Non-Self-Governing Territories, *supra* note 33, pp. 269 and 274.
129   Non-Self-Governing Territories, *supra* note 33, p. 273

In addition to the admission that full equality between wage earners of the two parties was not feasible, a further comparison of statistical figures released for Greenland and those available for Denmark, as well as of those concerning unequal salaries for Greenlanders and Danes in Greenland,[130] would have revealed dramatic differences between the two countries.

Despite the presence of these disparate economic and social factors which should have indicated inevitable problems of achieving an actual integration on equal footing, GA Resolution 849 (IX) approved the integration move without reservation.

15. Educational Advancement

Article 73a of the Charter stipulated the duty of administering powers to promote education in the non-self-governing territories. Not directly referred to in the lists of factors, the education requirement is closely related to, if not a prerequisite for, the terms "informed … processes" and "due knowledge" used in describing factors like "opinion of the population" and "political advancement".

Danish explanations and reports to the United Nations showed clearly that the educational situation in Greenland was far behind that in Denmark. A Danish diplomat observed in a 1950 meeting of the Committee on Information that "the standard of general education" in Greenland was less than satisfactory. He added that "in 1949 of a total of 207 Greenlanders studying in Denmark, none had taken the full university course". It was the hope of his Government that:

> "that situation would improve and that a larger number of Greenlanders would receive higher education enabling them to occupy leading positions in their own country."[131]

In light of the legal changes being introduced, as noted above, the lack of Greenlandic lawyers is not an unimportant consideration. In the 1953 annual report, recognizing that "the scope and quality of education is not uniform", Danish policy was still focusing on the same objective:

> "Denmark has considered it to be one of her most important objects to impart such cultural and technical knowledge which will enable the population to participate to an increasing degree in the economic and technical development of Greenland."[132]

Interestingly, it looks as if the remarks on economic, social and educational conditions in Greenland were prepared by other officials than those providing the political information. The former confirmed that the situation was still unsatisfactory for popular participation in

---

130 Non-Self-Governing Territories, *supra* note 33, p. 274.
131 UN document A/C.35/SR.15, pp. 5-6.
132 Non-Self-Governing Territories, *supra* note 33, p. 276.

key sectors of the society, while the latter kept saying that all the factors had been fulfilled and that the Greenlanders had freely expressed their informed and democratic political opinion. The "arbitrators" who produced GA Resolution 849 (IX) apparently considered these discrepancies insignificant.

16. Other Factors

General Assembly Resolutions 567 (VI), 648 (VII) and 742 (VIII) listed geographical, ethnic and cultural considerations among the factors affecting cases involving integration, including separation by sea, as well as ethnic and cultural considerations, including different race, language, religion, and distinct cultural heritage, interests or aspirations.

Greenland is geographically far away and overseas from Denmark and distances have affected and will necessarily continue to affect the relations between Nuuk and Copenhagen. The Inuit, notwithstanding a certain amount of sexual interaction, are racially different from the Danes. The cultural heritage of the Inuit, notwithstanding impositions by Denmark, is fundamentally different and distinct from Danish traditions.

These distinctions existed in 1953, and they hold true today. In a contemporary book by Schultz-Lorentzen, edited and published in 1951 by the Danish Prime Minister's Office, it was observed:

> "When speaking about the Greenlandic people, it is not just a geographical denota-
> tion comprising the groups of human beings who have their home on the coasts of
> Greenland. They are a people in the actual meaning, a national unit. They have their
> own language, independent of their closest surroundings. They have their own his-
> tory going back thousands of years, a history which is difficult to trace. They have
> a way of life which has been developed in a victorious fight against the hard, arctic
> conditions. They have a tradition, inherited from ancestors, a tradition which can
> not only be remembered and recorded, but one which is a web of threads which
> penetrate the mind and determine customs and ways of thinking".

The author went on to say that the encounter with the white man had not led to the abandoning of the primitive characteristics of the Greenlanders.[133]

The presence of these factors, as well as practically all the others enumerated in the Charter and in the three lists of factors, did not prevent the General Assembly in Resolution 849 (IX) from approving the integration of Greenland into Denmark. This gives good reason for the application of multiple grounds for challenging a decision which is contrary to substantive and procedural regulations, contains essential errors, and is manifestly unjust and unreasonable.

---

133 C.W. Schultz-Lorentzen, *Det grönlandske folk og folkesind*, Copenhagen: The Prime Minister's Office, 1951, p. 1.

17. New Evidence

With the "tribunal" in existence and still dealing with questions concerning non-self-governing territories and with the party requesting revision not being at fault for not submitting the information, new evidence can be brought to the attention of the tribunal if the evidence discovered is "of such a nature that it would have produced a change in the tribunal's views had it known thereof."[134] The evidence presented by Denmark to the General Assembly of many of the items mentioned above was not only unilateral and insufficient but also misleading and even fraudulent, and there is good reason to believe that the introduction of more impartial and complete evidence would have had a decisive influence on the award.

New Legal Developments

The law of political decolonization had in 1954 already been evolved through the UN Charter, general and specific General Assembly resolutions and a limited amount of State practice. Since then, it has taken on a more consolidated and definitive form, establishing beyond dispute the right of overseas colonial entities to external self-determination and the competence of the Assembly to determine when such a situation arises. GA Resolutions 1514 (XV) and 1541 (XV) and common Article 1 of the two International Human Rights Covenants come to mind as good examples of codification of these practices. If the Greenland case were to appear before the International Court of Justice or to reappear on the agenda of the General Assembly, it is quite possible to maintain that Greenland's status could be revisited, on both the basis of the law at that time, which has only been strengthened since, and new law.

During a 1980 meeting in the Human Rights Committee under the International Covenant on Political and Civil Rights, questions were thus raised concerning "the political maturity of the people of Greenland at the time of the referendum", referring to the 1979 referendum about the introduction of home rule. Denmark was also asked for clarifications about her "general policy ... on the question of self-determination". In a report to the Committee, which formed the basis for the discussion, Denmark had emphasized the constitutional integration of 1953 and GA Resolution 849 (IX). In describing the 1979 home rule arrangements, Denmark in her State report had stated that:

> "a condition of overriding importance for this system is the continued existence of national unity, which has the legal consequence that Danish constitutional rules and principles shall in their entirety continue to apply also in Greenland".

A Danish representative further mentioned that, "as far as the independence of Greenland was concerned, the decision of the unity of the realm had never been contested."[135]

---

134   Carlston, *supra* note 63, p. 232.
135   UN documents CCPR/C/1/Add. 19, pp. 2-3, and Add. 51, pp. 32-34 and Press Release HR/2011, pp. 2-3.

Indicative of Danish attitudes to self-determination for the Greenlanders may be the fact that, in her reports over the years to the Human Rights Committee, the portion on Greenland has been dealt with under both Articles 1 and 27 of the Covenant, about the right of self-determination and minority rights. The ambiguities persist. When Denmark ratified the Framework Convention for the protection of National Minorities, it did not list the Greenlanders, neither in Greenland nor those in Denmark proper, as a minority for the purposes of that treaty.[136]

The preference of the Danish Government is clearly to treat the Greenlanders, or the Inuit, as an indigenous people in Denmark. This was expressly the purpose of its ratification of ILO Convention No. 169 concerning Indigenous and Tribal Peoples in Independent Countries. Indigenous rights, however, are relevant only as long as Greenland remains under Danish jurisdiction. The Greenlanders as a people can of course also constitute an indigenous people, but they do not need protection as an indigenous group if and when they are the majority in a country of their own. Recognition as a people, with full control over their own affairs, is obviously the best method of ensuring continued identity, dignity, equal worth and quality of life. As to providing assistance and showing solidarity with other indigenous peoples, the Greenlanders are in a better position to accomplish that as a fully-fledged people.

It is argued that the Greenlandic people has a number of options which they can claim and exercise, now or later, based on a free and informed choice, for themselves and by themselves:

a)   Independent, sovereign State, in charge of internal and external matters, with full membership in international and regional organizations.

b)   Sovereign State in personal union with the Danish Crown. Such an arrangement could bring about Greenlandic membership in international and regional organizations and competences in foreign affairs, but the details of the relationship and any division of labor, as well as means of amendment and termination, depend on the deal made by the parties.

c)   Free association or commonwealth with Denmark (or another State). In the UN listing of minimum options which should be made available to colonial countries and peoples, free association is a middle station between independence and integration. It can lead to a variety of arrangements, including membership in selected international and regional organizations, but the people concerned maintains the right of external self-determination.

d)   Integration into Denmark as the administering power (or into another country). If all the substantive and procedural regulations are followed, the chances are that the integration will be seen as final.

e)   Federation means the coming together of two or more entities for the creation of a federal State where federal institutions are shared and where a number of joint powers

---

136   See the website of the Council of Europe at "www.coe.int" for the Danish declaration, the state report, and the comments of Advisory Committee and of the Council of Ministers.

exist, while provinces maintain significant control over local affairs. Federation is between equals while expanded self-government essentially indicates that a district or a group is subsidiary to a central government. And

f)   Expanded self-government, within Denmark, comes with any number of possible variations in terms of both additional institutions and delegated powers or functions, including the judiciary, police, natural resources, certain limited foreign dealings, etc., but such self-government is basically granted to minorities and indigenous peoples within and as part of independent States.

Concluding Observations

Many legal arguments have now been presented, drawing on elements in the history of Danish constitutional law developments and in the work of the United Nations. These elements confirm that the Greenlanders are a people under public international law whose colonial status has never been brought to a proper end. A people living in an overseas colonial possession has the right of external self-determination. On the other side, the Greenlanders are not a minority or an indigenous people within Denmark. Other research presented in this book and especially in the book called "Sources to the History of The Faroe Islands and Greenland" (In Danish: "*Kilder til Færøernes og Grønlands historie*") about Danish policy towards not only Greenland but also the Faroe Islands supports the same conclusions.

A summing up of the arguments presented above constitutes, indeed, a long list. The Greenlandic requests after World War Two for increased self-government and better living conditions were not aimed at and did not necessitate full integration into Denmark. Denmark initiated and pushed through the constitutional amendment providing for the integration of Greenland. Denmark's motivation, according to all indications and with much foresight, was to hold on to Greenland in an era of political decolonization and to circumvent UN supervision of Greenland as a non-self-governing territory under Chapter XI of the Charter.

Despite the fact that a referendum and parliamentary elections were required for the enactment of the constitutional amendments in Denmark proper, a referendum was not held in Greenland. The Greenlanders did not have representatives in the Parliament when the amendments were approved. The Provincial Council of Greenland, to which the Danish Government referred the integration question in 1952, was, according to Danish legislation which dictated the Council's composition and competence, neither expected nor entitled to consider issues of a constitutional nature. Members of the Council had not been authorized by their constituents to approve a change in the country's constitutional and international status. The Danish Governor was the Council's chairman.

In 1952, Greenland and Denmark were far from being equal partners. The political, economic, social and educational situation was far less advanced than in Denmark. There were no political parties in Greenland. There were no Greenlandic lawyers, and the Provincial Council did not receive impartial expert advice on the constitutional and international implications of integration. The inhabitants of East and North Greenland, who were not represented in the Provincial Council, had no say in the integration process. The only choice granted to the Greenlanders was between status quo as a colony and integration as a province. No other options, such as independence and free association, were ever made available.

Finally, it is contended that, while the General Assembly in Resolution 849 (IX) had the competence to remove Greenland from its list of non-self-governing territories, it did not have the power to approve the final integration of Greenland into Denmark because this was an issue involving a potential dispute between two parties and because one of the parties was not properly represented in the Assembly. Even if the competence of the General Assembly to approve an integration move of this kind were recognized, there are in the instant case ample reasons to revisit the decision of the Assembly. The dispute continues.

4 – The Status of the Greenlandic Inuit

Are the Greenlandic Inuit a People, an Indigenous People, a Minority or a Nation? A Practical, Philosophical and Conceptual Investigation[1]

Mininnguaq Kleist

Introduction

In order to be able to answer the question that headlines this paper, it will be necessary to try to define or at least narrow down the meanings of the four concepts and terms: "people", "indigenous people", "minority" and "nation" (all these concepts and terms are understood in the context of peoples). What is it that differentiates them from each other and in what senses are they alike?

In the arena of international law and politics there are different definitions of the above concepts and terms. These are the definitions which are perhaps the most relevant in this context and can be the most influential for the lives of the people they affect – they generate different legal rights. There may be other definitions of these concepts within other fields such as sociology and ethnography, but the consequences and the weight they are given in the field of international law and politics appear to be secondary, even though the definitions you find in international law and politics hopefully are inspired by or originate from the definitions of sociology and ethnography. I write "hopefully" because these

[1]   I would like to thank the members of the Working Group for interesting and inspiring discussions, and for having read earlier drafts of this paper and commenting on them: Professors Lauri Hannikainen, Ole Espersen and Gudmundur Alfredsson, advisor Bogi Eliasen and our Working Group's Secretary, Sjúrður Skaale. I would also like to thank my close friend Allan Olsen for linguistic and clarifying suggestions. In spite of their help, any errors and views found in this paper are entirely mine.

Sjúrður Skaale (ed.), The Right To National Self-Determination, *95-122.*
© *2004 Koninklijke Brill NV. Printed in the Netherlands.*

two fields of scientific expertise are the ones which deal intimately on a scientific level
with peoples, indigenous peoples, minorities and nations. Therefore these fields of scientific expertise contain a more thorough knowledge of this subject than the knowledge possessed in international law and politics, which again have other objectives.

In this chapter I will, as the heading suggests, deal with the Greenlandic Inuit and not
so much with the Faroe Islanders. The reason for this is that the situation and status of the
Faroese has already been dealt with intimately in the White Book published by the Faroese
Government in 1999.[2] There is no reason to do the same piece of work again in this paper.
Still, I will bring in the case of the Faroese whenever it seems appropriate and helpful. One
of the conclusions in the White Book was that the Faroese qualify as a people under international law. The Greenlandic "*Selvstyrekommission*" ("Commission on Self-Determination")
recently (March 2003) published an extensive report[3] on different issues concerning the
development of Greenlandic society, including some of the same issues dealt with in the
Faroese White Book. What I shall do here is take a practical, philosophical and conceptual
approach to the subject of this paper, something which the *Selvstyrekommission* does not do.

"Rigsfællesskabet" – The Community of the Danish Kingdom

Some relevant features of the Danish Kingdom: within the Danish Kingdom,
"*Rigsfællesskabet*", the Greenlandic Inuit are a distinct group. They differ from the ethnic
Danish majority group, and in this sense the Inuit qualify, to some extent, both as a minority and an indigenous people. But the reality of the Danish Kingdom is a bit more complicated. We have the metropolitan state Denmark, which is situated just north of Germany
and south of both Norway and Sweden. The next entity of the Danish Kingdom is the
Faroes, which is situated in the North Atlantic between the UK and Iceland (approx. 1000
km northwest of Denmark). The last entity of the Danish Kingdom is Greenland, which
is situated between Iceland and Canada (approx. 3000 km northwest of Denmark), and is
geographically considered to be part of the North American continent. If the territory of
the Greenlandic Inuit was a geographically integral part of metropolitan state Denmark,
the Inuit would be a minority in the traditional sense. In this hypothetical situation they
might need the protection which is offered, or given, by ILO Convention no. 169,[4] in the
form of special protective rights. In that situation they would be an indigenous minority
who would need protective measures.

But the actual situation of the Greenlandic Inuit and the Faroese is that they form a
vast majority in their own, in many respects, secluded territories. In Greenland there is

---

2   "*Hvidbog – Om vigtige forudsætninger for etablering af en suveræn færøsk stat.*" Færøernes
     Landsstyre, Törshavn, 1999.

3   *Selvstyrekommissionen*: "*Betænkning afgivet af Selvstyrekommissionen*", March 2003, Greenland
     Home Rule.

4   The International Labour Organization Convention no. 169 will be explained and exam-
     ined in the following.

a *"seemingly well-functioning self-government"*,[5] as Lauri Hannikainen puts it. The same is the case for The Faroes. In both Greenland and The Faroes democratic principles are utilized in finding their own political leadership. Therefore, in the case of Greenland, when it comes to *internal* matters which need political action, it is today a dubious project to argue for special protective indigenous rights, in order to avoid injustices committed against the Greenlandic Inuit, because formally, in many areas, they *are* the people in power. In *internal* Faroese matters, the Faroese do not need special protective minority rights either, in order to avoid injustices. Still, Denmark has some authority within internal Greenlandic and internal Faroese matters, mainly through the financial contributions (block grant) given to the two smaller economies.

The protective measures may have been needed earlier, when democracy was not the ruling principle in the respective islands. But this is not really the case anymore. Though as mentioned above, there may be exceptions to political areas where Denmark still holds the authority – directly or indirectly.

General remarks

The people of a sovereign state are constituted by the individuals who possess citizenship in that state. Within the body of the people, there may be smaller or larger groups of individuals who do not identify with the sovereign state they live in and the people of that state, even though they themselves are citizens of this particular country. Some of these groups may be indigenous people who only identify with their own often smaller group and the particular piece of territory they inhabit. The indigenous people may often view the rest of the population of the country as intruders and often also as oppressors. An indigenous people may have aspirations to create its own sovereign state.

Another group within the larger body of the people may be minorities. They may both identify with themselves and the larger body of the people, or only with themselves. In most cases, minorities are citizens of the country they inhabit.

The people of a sovereign state are either the (dominant) majority or the whole population. The people hold the dominant position in the sovereign state. In different conventions it is formulated that peoples have a formal right of self-determination.

Sovereign statehood entails citizenship. If Greenland and The Faroes became sovereign states, the peoples of these islands would become the citizens of these new states. As the situation is today they are citizens of Denmark.

Sovereign states are members of the UN and they are the core or "full-fledged" subjects of international law. They have a voice in the UN General Assembly. Indigenous peoples and minorities do not have any formal voice in the UN General Assembly.

---

5   Lauri Hannikainen: "The Status of Minorities, Indigenous Peoples and Immigrant and refugee Groups In Four Nordic States". Offprint from the Nordic Journal International Law, vol. 65, 1996, p. 6.

A fundamental principle in the international community is that all sovereign states are legally equal. Even though this may not be all true in reality, it is an important formal right proclaimed in the UN Charter. A sovereign state is not formally under the sovereignty of another state, and states are not allowed to interfere in other sovereign states' internal matters.

On the international scene there are many areas of interest where sovereign states are the only appropriate agents and entities, and as a consequence there are many international organisations, *viz.* the UN, NATO, the EU etc., where only sovereign states are allowed as members. If Greenland and The Faroes became sovereign states they would be able to become members of these organisations and pursue their interests within them.

The Categorizations

"Indigenous peoples"

Rodolfo Stavenhagen writes: *"If the word "indigenous" refers to "origins", all human beings are indigenous in some way. However, in the sociological and political vocabulary (and ever more often in the juridical usage as well), the term "indigenous" is employed as a reference to groups of the population that occupy a determined position in society as a result of specific historical developments."* And he continues *"One cannot deny the colonial roots of the present concept of "indigenous."*[6]

The indigenous peoples around the world count approximately 300 million people[7] spread all over the globe. The NGO-organization IWGIA (International Work Group for Indigenous Affairs – co-operates with the UN) reports on its homepage[8] that at least 350 million people worldwide are considered to be indigenous, and according to IWGIA the indigenous peoples are divided into at least 5000 peoples.

The term "indigenous peoples" covers widely peoples with indeed very different cultures, religions and languages etc. Indigenous peoples are always closely connected to a particular area or piece of land. They are considered to be the peoples that originally inhabited a certain particular territory, a certain particular country and/or a part of the world, before immigrants from other parts of the world came and gradually became the dominant people, thereby threatening the indigenous peoples' culture and land rights. In the creation of modern states around the world the indigenous peoples often became marginalized, and in many cases they have even been forced to move from their original land.

---

6   Article by Rodolfo Stavenhagen: "Indigenous Rights: Some Conceptual Problems" pp. 14-15 in W.J. Assies and A.J. Hoekema (ed):"Indigenous Peoples' Experiences with Self-Government", IWGIA Document no. 76, Copenhagen, 1994. Stavenhagen is working from El Colegio de Mexico and Instituto Interamericano de Derechos Humanos, Cuidad de Mexico, Mexico.

7   Source United Nations – www.un.dk (as of 2002-2003).

8   www.iwgia.org (as of 2002-2003). IWGIA is an independent international membership organization staffed by specialists and advisors on indigenous affairs.

Negotiating in present time with the "new" dominant group in the country some indigenous peoples have reached fairly good results, but mostly indigenous peoples still struggle for recognition. The historical developments (politically, culturally, economically, linguistically etc.) of the different indigenous peoples have differed a lot. Today, some live a modern (western) life in big multicultural cities and others may still be nomadic or hunters etc. But the common denominator is often the strongly kept connection to their old culture, and a special relation to the land. European colonialism has been one of the greatest sources of the above-mentioned situations in the Americas, Africa, Oceania and Asia.

Even though the above might seem like a wide definition of indigenous people, it is just an introduction to the topic. There is no authoritative definition of this concept or term which everybody explicitly would accept. Still, there are some attempts to describe indigenous people which are very widely accepted and these are the ones which I will present here. Both the UN and IWGIA point at the definition used in International Labour Organization (ILO) Convention no. 169 from 1989 and the almost same sounding definition formulated by Special Rapporteur for the Sub-Commission,[9] José Martinez Cobo, in the "Study of the Problem of Discrimination Against Indigenous Populations."[10]

ILO Convention no. 169 concerning Indigenous and Tribal Peoples in Independent Countries, 1989, defines in Article 1 the objects of the Convention:

"Article 1

1. This Convention applies to:

(a) tribal peoples in independent countries whose social, cultural and economic conditions distinguish them from other sections of the national community, and whose status is regulated wholly or partially by their own customs or traditions or by special laws or regulations;

(b) peoples in independent countries who are regarded as indigenous on account of their descent from the populations which inhabited the country, or a geographical region to which the country belongs, at the time of conquest or colonization or the establishment of present state boundaries and who, irrespective of their legal status, retain some or all of their own social, economic, cultural and political institutions.

2. Self-identification as indigenous or tribal shall be regarded as a fundamental criterion for determining the groups to which the provisions Convention apply.

---

9 The UN Sub-Commission on Prevention of Discrimination and Protection of Minorities.

10 José Martinez Cobo: "Study of the Problem of Discrimination Against Indigenous Populations", United Nations Publication, New York, 1987, (E/CN.4/Sub.2/1986/7/ Add.4).

3.   The use of the term *peoples* in this Convention shall not be construed as having
any implications as regards the rights which may attach to the term under international law."[11]

Note that "self-identification" as indigenous or tribal is regarded as a fundamental criterion
for being indigenous (or tribal).

Denmark has ratified ILO Convention no. 169 and it is applicable to the Inuit in
Greenland. "*Denmark does not consider the Faroese people neither as an indigenous or a tribal
people.*"[12] The working definition formulated by José Martinez Cobo, in the report: "Study
of the Problem of Discrimination Against Indigenous Populations"[13] states: "*Indigenous communities, peoples and nations are those which, having a historical continuity with pre-invasion and
pre-colonial societies that developed on their territories, consider themselves distinct from other sectors
of the societies now prevailing in those territories, or parts of them. They form at present non-dominant sectors of society and are determined to preserve, develop and transmit to future generations their
ancestral territories, and their ethnic identity, as the basis of their continued existence as peoples, in
accordance with their own cultural patterns, social institutions and legal systems.*"[14]

The term "a historical continuity" is key to the definition of indigenous peoples. The
historical continuity must be of an extended period of time which reaches into the present,
and consists of one or more of the following factors:
1)   Occupation of ancestral lands (or at least part of them);
2)   Common ancestry with the original occupants of these lands;
3)   Culture in general, or in specific manifestations;
4)   Language;
5)   Residence in certain parts of the country, or in certain regions of the world;
6)   Other relevant factors.

José Martinez Cobo also regards "self-identification" as an important part of his working
definition of indigenous peoples. An individual person is one who belongs to a given indigenous people through self-identification as indigenous (group consciousness), and is recognized and accepted by the group as one of its members (acceptance by the group). This
preserves for these communities the sovereign right and power to decide who belongs to
them, without external interference.[15]

---

11   International Labour Organization, Convention No. 169, Indigenous and Tribal Peoples
      Convention, 1989.

12   Lauri Hannikainen: "The Status of Minorities, Indigenous Peoples and Immigrant and ref-
      ugee Groups In Four Nordic States". Offprint from the Nordic Journal International Law,
      vol. 65, 1996, p. 63.

13   This is a working definition and not an official UN authorized definition, even though the
      UN in some cases may use it unofficially and non-bindingly.

14   "Study of the Problem of Discrimination Against Indigenous Populations" pp. 29, paragraph 379.

15   The presentation of the relevant parts of José Martinez Cobos' report is to some extent
      directly taken from the UN's and IWGIA's homepages.

Self-identification is also one of the elements that the UN points at when trying to define indigenous peoples. Other important elements are language and geographical area.[16]

It is not unproblematic to talk about definitions of indigenous peoples. Tapan Bose writes: "*The Draft Universal Declaration on the Rights of the indigenous Peoples prepared by the Working Group, which had been set up by the UN to work on this subject, does not include a definition of indigenous peoples or populations. This omission has been justified by the Chairperson – Rapporteur of the Working Group, Erica-Irene Daes – on the ground that "historically, indigenous peoples have suffered, from definitions imposed by others" and as a result, in certain countries many indigenous peoples have been declassified.(…) (E/CN.4/Stib.2/AC.4/1995/3, page 3).*"[17]

Erica-Irene Daes does not believe that a universal definition of the concept "indigenous" can be formulated, but on the other hand she recognizes that there are a number of factors which can be mentioned when attempting to develop an understanding of this concept. In different regions and national contexts these factors are present to a greater or lesser degree. These factors should only be viewed as general guidelines:

"*a.   priority in time, with respect to the occupation and use of a specific territory;*

b.   the voluntary perpetuation of cultural distinctiveness, which may include the aspects of language, social organization, religion and spiritual values, modes of production, laws and institutions;

c.   self-identification, as well as recognition by other groups … as a distinct collectivity; and

d.   an experience of subjugation, marginalization, dispossession, exclusion, or discrimination, whether or not these conditions persist."[18]

One may add as a comment, as Lauri Hannikainen does, that (to some extent) indigenous peoples are "'*endangered peoples', i.e. their survival as separate peoples is uncertain.*"[19] But in the

---

16   The www.un.dk homepage (as of 2002-2003).

17   Tapan Bose: "Definitions and Delimitation of the Indigenous Peoples of Asia", published in IWGIA Document no. 80, 1996. Also to be found on www.iwgia.org (as of 2002-2003). Note that the reference in brackets at the end of the text is a reference to a UN document. Tapan Bose is the Secretary of the organization "The Other Media" in Delhi. He is a leading human rights activist, film-maker and author.

18   Tony Simpson: "Indigenous Heritage and Self-Determination", Document IWGIA No. 86, Copenhagen, 1997, p. 23. The text piece is taken from a paper Erica Irene Daes presented at Suva, Fiji, 1996 on the "Pacific Workshop on the United Nations Draft Declaration on the Rights of Indigenous Peoples". Both the "Principles and Guidelines for the Protection of the Heritage of Indigenous Peoples" elaborated by Dr. Erica-Irene Daes and the "Draft Declaration as Agreed upon by the Members of the United Nations Working Group on Indigenous Populations at its Eleventh Session" can be found in Simpson.

19   Lauri Hannikainen: "The Status of Minorities, Indigenous Peoples and Immigrant and refugee Groups In Four Nordic States". Offprint from the Nordic Journal International Law, vol. 65, 1996, p. 3.

case of the Inuit of Greenland, who are under the sovereignty of Denmark, they *"form an overwhelmingly majority of the population of Greenland and exercise a seemingly well-functioning self-government."*[20] With approximately 50.000 Greenlandic Inuit this particular people is not likely to become extinct.

"Minorities"

Rodolfo Stavenhagen writes: *"The notion of minority can be taken in its numerical sense, as a population whose number is "inferior to the majority." Assuming that we live in a time where "majorities" govern (this being the founding idea of democracy) the identification of one or another ethnic group as a "minority" would put them in a permanently disadvantaged situation in relation to the "major-ity," particularly when that majority controls the state apparatus. The notion of minority can also be understood in a sociological sense, as a marginalized, discriminated, excluded or disadvantaged group, independently of its demographic weight. (I do not refer here to privileged or "dominant minorities" which generally do not need special instruments for the juridical protection)."*[21] (The last comment in brackets is not mine but Stavenhagen's. I found it important to include it here).

Lauri Hannikainen writes: *"By the term 'minorities' the international community has under-stood such national, ethnic, religious and linguistic groups which (1) differ from the rest of the popula-tion, (2) are numerically inferior to the leading nationality or nationalities, (3) are in a non-dominant position, (4) have a mutual sense of solidarity, (5) are well-established, including having deep roots in their country of residence and, according to the leading view, their members are citizens of their coun-try of residence. The residence of fifty years has not been considered to be enough, but a hundred years has been regarded as sufficient. International law grants certain basic minority rights to the members of minorities and basic protection to minorities as collective entities."*[22]

And Hannikainen continues: *"In the Nordic States the prevailing view has been that only persons belonging to well-established minority groups can have international minority rights, but there have been cases displaying reluctance even to recognize this."*[23]

Hannikainen adds, that under the Organization for Security and Cooperation in Europe (OSCE), *"[t]he term 'national minority' means such minorities which are well-established and clearly conscious of their status as a separate group; apparently their members must be citizens of the State where they live. These instruments appear to want to confine minority rights to unquestion-ably well-established minorities."*[24]

The High Commissioner on National Minorities of the OSCE, Max van der Stoel, stated at the OSCE Minorities Seminar in Warsaw, 1994: *"(...) I won't offer you* [a defini-

---

20   *Ibid.* p. 6.

21   Rodolfo Stavenhagen: "Indigenous Rights: Some Conceptual Problems" pp. 21.

22   Lauri Hannikainen: "The Status of Minorities, Indigenous Peoples and Immigrant and ref-
      ugee Groups In Four Nordic States". Offprint from the Nordic Journal International Law,
      vol. 65, 1996, p. 3.

23   *Ibid.* p. 5.

24   *Ibid.* p. 13.

tion] *of my own. I would note, however, that the existence of a minority is a question of fact and not of definition. In this connection, I would like to quote the Copenhagen Document of 1990 which (...) states that 'To belong to a national minority is a matter of a person's individual choice.' (...) I would dare to say that I know a minority when I see one. First of all, a minority is a group with linguistic, ethnic or cultural characteristics, which distinguishes it from the majority. Secondly, a minority is a group which usually not only seeks to maintain its identity but also tries to give stronger expression to that identity."*[25]

The High Commissioner's words are without legal consequences for minorities, but they are not without a certain weight, coming from a leading expert on minority rights with a formal status in one of the larger European governmental organizations.

In the Council of the European Bureau of Lesser-used Languages Greenland and The Faroes are not represented as linguistic minorities in Denmark. Even though their populations are small, and thus only a few people speak Greenlandic and Faroese, they do not qualify, because they have both chosen to stay outside the EC/EU.

Still, the Greenlandic Inuit and Faroese people living permanently in the metropolitan state of Denmark form minorities. There are approximately 10.000 Inuit and 15.000 Faroese living permanently in Denmark.[26] Ethnically and culturally they differ from the Danish population; they are numerically inferior to the leading nationality; they are in a non-dominant position; they have a mutual sense of solidarity (there are several Greenlandic Community Houses and Faroese Community Houses to be found in Denmark where people meet each other, as well as several social clubs formed all over Denmark); many of the Greenlandic Inuit and Faroese people living in Denmark have deep roots in Denmark. They may have been born and raised in Denmark, married to a Dane, have children who have been born and raised in Denmark. They cannot readily move to either Greenland or The Faroes. It goes without saying that both groups are citizens of Denmark.

The only criterion for minorities which the Greenlandic Inuit living in Denmark do not seem to meet is in the period of time in which they formed a well-established group in Denmark (of course, this depends on where you place the line of demarcation when considering time). The Faroese in Denmark have been a well-established group in Denmark for more than a century. The two minorities need the basic minority rights and the basic protection of minorities as collective entities. Those rights and instruments are something especially the Inuit in Denmark are in need of. Many Inuit in Denmark constitute parts of the lowest social segment in Denmark, and thus live under very poor living conditions.

"Peoples"

In the UN International Covenant on Civil and Political Rights, adopted in 1966, the first two paragraphs of Article 1 read as follows:

---

25   See the OSCE homepage: www.osce.org (as of 2002-2003).

26   The numbers can differ according to how you define the Greenlandic Inuit and the Faroe Islanders.

1. All peoples have the right of self-determination. By virtue of that right they freely
    determine their political status and freely pursue their economic, social and cultural
    development.

2. All peoples may, for their own ends, freely dispose of their natural wealth and
    resources without prejudice to any obligations arising out of international coopera-
    tion, based upon the principle of mutual benefit, and international law. In no case may
    a people be deprived of its own means of subsistence.

Rodolfo Stavenhagen's comment to the above is: "*Article 1 of the international conventions is
clear:"All peoples have the right to self-determination…."The international human rights system is
supported by two pillars: individual rights and peoples' rights. However, for reasons already discussed
the concept of "peoples' rights" has been given less attention than that of individual human rights.
Quite often the notion of "people" is quite simply equated with that of "nation" (do we not speak of
"United Nations"?) which in turn is confounded with the state. (States have a seat in the UN). States
are very jealous in claiming all sorts of rights for themselves (sovereignty, equality, non-intervention,
territorial integrity).*"[27]

After reading Rodolfo Stavenhagen's critical comment one just needs to look back at
ILO Convention No. 169 in order to realize that he is not completely wrong. It says:

"*3. The use of the term peoples in this Convention shall not be construed as having any implications as regards the rights which may attach to the term under international law.*"

This means that so-called indigenous peoples are not granted the same rights according to international law (e.g. the Human Rights Covenant) as a consequence of this particular convention. They do *not* qualify legally as a full-fledged people on the international
political and juridical scene through the ILO Convention, and they are certainly *not* full-
fledged subjects under international law. One of the reasons why is that they do *not* hold
the power of their countries – they are *not* the people of a separate sovereign state. They
have been called the same as peoples, but without any of the legal consequence linked to
this. There has been a need to emphasize that…and this "need" has not been one felt by the
indigenous peoples, for sure. This is embarrassing for the "full-fledged peoples" – to put it
mildly.[28]

Stavenhagen continues: "*International practice accords the right to self-determination to the
peoples of colonized territories but not to minorities. Indigenous peoples have good arguments to show
that they are or have been colonized. For this reason they demand that they be considered "peoples" and
claim the right to self-determination.*"[29]

---

27   Rodolfo Stavenhagen: "Indigenous Rights: Some Conceptual Problems" p. 23.

28   The indigenous peoples are obviously not interested in having their political and legal
      status impaired or having their rights limited in any way. On the other hand, the full-
      fledged peoples (those who hold state power) have an interest in that being the case,
      because they stand to lose authority, land and its resources, if the indigenous peoples
      obtain full political and legal rights.

29   *Ibid.* p. 23.

Even though Stavenhagen believes that indigenous peoples should demand to be considered as "peoples" and through this, claim the right of self-determination, this categorization, in my humble opinion, should not in any way be considered as being a sure road for a *realization* of the right of self-determination. Our Working Group's talks with UN officials indicated this point very clearly. For example, the Kurdish people, the Palestinian people and the Tibetan people[30] are commonly considered to be distinct peoples by the world society, yet they do not possess their own sovereign state. They possess only very limited degrees of self-determination, if any at all. This is in all three cases due to the given metropolitan states. The metropolitan states exclusively decide whether or not the above-mentioned peoples should possess their own sovereign states. There is no existing international organ which can order (with any authority or muscle, so to speak) a metropolitan state to give or grant another people its own sovereign state. It does not matter whether or not the given people in question are commonly considered to be a people with an "s", in plural.

Furthermore, "the right of self-determination" has not been defined by any authority with which the metropolitan states have to comply. Does "the right of self-determination" entail both internal and external self-determination or only the former? The decision lies solely in the hands of the metropolitan state (still, one can try to influence the decision). If Greenland demands a higher degree of self-determination by saying they have the right to this through being a people, Denmark could answer (I am not saying they will); you already possess a form of self-determination (Home Rule) and we find it to be sufficient.

None of the above-mentioned international governmental organizations or conventions could force Denmark to change this opinion. On top of this, there are more urgent "hot spots" with grave violations of human rights around the world, which demand more attention from the international community. Bloodshed and massacres do not occur in the relationship between Greenland and Denmark, and fortunately so!

In present day international law the entities which constitute "peoples" are the peoples who happen to be in power of their own territory and through this being an individual sovereign state and recognized by its neighbours (and to some extent the world community) as such.[31] Therefore, the Human Rights Covenant, and other conventions proclaiming the same, should be taken with a pinch of salt. It is the metropolitan states which decide how far self-determination should go – the sovereign states possess the rights. This may be a cynical interpretation, but I believe it is not far from the truth. Our UN meetings support this interpretation.

---

30 My examples, and not necessarily the same examples UN officials would use.

31 Erica Irene Daes also touches on this issue in her: "The Spirit and Letter of the Right to Self-Determination of indigenous Peoples: Reflections on the Making of the United Nations Draft Declaration" in Pekka Aikio and Martin Scheinin (ed): "Operationalizing the Right of Indigenous Peoples to Self-Determination", Åbo Akademi University, Turku/ Åbo, Finland 2000.

"Nation"

About the term "nation", Stavenhagen writes: "*A second accepted view refers to a combination of features that characterize a human group in territorial, historical, cultural and ethnic terms which give them a sense of identity that may find its expression in nationalist or ethnic ideologies. In this second acceptation the term "people" is similar to "nation," the only distinction being that the term "nation" is generally used in relation to the ideology and politics of "nationalism" which ties it to the constitution of a state, whereas the term people can be used without necessary reference to the control of state power. It follows that the use of one term or another corresponds to conventions and is not intrinsic to the social and historical phenomena to which it refers.*"[32]

This means that a "people" can actually constitute a "nation" without it being recognized as such by international conventions. In international law the recognition of one or the other concept as applying to a certain entity is a matter of convention, political will, interests and morality. The lack of the last two is sufficient to keep a "people" from being recognized as a "nation'. This is not uncommon.

Stavenhagen adds: "*There are good and valid reasons to consider the indigenous peoples of the Americas and elsewhere as "peoples" and subjects of human and legal rights in the sense the UN employs the term. Some would even say that the use of the term "nations" would be justified. The North-American Indians, for instance, refer to themselves as "nations," partly because in the past they have been denominated as such by the North-American governments. The indigenous Latin-Americans, by contrast, have in their recent encounters and conferences insisted on the use of the term "peoples".*"[33]

Here the two terms "peoples" and "nations" are used in the same way by the Latin-American Indians and the North American Indians. Both the Latin-American Indians and the North-American Indians are evenly "indigenous", if you can say that. There is nothing, in principle or intrinsically, which differentiates the two groups of peoples. Still, they use different terms in characterizing themselves. Firstly, this may reflect a habitual "term using" – you have been categorized as being such and such, by outsiders and/or yourself, and you keep on using this categorizing term. Secondly, it may to some extent reflect the aspiration of a given people – the use of a specific term gives you more or less specified rights and opportunities.

Does this usage of different terms in these two cases have any consequences in international law? The answer is yes, but no matter what the Indian populations call themselves, there are no sovereign states today, on the American continents, that you can call sovereign Indian states. I could go further into the cases of the Indian peoples, but that would miss the objective of this paper. The cases of the Indian peoples and the Greenlandic Inuit differ too much.

The above shows to some degree that the use of one or the other term, in order to categorize a given people, is not the only criterion to consider when considering whether or not a given people should be granted full self-determination. History and practicalities

---

32   Rodolfo Stavenhagen: "Indigenous Rights: Some Conceptual Problems" p. 24.

33   *Ibid.* p. 24.

also have to be considered, and if they point in a direction which does not look promising enough, it does not matter what you call yourself. It is of course up for discussion when the picture, on the whole, looks too grim. How you place yourself in such a discussion also depends largely on the perspective from which you enter the discussion. This does not necessarily mean that you are biased, though it could mean exactly just that. But it may also be that you view things differently.

The term "nation" is the root of the term "nationalism", which is a term that is loaded with very heavy negative associations. Movements of nationalism around the world have often led to clashes between ethnic groups, discrimination and, in some extreme instances, ethnic cleansing and genocide. Nationalism appeals to your emotions, and as emotions are irrational, they may lead to people placing their own culture on a pedestal in such a way that they lose respect for other nationalities. This means that the term "nation" is often reluctantly used and is becoming more and more uncommon in connection with state-building.

Discussion

In the following discussion, I will deal with Greenland and, whenever it seems relevant and fruitful, I will include The Faroes in relation to the subjects already dealt with in the above.

Greenland

The Greenlandic Inuit are recognized as and considered to be an indigenous people by themselves, Denmark and the international community. The Greenlandic Inuit consider themselves to be indigenous, because the interpretation of the concept "indigenous" is that by being indigenous you were and are the first people, the original people, of the land – Greenland. The Greenlandic translation of the concept "indigenous people" is "*nunap inoqqa-avi*", which again could be translated as "the lands first/original people". It has importance to the Greenlandic Inuit to explicitly state this. By this the Greenlandic Inuit can morally and consistently claim Greenland as being their land. They did not take the land from another people. They were here first (the arctic area of the North American continent – the northern part of Canada, most of Alaska, and Greenland can be said to be "Inuit land").

The importance for the Inuit to explicitly state this is most likely due to the colonization of the Greenlandic Inuit by the Danes. The Danes have never been numerically superior to the Inuit, i.e. in Greenland. Still, Greenland and the Inuit entered the Danish Kingdom and came under Danish rule (even though Greenland has its Home Rule it is not a sovereign state – not even a state within Denmark). This may cause some doubt, and not strangely, about whose country it is (to put it simply). By this you may as an Inuit want to remind the Danes and others that you were the first to be here. By saying that you are the indigenous people of the land you state this, and by stating this you can morally claim the country to be yours. Unfortunately, there may be a downside to the emphasis laid upon the indigenousness of your people. If you are not careful it may cause problems for you if you want to strive for higher political and juridical status on the international scene. The following will show this.

ILO Convention no. 169 states that with this Convention, or using this Convention, indigenous peoples cannot achieve full status as "peoples". The Convention gives indigenous peoples a lot of protection against encroachment from outside, but it does not grant them the right to be a people with an "s" (remember indigenous peoples' rights are more limited than peoples' rights, which again have a more limited status than peoples with their own sovereign state; sovereign states are the full-fledged subjects of international law). The categorization "people" would *formally* open the door (note: "formally" – you would still have to take the steps towards and through the door for full internal and external self-determination yourself) for some indigenous peoples' aspirations to build up their own sovereign states with full internal and external self-determination, thus full autonomy. In many cases the peoples, those who possess their own sovereign state, have a strong interest in this not happening. Many sovereign states have indigenous populations within their territories, and these states are not interested in giving away land (or the control of it) – the reason often given is that it would create instability on the international scene if all the indigenous peoples of the world would achieve sovereignty of their lands. This might be true, but it is very unlikely that all the approximately 5000 different indigenous peoples would want to create their own sovereign state. In many, if not most, cases it would not even arise as a question because of the small sizes of the given indigenous population. Other practical obstacles may also be present, which make other arrangements than sovereign statehood more attractive. Running a state is not even consistent with some indigenous ways of life.

One must admit that the 20th century saw a lot of "new" sovereign states emerging. But most of these were either former colonies or nations, which in some point in time had been illegitimately annexed by another country – often by a totalitarian state. The secession by either a colony, or a nation from a totalitarian state can hardly be used as reasons to oppose the notion of secession. Staying as a colony and staying within a totalitarian state is *ceteris paribus* a much greater evil than secessions.

Also, the argument that a lot of new states would create anarchy and disturb the world order is very weak. Yes, it might become more difficult to agree on international issues. But if a nation becomes independent this does not mean that it places itself outside any framework of moral thinking. If entities become independent this does not mean that they become unrestrained and run amok.[34]

Furthermore, as stated above, international practice does accord the full right of self-determination to former colonized peoples,[35] in some cases even becoming sover-

---

34   This is a point which the philosopher Allen Buchanan presents and elaborates in his "Secession – The Morality of Political Divorce from Fort Sumter to Lithuania and Quebec", pp. 102-104, Westview Press, Boulder, 1991.

35   See Stavenhagen above, and Sir Robert Jennings & Sir Arthur Watts (ed): "Oppenheim's International Law – Ninth Edition – Vol. I – Peace", pp. 281-295, Longman, Harlow, England, 1992.

eign states (many of the African states are examples of this). This gives indigenous peoples a chance to achieve self-determination, if they work hard enough for it. Still, you have to bear in mind that there are different degrees of self-determination (this is a question which will be dealt with elsewhere in this report) and only some of them will lead to a sovereign state. In every single case the involved parties will have to decide on which arrangements will be the most appropriate.

With its Home Rule Greenland has achieved internal self-determination on many areas, but the exceptions are; the police force which does its' policing according to Greenlandic laws, but is under the authority of the Danish police force and the whole force is directly financed by the Danes; the currency used in Greenland is the Danish Kroner; the judiciary system is ultimately under Danish authority, but the Greenlandic Parliament has the competence to make the internal laws; and, Denmark has a lot to say when it comes to the Greenlandic economy because of the financial contribution given. When it comes to international matters Greenland's authority is very limited even though current developments point towards gaining more and more authority. Still, when it comes to the security and defence of Greenland Denmark has the final say and Greenland is not allowed to manoeuvre on its own. This is an area of great importance for Greenland because of the military and geo-political importance Greenland has for the only super power in the world – the US. When the US and Denmark meet and negotiate issues which involve Greenland, it is not strange that Greenland wants to have a say. Fortunately, Denmark has opened up and recognized the Greenlandic wishes and has begun to work together with Greenland on exactly this matter. The US is the party which has to be convinced of the reasonableness of the Greenlandic wishes.

Denmark is a member of the EU, Greenland is not. In cases where Danish interests are not compromised or when the Greenlandic interests are not directly contrary to those of Denmark, Greenland is allowed to manoeuvre in its own foreign policy, but still with the limitation of not being a full subject under international law. A strengthening of Greenland's international personality and political profile would get Greenland closer to becoming a full subject under international law. Furthermore, ever-continuing negotiations with Denmark will also be needed until this aim is reached. Another important factor is to continue the internal development of the country, including strengthening the economy. In real-life informal politics, someone who cannot stand on their own feet economically will not get the same political recognition as someone who can.

It is the ambition of many, if not most, leading Greenlandic politicians to achieve full autonomy for Greenland. To some extent this is a wish the people of Greenland share too. I claim this because the people knew about this ambition prior to the last elections for the Greenlandic Parliament in December 2002, and the people to a great extent voted for parties and politicians with this ambition[36] (still, one must admit that there may be other

---

36   Still it seems that the Greenlandic population wants this to happen without lowering the standards of living too much – Gallup polls in Greenlandic newspapers have indicated this.

reasons why those politicians got elected, but one must also admit that such cardinal issues as Greenland's future political status cannot have been weighed lightly in the minds of the voters).

Greenland has through the years, and especially after the establishment of the Home Rule, achieved authority over areas such as health care, education, housing, the environment, infrastructure, finances (Greenland has its own tax system separate from the Danish, and even though it is economically self-sustaining (Denmark gives a substantial contribution yearly) it has much to say about how the money should be spent), social welfare, the cultural area, the fishing industry, agriculture, and businesses in general, to a large extent the subsoil etc. It is clear that there are limitations to how much further one can go in gaining authority in many more areas before the question of becoming a full subject under international law and sovereignty as a state will arise. This is the question which I will be addressing here, not to be confused with the more practical questions of how to become economically self-sustaining and how to lift the educational level of the Greenlandic population, which is much needed before the above status can be achieved. There may be practical reasons, such as those just mentioned, for not granting an indigenous people the status of subject under international law, but practical problems can be solved (mostly), and they will most likely not pose universal problems (not applicable to all; not relevant for all), but only local problems for a particular indigenous people. Practical problems have to be dealt with when looking closer into particular cases. The project of this article is not to deal with practical problems, such as economic, educational and social ones etc., but to deal with matters of principle, law, and to some extent morality (and yes, I deal with a particular case here, Greenland, but again on a level of principle).

In ILO Convention No. 169 a definition of indigenous peoples is given. In the same Convention it is said that this Convention cannot be used to grant indigenous peoples full rights under international law. In a way it can be said that this Convention both identifies and denies particular entities, namely the indigenous and tribal populations, full international legal rights.

In the following discussion, I will try to show that none of the defining characteristics of being an indigenous people under international law and practice actually distinguishes you from a people in any defining and legally relevant way. Through this I will try to show that *none of* the reasons given for not granting indigenous people and the Greenlandic Inuit the status of full subjects in international law are valid.

Borders

Now, let us look at the role borders play in defining peoples in international law. In international law what defines a people are not cultural characteristics, but geography. A people is the population of a given territory. This is also the case when boundaries are drawn. An example are the German people. Before the second world war they were one people. After the second world war, they became two, after the border was drawn. And in the nineties they became one again when the two Germanies were joined and the border erased. Before the border was erased the two German peoples constituted two full-fledged international subjects, and today they constitute only one.

Both the Greenlandic Inuit and the Faroese live on islands geographically far away from the metropolitan state Denmark. No new "artificial" borders would have to be drawn – nature has already taken care of that. Thus, seen from the perspective of borders nothing stands in the way of the Greenlandic Inuit and the Faroese attaining the international legal status of peoples. The same goes if they have further aspirations for creating their own sovereign states. The so-called "salt water theory"[37] is applicable in the cases of both the Greenlandic Inuit and the Faroese, which means that if they wish to go further in their political aspirations, that is, if they want to try to aim at a higher legal international status, the road seems to be open from here (this will be dealt with elsewhere in the report).

Thus, with respect to borders, there is nothing which stands in the way of the Greenlandic Inuit being considered as a people under international law. The same goes for the Faroese. There is a lot of salt water between Denmark and the Faroes, and even more between Denmark and Greenland…

In international law, the relevant criteria when claiming land are: that the land you claim to be yours is morally yours, that is, you were here first; that you are actually present in the territory; and that you exercise your sovereignty in the area in question. Beyond this, your actual relationship with the land in question does not really matter (that is, how you utilize it and how you make a living in the land).

Now, let us take another look at what differentiates indigenous peoples from peoples intrinsically (if anything at all).

Descendency from original inhabitants

In the definitions of indigenous people it is stated that to be considered as an indigenous people you must be the descendants of the original inhabitants of the territory who lived there prior to colonization and/or conquest. Colonization, or the fact that you have been conquered through violence (not the case in either the Inuit or the Faroese case) is not an

---

37   The salt water theory, also called the blue water thesis, is incorporated into General Assembly Resolution 1541, which states in the relevant part:

Principle IV

Prima facie there is an obligation to transmit information in respect of a territory which is geographically separate and is distinct ethnically and/or culturally from the country administering it.

Principle V

Once it has been established that such a prima facie case of geographical and ethnical or cultural distinctness of a territory exists, other elements may then be brought into consideration. These additional elements may be, *inter alia*, of an administrative, political, juridical, economic or historical nature.

I am guilty of almost copying this footnote from S. James Anaya: "Indigenous Peoples in International Law", p. 60, Oxford University Press, New York, 2000.

intrinsic matter, but something that happens to you as a group, it is imposed on you. It does not change the fact that you are a descendant of the original inhabitants.

Let us take a look at the Danes. Are they the descendants of the original inhabitants of their country? Without a detailed knowledge of the Danish pre-historical period the answer must be affirmative. If one looks deeper into the case one will find that the Danes (or their ancestors) have actually been in what is now known as Denmark for a longer period of time than the Inuit have been in Greenland and the Faroese in The Faroes. The only difference is the colonization and I will claim that having been colonized is not an intrinsic matter, and therefore it is difficult to argue that it is a fundamentally differing aspect between the peoples mentioned.

Whether or not colonization as a tangible thing imposed on you is enough grounds to be granted lesser political rights as a people can always be discussed. You might have to consider the cases at hand independently. One important factor to consider would be how traumatizing the colonization had been to the people in question. But one should keep in mind that very strong reasons indeed are needed to take away the rights of a people. To take away rights from a people is also almost always associated with punishment, and it does not make sense to punish a (former) colonized people. To withhold rights as some kind of protection against the different problems and dangers of the modern world does not make much sense either. I would rather say if protection is needed then enhanced rights should be given, should any special measures be required.

Culture

Now let us turn our attention to the concept "culture" (in a broad and general sense). This concept is not made relevant in the case of defining peoples in international law, but is made relevant in the case of defining indigenous peoples, and therefore I think it is relevant to take it up here. In saying that culture is not relevant in defining peoples in international law, you are not saying that it has nothing to do with a people, in fact all peoples have a culture.

In the definitions of indigenous peoples it is said that in order to be categorized as an indigenous people you must have a distinctive culture which can be recognized as your own and which is different from other cultures. This difference and distinctiveness can be to a greater or lesser degree. Of course you may have some similarities with other cultures – this is to some extent inevitable. But overall you have to be able to distinguish "you" from "them" culturally, and you have to be able to recognize that difference even after colonization has taken place.

As already stated above, in international law culture is not relevant as such in order for a people to be considered a subject. In common sense, in philosophy, and intrinsically it is another matter. One would like to think that a people has a culture – with its many aspects – which the individuals of this certain people share. This, among other things, keeps them together through better or worse (voluntarily as well as involuntarily – it is not easy to leave one's culture even if one wishes to). The individuals together constitute a people. It is hard if not impossible to try to imagine a people without it having a shared culture

– elements of a culture may be the language, traditions, clothing, institutions, symbols, cuisine, humour etc.

Do the Danes have a culture? The answer is yes (if I gave a negative answer to that question to a Dane, I would be in trouble and not just because it could be insulting to hear the claim that your people do not have a culture; my own common sense would protest too – as stated, it is hard to imagine a people without a culture). Is Danish culture distinct from that of the Swedes, the Germans and the Norwegians? The answer is again positive; the four mentioned nations have their own distinct cultures.

The difference between the cultures of indigenous peoples and peoples' culture is, again to a lesser or greater degree, that a peoples' culture has been influenced more from the outside. There has been more interaction with other peoples, and through this it might have been less static (to put it provocatively – there are of course peoples who have been isolated or isolationistic and indigenous peoples who have had plenty of interaction with other peoples). There are perhaps a greater variety of "life forms" to choose between as an individual within a people (again, to some extent, provocatively).

If there is this difference between indigenous peoples' and peoples' cultures, is it an intrinsic matter? And if there is a difference, is it relevant in the case of indigenous peoples' wish to attain the same legal rights as peoples?

The answer to the first question is negative. No, because culture is a product of ourselves and our surroundings. This goes for both indigenous peoples and peoples. Surroundings influence us and our cultures. At the outset, the nature of our surroundings is not up to us (of course, you can in some instances seek to change elements of the surroundings), and if we do not to some extent adapt we will not survive, and because of that it is not intrinsic.

It could be claimed that the answer to the first question could become positive, because these experiences (of our surroundings) shape us and become part of us through time both as individuals and as a culture. But the answer to that would be that this goes for both indigenous peoples and peoples. There is only an arbitrary difference in the surroundings and experiences which is actually also to be found when we exclusively consider the so-called "peoples". One almost feels the urge to sarcastically say that indigenous peoples and peoples are of the same species – they are all human beings…

I conclude that there is no intrinsic difference in the cultures of indigenous peoples and peoples, at least not a difference which justifies different international legal rights. There may be practical reasons for not granting indigenous peoples rights on the same footing as peoples, but they can be overcome through development and adaptation to the different requirements and duties with which peoples have to comply. There may be practical limitations to what an indigenous people can overcome, simply because many indigenous peoples' populations are too small. But this does not seem to be the case with respect to the Greenlandic Inuit who count approximately 50.000 individuals.

To have an own distinct language is one of the requirements in order to qualify as an indigenous people. The Greenlandic Inuit have their own languages distinct from Danish, so the Inuit qualify as an indigenous people. But this does not mean that they will thereby be "disqualified" from becoming a people under international law. In this respect, this would also qualify the Danes as an indigenous people, since they have their own language too. The Greenlandic Inuit languages are closely connected to the other Inuit languages in Canada, Alaska, and Chukotka in Russia. The Danish language is a Scandinavian language and is related to e.g. Swedish and Norwegian.

There are no international legal requirements language-wise in order for a subject to gain the full status, rights, and duties of a people. Many different peoples share the same language, but yet they are not necessarily considered to be the same. And at the other end of the spectrum a people in the international legal sense (a full-fledged subject) can consist of different language groups, as is the case with e.g. Switzerland, Belgium, India, China, Indonesia etc.

Do the Greenlandic Inuit have a culture which is distinct from that of the Danes? Without going into any cultural details the answer is a clear yes. For readers who are not familiar with the two peoples, here is a short introduction. The old Inuit formed a highly specialized hunting society based mainly on sea-mammals. Today, that is still part of the lives of the Greenlandic Inuit, but the main resources of the society now come from the fishing industry. The Danes have a culture which for a long time was based on agriculture, but which through time has become more and more specialized and industrialized. The Danes have also had a long tradition of fishing. Today, both industries are present, but many more industries have sprung up and developed, and they rely to a greater extent on human resources. Another relevant aspect for the difference between the two cultures is the impact the different climates have had, and still have. The Greenlandic Inuit live under harsh arctic and sub-arctic conditions, whereas the Danes live under a temperate climate, which enables more friendly living conditions.

The name "Greenland" has no root in the Inuit language. It originates from the Norsemen, who came to Greenland in the 10th century, staying in the country for about four centuries. The Inuit's name for Greenland is "*Kalaallit Nunaat*". The Greenlandic Inuit call themselves "*Kalaallit*"(*pluralis*), and "*nuna*" is the word for land, thus the Greenlanders' land. But the word "*kalaaleq*" (*singularis*) is an "inuitization" of a foreign word[38] which, in the author's opinion, is not a suitable name for the country of a nation. It is a question of dignity. But this is a debate which has to take place in Greenland. There have been suggestions to adopt the name "*Inuit Nunaat*". "*Inuit*" (*pluralis*) means people. "*Inuk*" (*singularis*) means human being. It could also be debated whether or not "Greenland" should be kept as the international name. There are many examples of nations changing the known official names of their states after having become independent, because the former names where given by the colonizers.

---

38   It is unclear whether the word "*kalaaleq*" has its root from the Norse "*skrælling*" or "*karel*", which in the first case is a condescending name, and the second is the name of someone coming from another part of the world – which is not very flattering either. The Greenlandic Inuit probably adopted the name not knowing its meaning. Habit and ignorance has kept it alive.

Self-identification

In all the three above-mentioned definitions (two, if we are strict) of indigenous peoples "self-identification" as "indigenous" is a fundamental requirement for being indigenous. This means that you as an individual identify yourself as being part of a group of people, who identify themselves as being the descendants of the original inhabitants of the territory (to some extent this group of people who identify themselves with the original descendants of the territory also have to identify you as an individual belonging to this group).

No importance is attached to the "outside" identification of a certain group as an indigenous people in order for it to qualify *as* an indigenous people, though there is an example which might cast some doubt on this: when part of the white population in South Africa tried to attain the status of indigenous people of South Africa, as protection against the vast black majority after the democratization in the country, the international community did not recognize this. Even though the white population had been in the country for three or four centuries, they were not descendants of the original inhabitants of the country. In this context their role, or place, was more like that of the descendants of the colonizers and conquerors.

The emphasis laid on self-identification means that you yourself hold the key for being considered either as an indigenous people, a people, or both. As shown before, you could argue that the Danes, and many other peoples as well, are just as "indigenous" in their territories as the Greenlandic Inuit are. The Danes are also the descendants of the original inhabitants of their territory. They have a culture and language which have roots all the way back to these first and original ancestors. And, they are full subjects under international law – mainly because they possess their own sovereign state. There are no full subjects under international law who do not possess their own sovereign state.

Colonization, subjugation, exclusion, marginalization, dispossession, discrimination and domination

Both ILO Convention no. 169 and Mr. Cobo's working definition of indigenous peoples mention that indigenous peoples are the descendants of the pre-colonial population of a given territory. I have already in the above established that this is the case for the Greenlandic Inuit.

The Inuit were in Greenland before the Danish colonization. The Inuit were in Greenland during the colonization, and they are still in Greenland – it is an established fact that Greenland was considered to be a Danish colony. Formally it is not that anymore, but you can question whether or not this is the case today. Greenland's status within the Danish Kingdom was changed (and you may even say Greenland's status was up-graded) when the Danish Constitution was renewed in 1953.

In order to be able to understand who the indigenous peoples are, and what they have undergone, Dr. Daes introduces the following concepts: "subjugation", "exclusion", "marginalization", "dispossession" and "discrimination," as relevant factors for being an indigenous people. If you follow Cobo you can add being "dominated" by another people.

Greenland was subjugated by Denmark before (and some would also say after) the implementation of the new Danish Constitution in 1953. It is of course up for discussion whether or not the concept "subjugation" is too strong a concept to utilize today in the relationship between Greenland and Denmark. But it is a fact that Denmark, in recent years, has overruled Greenlandic political wishes.

If Greenland begins to earn money on its subsoil, Greenland has to share the income with Denmark equally up to the first 500 mill. Danish Kroner. From thereon the two parties have to negotiate the next apportioning. To this, one has to add that this arrangement may to some extent be due to the financial contribution made by Denmark to the Greenlandic economy, so there seems to be nothing strange about this arrangement. Still, this arrangement might have to be renegotiated if Greenland is to become economically self-sustaining in the future.

Without going into details, the Greenlandic Inuit have experienced exclusion from important decisions concerning their lives and territory by various Danish governments. Examples involving the Thule Air Base and the crashing of a hydrogen bomb-carrying US B-52 bomber in the sixties clearly show this. That was over 30 years ago. In 2003, Greenland was excluded from the active negotiations between the US and Denmark, when it came to aspects involving the Thule Air Base. Morally, this is very hard to defend (not to say, morally reprehensible), but fortunately there is progress on this matter. Greenland is in the process of becoming an active party to the negotiations.

The Greenlandic Inuit have been and are still to a great extent dominated by the Danes within Greenlandic society. Today, the Greenlandic Inuit form the political elite in Greenland exclusively, still with the political limitations there are due to the relationship with Denmark. Most of the directors and high positioned officials in both the local and central administrations are Danes. Most entrepreneurs and businessmen are Danes.[39] Many teachers, if not most, in the educational system are Danes. This means that Danes do influence and dominate Greenlandic society to a much higher extent than what their numbers in Greenland justify (if you can say so). This is not necessarily a bad thing, because the general educational level of the Greenlandic population is still too low. Greenlandic society needs highly educated people, and Greenlandic society cannot provide these people on its own today. On the other hand, it is not necessarily a good thing that the Danes have such a strong position in Greenland. As a result of this strong position, many Danish norms and customs, ways of thinking and behaving etc. have been uncritically brought into Greenlandic society. On top of this, you can in many ways claim that in Greenland the Danish language is the language of power.[40] It goes without saying that this has, of course, caused problems for the Greenlandic Inuit on a societal level.

---

39   Peter Munk Christiansen & Lise Togeby: *"Grønlands elite"* pp. 84-86, in Gorm Winther (ed): *"Demokrati og magt i Grønland"*, Aarhus Universitetsforlag, Århus, 2003.

40   Gorm Winther (ed): *"Demokrati og magt i Grønland"*, article by Gorm Winther: *"Demokrati og magt i Grønland"*, p. 22, Aarhus Universitetsforlag, Århus, 2003.

I will not, in this chapter, go into any details about whether or not the Greenlandic Inuit have been marginalized, dispossessed or discriminated by the Danes (either before or today). I do not feel this is the place to go through these aspects which have been, and to some extent still are, aspects of the relationship between the Greenlandic Inuit and the Danes.

With respect to these above-mentioned aspects – colonization, subjugation, marginalization, dispossession, discrimination and domination – the Greenlandic Inuit qualify as being an indigenous people. Now, do these aspects *disqualify* the Greenlandic Inuit from becoming a full subject under international law with all the rights and duties this specific status brings with it? I do not see why this should be the case. Many peoples have experienced the above in their history and are today considered to be full subjects under international law. This is the case for many peoples of Africa, India, Oceania, etc. There are no rules or laws in international law which prevent you from becoming a people under international law, qua you being a people which have suffered under colonialism. What makes the Greenlandic Inuit different from the peoples who have become full subjects under international law is that the full subjects of international law have formed their own sovereign state.

The Greenlandic Inuit do not possess their own sovereign state. If they did they would become a full subject under international law. Can the Greenlandic Inuit become a full subject under international law on a formal line with Canada, Sweden and Luxembourg, without possessing their own sovereign state? No! Further negotiations with Denmark, and a strengthening of Greenlandic society (at all levels and in all aspects), and a stronger international personality would get them some of the way, but only secession would put them on a par with Canada, Sweden and Luxembourg. Do they want that or can they make do with less? That is for the Greenlandic Inuit to decide.

In ethnography it is rather clear that you can have different peoples living within the same sovereign state. The matter is a bit different when you deal with international law. One of the reasons why indigenous peoples and peoples have their own juridical status is that you cannot have two full subjects and agents (on the same level) under international law to represent one sovereign state. Who would be the signer of international treaties? Who would be the sovereign? And, the international society would not know where to place this particular state if its two subjects could not agree on differing issues.

Conclusions and Viewpoints

Both the Greenlandic Inuit and the Faroese have been denominated "folk" in Danish, "people" in English, by different Danish Governments and by the Danish Queen. The two entities are especially mentioned in the Danish Constitution. They possess all the characteristics needed to be considered peoples under international law, but still not full subjects under international law, since you need your own sovereign state to be recognized as such. They have gone most of the way in terms of attaining full internal self-determination, but there is still some way to go yet. For both islands external authority is very limited. Seen from the perspective of self-determination, there is still a good distance to go before they reach the full autonomy of a sovereign state. There may also be significant practical obstacles before they can attain this status, but these can be overcome. Both peoples and societies are in the process of developing well-functioning societies, which could in time become well-functioning sovereign states. The Faroes are a bit ahead of Greenland in this respect. Do the two populations want to become sovereign states? That is for them, and them only, to decide.[41]

Of course, you can be an indigenous people of your country and still be a full-fledged people under international law – nothing which has to do with "indigenousness" prevents this. The problem arises if you want to become a full-fledged subject under international law – you need to possess your own sovereign state to become that. Now, if you want to go for the highly proclaimed rights to self-determination attributed to peoples (with an "s') you could be advised to do the following: the right to self-determination for peoples has not been further specified by any authority with which sovereign states have to comply.[42] This means that it can range from very little to very much self-determination – it has not been specified what it has to include or entail.[43] Therefore, a good idea is simply to go for the specific and concrete rights and authorities such as the right to nullify laws and orders coming from the metropolitan state, and the authority to fully decide Greenland's exter-

---

41   I am supported by the philosopher Daniel Philpott on this view, who also believes that the population of the metropolitan state should not be involved in such a referendum. The legal scholar Lea Brilmayer has an opposing view. She argues that it is not clear from democratic theory why everyone in a state should not vote on the separation of a group within its borders. Philpott points at what would be the absurd result of Brilmayer's view; it would have allowed the English to vote on the independence of the American colonies and the Soviets on the fate of the Baltic states.

     Daniel Philpott: "In Defense of Self-Determination", pp. 362-363, Ethics, vol. 105, issue 2 (Jan. 1995), The University of Chicago Press, Chicago, 1995.

     Lea Brilmayer: "Secession and Self-Determination: A Territorial Interpretation", p. 185, The Yale Journal of International Law, Yale Law School, New Haven, 1991.

     What one probably has to distinguish between is how the seceding group's territory became part of the metropolitan state. If you are a colony or have been wrongfully annexed into the metropolitan state, then I think it is clear that the original members of the metropolitan state should not participate in the vote. Greenland was once a colony and the process which led to the annexation of Greenland into Denmark was highly dubious (see footnote 44 below). The annexation of the Faroe Islands into the Danish Kingdom suffers from the same dubiousness.

42   Daniel Philpott supports this view, too, in his paper: "In Defense of Self-Determination", p. 385, Ethics, vol. 105, issue 2 (Jan. 1995), The University of Chicago Press, Chicago, 1995.

43   L.C. Green points to this too, in his paper: "Aboriginal Peoples, International Law and the Canadian Charter of Rights and Freedoms", pp. 340-342, The Canadian Bar Review, vol. 61, 1983. This is a more than twenty-year-old paper, but the talks of our Working Group with UN officials indicate that the vagueness characterising this particular area is still the case.

nal manoeuvring, that is, the right to full external self-determination. In terms of rights and authorities, I believe, one should go for substance, rather than highly proclaimed (but vaguely specified) principles. Self-determination will automatically come with these more concrete rights and authorities.

If the Greenlandic Inuit insist on the non-concrete right to self-determination, then they should mention the fact that they were a former colony. With this status they have a right to a development pointing towards self-determination in its fullest sense. One should also point at the process which led Greenland from being a colony to an integral part of Denmark, as a highly dubious affair, where Denmark clearly made use of its upper hand.[44] If the Greenlandic Inuit choose to walk this path, they would still, further on in the process, have to demand more concrete rights than the ones mentioned above. Self-determination in itself is empty. The contents will in separate cases have to be established according to the conditions surrounding each case.[45]

As has already been stated, if the aim is to become a sovereign state, then the Greenlandic society will need to develop and strengthen in order to be able to stand on its own feet economically (there are also other areas, such as the social, educational and health care areas, which require strengthening, but the economy will be the crucial area).

Another thing the Greenlandic Inuit can be advised to do is to emphasize their indigenous status where it is needed and where it does not impede their cause. Bear in mind, that this could be done where the protective measures of this particular term would be helpful. For example, in the work done in connection with the International Whaling Commission, where indigenous peoples are given the right to hunt a certain number of whales, when it is part of the given indigenous culture. Other situations where the Inuit could emphasize their indigenousness could be in events where they want to show their solidarity with other indigenous peoples. But, if or when the Greenlandic Inuit obtain a higher juridical and political status, the need to utilize the term "indigenous people" will become more and more obsolete. A problem with the term "indigenous people" is that many peoples and states do not want to concede too much to indigenous peoples, especially when it comes to matters which can have constitutional implications. Some peoples and states will not even begin to meet or even start negotiations on an official basis with an indigenous people. The reason may be that as a consequence of such a concession (meetings and negotiations with indigenous peoples on certain matters would be a concession in itself) peoples and states may stand to lose authority over a given indigenous people and their territory. The Greenlandic Inuit could try to avoid this obstacle by emphasizing their plain "peoplesness",

---

44 In short: "*Landsrådet*" – "the Council of Greenland" – were given three days to decide whether or not you wanted to become part of Denmark. If not, you were on your own.

45 Daniel Philpott also points at the distinction of self-determination in connection with decolonization and the fact that self-determination has to be further specified in order to fit different cases: "In Defense of Self-Determination", pp. 353-354, Ethics, vol. 105, issue 2 (Jan. 1995), The University of Chicago Press, Chicago, 1995.

because on the other hand, if the Inuit keep on emphasizing their indigenousness, it might cause problems on the political scene.

They must transcend their indigenousness and begin to explicitly emphasize the characteristics of their people as a separate people distinct from the Danish, which in the long run qualifies for a higher status under international law. In that case, they would rarely need to emphasize their indigenousness.

Greenland is officially a former colony and since international legal practice accords full self-determination to former colonized peoples, the Greenlandic Inuit have a strong case in advocating for a development pointing in that direction. Actually, they do not need to ask anyone for permission – it is their right. Still, to keep up the good atmosphere it would be a sign of good faith to try to do this with the understanding and cooperation of Denmark. Of course, Denmark would have to be understanding and willing to cooperate.

If the Greenlandic Inuit became citizens of their own country, this would mean that they possessed their own sovereign state, and they would thus have become a full-fledged subject under international law. It is implicit that sovereign statehood means that your country possesses full autonomy. The fact that the Greenlandic Inuit form a majority in their own secluded territory speaks in favour of this development.

A short consideration: if you want to up-grade your political and international legal status, including achieving the sovereignty over your own country, you have to seek to become a subject under international law by getting recognized by other sovereign states. Sovereign states are the core subjects under international law, and these subjects are partly defined through the holding of sovereignty over territory. Other ways to strengthen yourself and your legal profile are to become more active internationally in as many spheres as possible and thereby become more internationally visible – that is, strengthen your international personality. The fact is that every time you become a member of an international (governmental) organization you become a subject of this organization, but it does not mean that you become a subject anywhere else. In order to become a subject in other organizations and spheres, you have to become member of these too. Lastly, you can strengthen your international personality through establishing permanent diplomatic connections with other countries.

As the situation is today, it is not very settling, for either the Greenlandic Inuit or the Faroese, to have in mind that the Danish Constitution does not necessarily prevent the unilateral repealing by Denmark of the Home Rule Acts of both countries. That is very unlikely to happen in reality, but the mere fact that it might be legally possible, is an uncertainty which ought to be eliminated.

This uncertainty is something which might have to be eliminated if you seriously want the Danish *Rigsfællesskab* to have a future.[46] It would not be enough for a leading politician or a leading law expert to proclaim that the above repealing could not happen in reality, but the following options are available to do the job. One option would be an uncertain road to walk (because you cannot predict the outcome): take the problem to the Danish High

---

46   The Danish *Rigsfællesskab* includes Denmark, the Faroe Islands, and Greenland.

Court and hope that they will rule that the two Home Rule Acts of both islands cannot be repealed either by the Danish Government or Parliament.

Another path to follow would be for the two countries to demand a constitutionally rooted *right of nullification* and/or a *right to veto*, and this demand was granted by Denmark. In this particular case the right of nullification would mean a right to nullify laws and orders issued by the metropolitan state's Parliament and/or Government. This would mean that laws and/or orders issued by the Danish Parliament and/or Government could be nullified by the Greenlandic and Faroese Governments and Parliaments, so that these laws and/or orders would not cover and would not be implemented in these two respective entities. The issued law and/or order would still count and be implemented in metropolitan state Denmark.

The right to veto would give any of the two smaller entities in the sovereign state of Denmark a right to veto any laws proposed by Denmark – laws intended to cover the whole *Rigsfællesskab*. Utilizing the right to veto would mean that the proposed law would be totally dismissed for the whole *Rigsfællesskab*. The right to veto would of course be a more extensive right.[47]

One or both of these two rights would have to be constitutionally rooted, but this would mean that the Danish Constitution would have to be changed. This will not be easy, even though Denmark has established a commission to work on a future new Danish Constitution. The right of nullification would naturally be the less difficult right to implement in a future Danish Constitution, because its consequences are less extensive.

The above-mentioned options would mean the decisive elimination of the possibility of the repealing of the two Home Rules.

The notion that Greenland's and the Faroes' representation in the Danish Parliament can work as some kind of parliamentary protection for Greenlandic and Faroese interests is very weak. The Faroes and Greenland have each two seats, thus four seats/votes put together. There are in total 179 seats in the Danish Parliament. On issues where fundamental conflicts of interest between Greenland and The Faroes on the one side and Denmark on the other arise, the value and weight of the Greenlandic and the Faroese representation in the Danish Parliament is only symbolic and without political weight. Furthermore, where conflicts of interests arise Greenland and The Faroes can only count on the support of the far left of the Danish political spectre (this is an ally who has only very limited political strength). In such cases Danish interests are often bullied through. Examples which show the truth of this claim can be found in cases concerning military and security policy.[48]

In our Working Groups' meetings with UN officials it was clearly said that only symbolic political representation is not considered to be enough when issues such as the above arise. The political representation has to be real, that is, to be strong enough to protect

---

47   For a more elaborate account of the right of nullification and the right to veto, one place to look could be in Allen Buchanan's "Secession – The Morality of Political Divorce from Fort Sumter to Lithuania and Quebec" Westview Press, Boulder, 1991.

48   This is an aspect which is also presented in the Faroese White Book.

ones interests. An implementation of the right of nullification (a right to veto would also do the job, but would still leave us with the problem of one people being able to decide for another people) would lead to a more egalitarian relationship between the entities. The Greenlandic Inuit and the Faroese as nations need much more than a symbolic political representation in the highest political organ in the Kingdom, if proper respect is to be shown towards the two nations.

Political rights and human rights are very closely connected. If a people has lesser political rights, it will have consequences for the individuals of the given people in question. The individuals of this people would have lesser human rights than the individuals of peoples with full political rights. If an external people has the right of decision-making in political matters which actually only concern your people and/or territory, then your political rights are impeded. When your political rights have been impeded, then it is obvious that your human rights have been violated. In connection with the Greenlandic Inuit and the Faroese population this does not look good for Denmark.

As a consequence of the above you may with much plausibility infer that within the Danish Kingdom or the sovereign state of Denmark, if you please, the Greenlandic Inuit and the Faroese people only possess some kind of second-class citizenship, through being members of marginalized entities. Now, formally there are no different levels of citizenship, but in reality the Greenlandic Inuit and the Faroese people have lesser political rights within the state of Denmark: they are not citizens of the country they identify with; their Home Rules can be overruled and might even be repealed by the supreme political institution of the state (the Danish Parliament); an external people has a say in matters which otherwise only concern the Greenlandic Inuit and the Faroese; and finally the two North Atlantic entities have only a very insignificant representation in the supreme political institution of the state, with the great disadvantages this brings where conflicts of interest arise.

Now, why do the Greenlandic Inuit and the Faroese not just secede unilaterally from Denmark? Why all this talk? The thing is that both Greenland and The Faroes wish to keep up a good relationship with Denmark, because in spite of the political and cultural differences, history has created many bonds between the three entities. You do not want to slam the door behind you, but the problem is, if you read between the lines of statements coming from Danish officials, that: *If you want to secede, you will be slamming the door behind you. If you do not want to slam the door behind you when seceding, Denmark will do it for you.* You do not want this to happen. You can try to prevent this from happening in your work for a greater degree of autonomy within the Kingdom, or even secession, if you walk this path in a common agreement with Denmark.

To want to become legally and politically independent from Denmark is not to say you do not want to have anything to do with Denmark, nor that you dislike Denmark and its citizens. It means that you want to decide for yourself in matters which only concern you, as the Danes do in Denmark. It means that you want to meet Denmark on a legally and politically equal footing. This is not the case today.

5 – The Faroes as a Non-Self-Governing Territory

Bjørn Kunoy

Introduction[1]

Ubi societas ibi jus. Every community needs a legal order. This is true for the international community, as it is for every other community. As in every municipal law system, international law is characterized by the attribution of subjects to diverse entities. The notion "international legal personality" is a synonym of "subject" in international law. An international legal subject is directly entitled to rights and has obligations under international law. As a preliminary illustration it can be interesting to see which entities are subjects under international law before examining whether The Faroes can be deemed to be such a subject.

Max Huber, in his famous arbitral award "The Palmas Islands", in 1928 established that international law was the legal order of inter-state relations. This is not true in contemporary international law. A profound modification has occurred during the second half of the twentieth century. The subjects of the international legal order include not only states but, by extension, international organizations.[2] Furthermore, a new international legal subject, attributable to individuals, has emerged and is today undeniable. The International Court of Justice explicitly affirmed this in the "LaGrand"[3] Order. Colonial people can also be considered as international subjects as they dispose of rights and have obligations in international law separate from the metropolitan states.

This chapter will examine whether The Faroes can be considered as a colonial known territory and if so, whether it can become a subject in international law and is entitled to inherent rights under public international law.

---

1   I am grateful to Mr. Bárður Larsen and Mr. Martin Martinez Navarro for their remarks on the manuscript.

2   ICJ Report, 1949, "Reparation for Injuries Suffered in the Service of the United Nations", Advisory Opinion, 11 April 1949, Rec. 1949, p. 179.

3   ICJ Report 2001, (Germany *v.* United States of America), p. 104, para. 77.

Sjúrður Skaale (ed.), The Right To National Self-Determination, *123-137.*
© *2004 Koninklijke Brill NV. Printed in the Netherlands.*

This chapter does not pretend to furnish a complete and exhaustive examination of the existing literature concerning self-determination and studies analyzing the (very important) issues in question. Its objective is to initiate a debate about whether international customary law provides criteria to determine which territories can be considered as non-self-governing territories and whether The Faroes fulfil these conditions. If this appears to be legally founded one can state that Denmark has an international obligation to register The Faroes as a non-self-governing territory pursuant to Chapter XI of the UN Charter. First, though, it seems pertinent briefly to recall some legal elements concerning self-determination in positive international law.

Self-determination[4] in *jus positum*

Under international law some peoples are considered as international legal subjects and are attributed with an inherent right to self-determination.[5] Before examining whether The Faroes can be considered as having a right to exercise self-determination, it will be established that "all peoples", as provided in diverse international instruments, shall not be interpreted as if all peoples are legal subjects entitled to a right to external self-determination.[6]

Self-determination is not provided for by the text of the UN Charter, in the context that it has generally been used since the adoption of UNGA Resolution 1514 (XV), on 14

---

4   The principle of the right of self-determination is generally subdivided into external and internal. This article refers predominantly to the external sense.

5   The literature on this subject is very rich and the following references are not to be interpreted as an exhaustive list. For a thorough understanding of self-determination, see: Cassese A., *Self-Determination of Peoples: A Legal Reappraisal*, Cambridge, Cambridge University Press, 1995, 375 pp.; Crawford J., *The Creation of States in International Law*, Oxford, Oxford University Press, 1979, 500 pp.; Christakis T., Danspekgruber W., Watts A., *Self-Determination and Self-Administration – A Sourcebook*, Boulder/London, Lynne Reiner, 1997, 512 pp.; Duursma J., *Fragmentation and the International Relations of Micro States*, Cambridge, Cambridge University Press, 1996, 461 pp.; Franck T., *Fairness in International Law and Institutions*, Oxford, Clarendon Press, 1995, 500 pp.; Gayim E., *The Eritrean Question. The Conflict Between the Right of Self-Determination and the Interests of States*, Uppsala, Swedish Institute of International Law, 1993, 716 pp.; Higgins R., *Problems and Process: International Law and How We Use It*, Oxford, Oxford University Press, 1994, 274 pp.; Jennings R.Y., *The Acquisition of Territory in International Law*, Manchester University Press, 1961, 126 pp.; Kohen M.G., *Possession contestée et souveraineté territoriale*, Paris, PUF (Publications de l'Institut Universitaire de Hautes Études Internationales, Genève), 1997, 579 pp.

6   External self-determination can be exercised by three different procedures: independence, association and integration. Internal self-determination on the other hand is understood as the right of every people to exercise their political, civil, economic, social and cultural rights within their state. For a thorough understanding of this latter see: Christakis, T., *"Le droit à l'autodétermination en dehors des situations de décolonisation"*, Paris, Documentation Française, 1999, 476 pp.

December 1960. The principle of self-determination is twice articulated in the Charter of the United Nations: in Article 1, Paragraph 2: "The Purposes of the United Nations are … to develop friendly relations among nations based on respect for the principle of equal rights and self-determination of peoples"; and Article 55: "With a view to the creation of conditions of stability and well-being which are necessary for peaceful and friendly relations among nations based on respect for the principle of equal rights and self-determination of peoples". The formula "*equal rights and self-determination*" appears in these two articles; the sense seems to be that the rights of the peoples of one state should be protected from interference by other states. This interpretation can also be understood in relation to the fact that in 1945 it was the rights and obligations of the sovereign Member States that was the main preoccupation.[7] It was not conceivable to consider the rights of those not yet independent. What was being provided for were the equal rights of states, not of individuals.[8]

The decisive Declaration on the Granting of Independence to Colonial Countries and Peoples – UN General Assembly Resolution 1514 (XV) – was adopted by a clear majority and reflects the anti-colonization sentiments prevalent throughout the 1950s and confirms the formation of an external right to self-determination of colonized peoples as a general principle of law.[9] Principle 2 of the Resolution states this right, but this revolutionary right concerns only some peoples, *in concreto* the territories registered under the obligations of Article 73 (e), Chapter XI in the UN Charter.[10] Chapter XI is entitled *Declaration Regarding Non-Self-Governing Territories,* and covers those colonial territories for which the respective Member States (Administrating Powers) have or assume responsibility in compliance with Article 73 (e).

Following this conclusion, it was not intended, during the adoption of Resolution 1514 (XV) on 14 December 1960, to crystallize the right of self-determination to all universal peoples. In this context, we should also recall that Principle 6 of Resolution 1514 (XV) proclaims the sovereign rights and territorial integrity of all Member States, which demonstrates the restrictive application of the announced "inalienable right" of all peoples. Unlike Greenland, The Faroes were not registered as a non-self-governing territory under Chapter XI of the UN Charter.

In the context of the examination of Faroese self-determination, one might be tempted to induce an autonomous source for this inherent right. The Danish Government has on several occasions unilaterally declared that the Government would respect a decision by the Faroese people to change their constitutional or international legal status. We

---

7   Higgins R., *Problems and Process: International Law and How We Use It*, Oxford, Oxfort University Press, 1994, p. 111.

8   The *travaux préparatoires* of the Charter confirm this understanding of the phrase: see VI UNCIO 300.

9   Cassese A., *Self-Determination of Peoples: A Legal Reappraisal*, Cambridge, Cambridge University Press, 1995, p. 171.

10   *Ibid.*, pp. 69-72.

should recall that a unilateral act is defined as an act imputable to one sole subject of international law.[11]

Unilateral acts are not stipulated as a source in international law in Article 38 of the Statute of the International Court of Justice. The Permanent International Court of Justice (PICJ) and the ICJ have, however, recognized voluntary formation of law as an autonomous source of international law.[12] In the East Greenland Case, 5 April 1933, the PICJ recognized that a verbal declaration of 19 July 1919, by the Norwegian Minister of Foreign Affairs, *Ihlen*, to the Danish Ambassador had binding legal effects for Norway.[13] The Danish unilateral declarations towards the Faroese people cannot, nevertheless, be interpreted as binding on Denmark, on the legal basis of a voluntary formation of law, because these declarations have been expressed internally in the Danish Realm and exclude, therefore, any auto-normative formation in positive international law.

International law being a normative legal system, other subjects than the colonized people became entitled to self-determination. UN General Assembly Resolution 2625 (XXV), adopted on 25 October 1970, has been recognized as one of the most significant pronouncements on the right of self-determination approved by the UN General Assembly. Not only are non-self-governing territories granted the right to external self-determination, but peoples subject to military occupation are also attributed this right. Principle (e) of Resolution 2625 (XXV) specifies that "self-determination being possible in situations of colonialism, and the subjection of peoples to alien subjugation, domination and exploitation." This provision has a rigid connotation, and shall be interpreted as occupied territories[14] upon the termination or suspension of military hostilities.[15]

The international jurisprudence, even visionary and progressive in these specific cases, also provides conclusions to a rather strict interpretation of "self-determination of all peoples". By 1971, the ICJ, in the *Namibia Opinion*, made clear the normative role of international law and affirmed that the subsequent development of international law in regard to non-self-governing territories,[16] as embodied in the Charter of the United Nations, made the principles of self-determination applicable to all of the non-self-governing territories.[17] To illuminate this interpretation, reference can also be made to the Separate Opinion of Judge Hardy Dillard in the *Western Sahara* Advisory Opinion of 6 October 1975, which noted that:

---

11   Daillier P., Pellet A., *Droit International Public*, Paris, LGDJ, 2002., p. 362.

12   PICJ, *East Greenland Case* (1933), Series A/B, number 53, p.69; ICJ, *Nuclear Essays* (1974), Rep. 1974, p. 268, para. 43.

13   Daillier P., Pellet A., *op. cit*, p. 359.

14   See General Assembly Resolution 3236 (XXIX) 1974 (Palestine); General Assembly Resolution 2144 (XXV) 1987 (Afghanistan).

15   Cassese A., *op. cit.*, p. 72-76.

16   Higgins R., *op.cit.*, p. 116-118.

17   Legal Consequences for States of the Continued Presence of South Africa in Namibia notwithstanding Security Council Resolution 276 (1970), Advisory Opinion, ICJ Reports (1971) 16 at 31.

".... norm of international law had emerged regarding non-self governing territories under the aegis of the United Nations."[18]

Nevertheless, many rebel movements have proclaimed their right to self-determination, notwithstanding their respective peoples neither being notified under Chapter XI of the UN Charter, nor militarily occupied. Illustrative examples can be made to the unilateral independence declarations of Chechney (2 November 1991), Nagorno Karabakh (6 January 1992), and the Serb population of Bosnia-Herzegovina (9 January 1992).

Article 1 of the International Human Rights Covenants[19] has in many cases served as legal reference for these demands for independence. These two international instruments were adopted after the decision was taken to advance the Universal Declaration of Human Rights, adopted on 10 December 1948, through a series of international treaties which were eventually adopted on 16 December 1966.

The Danish Government has, in accordance with the International Covenants on Civil and Political Rights, and the Covenant on Social, Economic and Cultural Rights, reported[20] the implementation of the human rights provisions in what concerns The Faroes under Article 1, "all people have a right of self-determination."[21] Could one conclude that this Danish conduct was a constitutive act recognizing the Faroese external self-determination? Conform to Article 32 of the Vienna Convention on the Law of Treaties[22] "recourse may be had to supplementary means of interpretation, including the preparatory work of the treaty and the circumstances of its conclusion, in order to confirm the meaning resulting from the application of article 31 "to determine the exact interpretation of a treaty provision. Taking into consideration the *travaux préparatoires* and the international legal doctrine,[23] this provision of the Covenant, apart from occupied territories and non-self-governing territories,[24] entitles only internal self-determination, to be understood as the internal promotion of political and civil rights,[25] which also prevails for the Faroese people.

To confirm the latter, it is interesting to note the Second Opinion of the European Community Arbitral Commission, called the *Badinter Commission*, during the armed conflict

---

18   ICJ Reports (1975), 12 at 121 – 122 (sep. op. Judge Dillard).

19   The Covenant relative to Civil and Political, and the Covenant relative to Social, Economic and Cultural Rights were signed 16 December 1966 and entered into force on 23 March 1976.

20   Article 40 and 16 oblige the Contracting Parties to report to the Human Rights Committee the implementation of the provided provisions.

21   UN Doc CCPR/C/DNK//99/4 of 22 February.

22   The Vienna Convention on the Law of Treaties, 23 May 1969, 1155 UNTS 331.

23   Cassese A., *op. cit.*, pp. 54 -56.

24   Franck T., *Fairness in International Law and Institutions,* Oxford, Clarendon Press, 1995, p. 156.

25   Crawford J., "State Practice and International Law in Relation to Secession", *British Yearbook of International Law*, 1998, pp. 92-96.

in the Balkans. According to this Opinion (11 January 1992), the interpretation of Article 1 of the Covenants shall be understood as the right of every individual in the Serbian part of Bosnia-Herzegovina to belong to any religious, ethnic or linguistic community.[26] In other words, it promotes the interpretation of this provision as an internal self-determination right.

A source of confusion, however, is that no provision in the Covenants is addressed to contravene a possible broad interpretation of Article 1, as for example Principle VI[27] in the UNGA Resolution 1514 (XV). Another analogy can be made with the Helsinki Declaration, concluded, under the aegis of the Conference on Security and Co-operation in Europe, on 1 August 1975, which in its Principle VIII treats equal rights and self-determination of peoples. Principle IV provides that the territorial integrity of all States is inviolable and avoids *in fine* a loose interpretation of Principle VIII.[28]

If we recapitulate these legal facts, one can say that The Faroes do not constitute a subject in international law, because this territory is not subscribed under the obligations of Article 73 (e) of the UN Charter and the Faroese people are not in a situation of colonialism and subjection of peoples to alien subjugation, domination and exploitation.

However, the fact that Article 1 in the Covenants is not contravened by provisions proclaiming the principle of territorial integrity makes it interesting to analyze closely the prevailing political circumstances during the adoption of this "dynamite provision"[29] with particular emphasis on the Danish position.

Adoption of Article 1 in the Human Rights Covenants

During the drafting of the Human Rights legal instruments, the entire issue was obfuscated by the then prevailing antagonism between Eastern and Western bloc countries, where the Western powers as a general rule did not vote for resolutions proposed by countries from the Eastern bloc and *vice versa*. The provision governing a people's right of self-determination became a focal point in this on-going confrontation and a strong opposition occurred to the draft proposal to insert the current Article 1 in the Covenant. On 5 February 1952, a vote was held to determine which version of common Article 1 should be inserted in the two Covenants. The main point of opposition to this provision was the vague definition of "people"[30] causing some countries to vote against the language of Article 1.

---

26   *Ibid.*, pp. 103-104.

27   Principle VI: "Any attempt aimed at the partial or total disruption of the national unity and territorial integrity of a country is incompatible with the purposes and principles of the Charter of the United Nations."

28   Cassese A., *op. cit.*, pp. 285-288.

29   British Delegate: UN Doc. A/C.3/SR.644 (1955) P. 101, para. 15.

30   Duursma J., *Fragmentation and the International Relations of Micro States*, Cambridge, Cambridge University Press, 1996, p. 31.

For some States, the perception of self-determination was considered too nebulous to be included in an international conventional instrument.[31] The opposition bloc[32] also argued that the UN Charter only provided for self-determination as a principle and not as an inalienable right of peoples.[33] Facing this vigorous opposition, the UN General Secretary proposed to attach Article 1 as a declaration to the Covenant.[34] Denmark was among the colonial Member States opposing the procedure for self-determination provided for in the Covenant. Denmark considered the controversial common Article 1 as granting the right to secession to peoples within Member States[35] and thus voted against UN General Assembly Resolution 545 (VI) to incorporate the current Article 1 into the Covenants. It would appear that the Danish position was that a people's right of self-determination was too complex an area to be inserted in international legal instruments that were to be given binding effect[36] and held the view that the construction "every people" was too broad[37] and unnecessary. This was not a solitary interpretation, but was shared with the colonial empires.[38]

Can the Danish opposition to the insertion of the current Article 1 possibly be interpreted as action to prevent further territorial diminishment? This may be the case, given Denmark's overseas territories, The Faroes and Greenland, whose geostrategic importance cannot be ignored as a factor in Danish geopolitical strategic policy during the Cold War. Maintaining these two overseas territories in the Danish Realm, Danish political influence in policy-making in international relations was unquestionably increased.

The Faroese Home Rule Act, implemented on 1 April 1948, refers to "*det Færøske folk*"[the community of the Faroese people] and "*et selvstyrende folkesamfund*" [a self-governing people's society]. It is not inconceivable to state that these provisions were in the mind of the Danish delegation and *ipso facto* influenced the Danish opposition to the adoption of Resolution 545 (VI), *inter alia* because no definition of "people" was in the provision.

---

31   Denmark (A/C.3/SR.644, para. 2).

32   The following countries represented the negative votes when UN General Assembly Resolution 545 (VI) was adopted, Australia, Belgium, Canada, Denmark, France, Holland, the United Kingdom.

33   The French and English versions of Article 1, paragraph 2 of the UN Charter are different. The English version of the purposes of the United Nations is: "To develop friendly relations among nations based on respect for the *principle* of equal rights and self-determination of peoples," ... "*Développer entre les nations des relations amicales fondées sur le respect du principe de l'égalité de droits des peuples et de leur droit à disposer d'eux-memes, ...*". (Emphasis added).

34   UN Doc. A/C.3/SR.633 (1955).

35   UN Doc. E/CN.4SR.369 (1953) P.5, 16; UN Doc E/CN.4/SR.370 (1953) & UN Doc. A/C.3/SR.642-670 (1955) pp. 90, 94, 124 – 126, 143, 225 & 231.

36   UN Doc. A/3077 (1955) p. 12, para. 31.

37   UN. Doc. A/C3/SR.676 (1955) p.262.

38   Duursma J., *op.cit.*, p. 31 (including Australia, Belgium, France, and the United Kingdom).

Denmark has experienced a number of territorial diminishments. After the Napoleonic Wars, Danish-controlled Norway, a part of the Regal Monarchy Union, was ceded to Sweden by the Convention of Kiel (14 January 1814) in what can be considered as a territorial relinquishment. In Bismarck's attempts to unify Germany, Schleswig and Holstein were wrested from Denmark in the second war of Schleswig (1864). Denmark was a signatory party to the Peace Treaty of Vienna on 30 October 1864, and ceded the Danish King's sovereignty over these regions. The West Indies were sold to the United States on 4 August 1916, Iceland established its independence on 1 December 1918 after having signed a bilateral agreement with the Danish Government, which was adopted by the Assembly on 30 November 1918. Most important in this context is that The Faroes had a *sui generis* government while Denmark was occupied by Germany during the Second World War.

After the war, lengthy negotiations were held between Faroese officials and the Danish Government about the future constitutional status of The Faroes. A referendum was organized on 14 September 1946, in which a small majority voted in favor of independence. The Faroese Assembly then confirmed this plebiscite, which resulted in the dissolution of the Faroese Chamber on 24 September 1946 by the Danish Government. This disregard for the referendum happened in spite of the prior declarations of Prime Ministers Vilhelm Buhl[39] and Knud Kristensen,[40] pronouncing the constitutive value of an eventual referendum surrounding the Faroese constitutional issue in the Danish Realm.

Arguably, one can claim that since the Danish Government was already ready to accept an eventual secession of The Faroes during the bilateral negotiations in 1945 and 1946, it seems unreasonable of Denmark in 1946 not to register The Faroes as a non-self-governing territory. This latter is also grounded in other historical facts concerning the integration of The Faroes to Denmark.[41]

In spite of the fact that The Faroes were not registered as a UN Chapter XI subject, one can nevertheless not exclude the study of The Faroes as such an entity. Some territories have notably been registered by the General Assembly as non-self-governing territories despite the exclusion of these territories when the colonial empires in 1946 unilaterally registered which territories were to be considered as non-self-governing territories.

This procedure has been legally founded on Resolution 1541 (XV), which enunciates some principles to determine this question. In this context, it can be considered as pertinent to examine whether these enunciated principles reflect international customary law

---

39   Declaration of Vilhelm Buhl in the Faroese newspaper, *Dimmalætting*, 27 October 1945.

40   Danish proposal for the negotiations procedure between the Faroese official representatives and the Danish Government during the negotiations in January to March 1946. My translation: "The Ministeries Delegation has expressed that, if the Faroese people aspire to independence and dissolution with the historical relations to Denmark, this decision will be respected." "*Ministeriets Delegation har givet Udtryk for, at man, hvis Færingerne måtte ønske den fulde Selvstændighed og Ophør af det Historiske Samhørsforhold med Danmark, fuldt ud vil respektere dette Ønske...*"

41   See *infra*.

and whether The Faroes can be considered as concerned by these criteria in spite of not having been registered as a non-self-governing territory by Denmark.

The Principles Enunciated in Resolution 1541 (XV) and Their Binding Character

As previously described, the non-self-governing territories only became entitled to the external right to self-determination under positive international law after the adoption of Resolution 1514 (XV). To ensure that a people's right to self-determination could not be usurped, guidelines regarding non-self-governing territories were promulgated by the UN General Assembly.

UN General Assembly Resolution 1541 (XV) deals with "Principles which should guide the Members in determining whether or not an obligation exists to transmit the information called for under Article 73 (e) of the Charter." This Resolution was adopted on 15 December 1960 with the aim to ensure that territories that were *de facto* colonies and fulfilled the cumulative criteria in the resolution, could be attributed with the right to self-determination in spite of a refusal by the colonial state to register its colonies as non-self-governing territories. Resolution 1541(XV) was adopted with a view to recognizing the Portugese and Spanish colonies as non-self-governing territories; these two latter states entered the United Nations only in 1955 and refused to register their colonies pursuant to Chapter XI of the UN Charter.

As previously explained, the year after the ratification of the UN Charter, the General Assembly adopted Resolution 66 (I) encouraging all Member States to register their colonies as subjects according to Chapter XI of the UN Charter. The modest Article 73 of the UN Charter refers only to *self-government*, and not independence. The colonial empires decided herein unilaterally which national territories were to be registered. Denmark was one of the eight colonial Member States who registered an overseas territory. Denmark chose only to register Greenland as a non-self-governing territory.

Before we enter the discussion concerning the normative value of Resolution 1541 (XV), we must not forget that, in conformity with Article 13 of the UN Charter, the resolutions of the UN General Assembly are only recommendations. However, the principles of these "non-binding" resolutions can become part of the international *corpus juris*. Article 38 (1) (b) in the Statute of the International Court of Justice recognizes international customary law as an official source in international law. Quite interestingly, the Statute does not, however, establish which components shall be established in determining the existence of an international customary norm. Article 38 (1)(b) originated in the Statute of the Permanent Court of International Justice and was drafted in the League of Nations Advisory Committee of Jurists in 1920. What does appear from the drafting history is that those responsible for Article 38 (1) considered that there were two elements which made up customary law: state practice, the objective element, and the attitude towards that practice, termed the subjective element or *opinio juris*.[42] Whose practice counts? It is

---

42   Mendelson M.H., *Recueil des Cours*, 1998, p. 195.

not just the practice of states which contributes to the development of customary rules. The practice of international organizations can also create customary rules.[43] In voting for or against a resolution of the UN General Assembly, states are engaging in a form of state practice and are making manifest their subjective attitude about the rule in question.[44] The role of international organizations in generating international customary rules cannot be underestimated.

To constitute a viable *usus* element, the practice has to be uniform. In the Fisheries Case[45] the ICJ emphasized that although a ten-mile closing line for bays had:

> "...been adopted by certain States...other States have adopted a different limit. Consequently, the ten-mile rule has not acquired the authority of a general rule of international law."

In the North Sea Continental Shelf Case the Court demanded the practice in question to be, not only uniform, but also extensive and the practice should include that of "States whose interests are specifically affected."[46] This is, of course, not pertinent in determining local customs, but highly relevant when finding general rules of international law binding on all members of the international community.

The Court itself often seems to approach the question of sources with a certain looseness. In some judgments and opinions, UN General Assembly resolutions are referred to without any clear indication as to what legal purpose their invocation serves.[47] Are those resolutions mere historical events, or evidence of practice, or do they carry some normative weight? The Nicaragua *v.* United States Case is a clear illustration of the Court using General Assembly resolutions as *opinio juris*. Referring to certain General Assembly resolutions and in particular Resolution 2625 (XXV),[48] the ICJ said that the effect of consent to the text of such resolutions must be understood "as an acceptance of the validity of the rule set of rules declared by the resolutions by themselves."[49]

The same postulate can be stated about certain provisions, and most particularly point 4, in General Assembly Resolution 1803 (XVII) (14 December 1962) concerning the sovereignty of natural resources. This can be grounded in the conclusion of the sole arbitra-

---

43   ICJ Advisory Opinion, "Reservations to the Genocide Convention", ICJ Reports, 1951, p. 15.

44   Mendelson M.H., *op. cit.,* p. 202.

45   Fisheries Case, ICJ Reports 1951, p. 116 at 131.

46   North Sea Continental Shelf, ICJ Reports, 1969, p. 43, para. 74.

47   Higgins R., *op. cit.,* p. 37.

48   See UNGA Resolution 2535 (XXIVB) 1970 and 2672-C, 1970; UNGA Resolution 3236 (XXIX) 1974 (Palestine); UNGA Resolution 2144 (XXV) 1987 (Afghanistan).

49   ICJ Reports (1986), *Military and Paramilitary Activities in and against Nicaragua*, p. 14 at 100.

tor, Professor René-Jean Dupuy, in the Texaco Award.[50] Professor Dupuy assessed that the international customary legal value of the provisions was clear. He grounded this conclusion essentially in the broad General Assembly vote[51] and secondly in the relative practice of the upstanding Resolution. As an analogy, it can be mentioned that Resolution 1541 (XV) was adopted with a very broad majority[52] receiving support from different countries from different blocs. Following this reasoning, one could postulate that an *opinio juris* is present in this case. But what was the Danish position to this indeed very significant Resolution?

Denmark voted positively to Resolution 1541 (XV) and apparently distinguished itself from other colonial Member States, such as the United Kingdom, France and Australia, who abstained. It was even Ambassador Boeg, the Danish representative to the Fourth Committee of the UN, who submitted Resolution 1541 (XV) before the General Assembly.

Furthermore, Resolution 1541 (XV) has been very explicitly practised granting independence to *inter alia* Mozambique, East Timor and Angola, as the adoption of Resolution 1542 (XV)[53] applying these principles to Portugal and Spain proves. Denmark voted in favor also of this latter Resolution, which was, arguably, approved by the concerned states conforming to the stipulated demands in the North Continental Shelf Case. The respect and conduct of Resolution 1542 (XV) can be considered as having legally qualified Resolution 1541 (XV) as international customary law by assimilating these territories to the non-self-governing territories, regardless of whether or not such registration had been submitted by the metropolitan Administrating Power. Also General Assembly Resolution 41/41A[54] has applied Resolution 1541 (XV) when recalling that New Caledonia shall be considered as a non-self- governing territory in spite of the French negligence of its obligations since the register in 1946 of this island as such a territory.

---

50   Texas Overseas Petroleum Co/California Asiatic Oil Co. *v.* Government of the Libyan Arab Republic, 17 ILM 3, 29 (1978), 53 ILR 389 (1979).

51   *Ibid*, para. 87. *"En fonction des conditions de vote précédemment évoquées et traduisant une opinio juris communis, la résolution 1803 (XVII) paraît au tribunal de céans refléter l'état du droit coutumier existant en la matière. En effet, à partir du vote d'une résolution constatant l'existence d'une règle coutumière, les Etats expriment clairement leur opinion. L'acquiescement en l'espèce d'une majorité d'Etats appartenant aux différents groupes représentatifs indique sans ambiguïté la reconnaissance universelle des règles incorporées..."*

52   Resolution 1541 (XV) was adopted with 69 affirmative votes, 2 negative and 21 abstentions.

53   In Resolution 1542 (XV) of 15 December 1960 the General Assembly recalled "differences of views …concerning the status of certain territories under the administrations of Portugal and Spain and described by these two States as *overseas provinces* of the metropolitan State concerned." Moreover, the General Assembly stated that it considered that the territories under the administration of Portugal, which were listed therein were non-self-governing territories within the meaning of Chapter XI of the Charter. Portugal accepted this position in 1974.

54   UNGA Resolution 41/41A, 2 December 1986, was affirmatively voted and placed *de jure* New Caledonia as a non-self-governing territory, pursuant to Chapter XI of the Charter.

One might reasonably state that Resolution 1541 (XV) reflects international customary law, as an *opinio juris* does exist. A temporal argument can also be presented to found this postulate. Resolution 1541 (XV) was adopted the following day after the adoption of the decisive "Declaration on the Granting of Independence to Colonial Countries and Peoples" which, together with the broad affirmative majority, reflects the sincere attitude of the states in what concerns the subjective *opinio juris* question of this Resolution. Having confirmed the binding character of Resolution 1541 (XV) for all states in the international community, it is left for us to examine whether The Faroes can be considered as fulfilling the criteria.

To determine if Denmark is under an international obligation to register The Faroes as a non-self-governing territory, we shall turn to the guidelines in the Annex to the Resolution 1541 (XV) which in Principle I establishes that Chapter XI of the UN Charter is applicable for colony known territories; meanwhile, Principle IV enunciates that there "*prima facie* is a obligation to transmit information in respect of a territory which is geographically separate and is distinct ethnically/and or culturally from the country administering." Principle V[55] concerns the bilateral administrative, political, economic and historical relations. Principle VIII deals with the integration procedure, and states: "Integration with an independent state should be on the basis of complete equality between the peoples of the erstwhile non-self-governing territory and those of the independent country with which it is integrated..."

First of all, it could be pertinent to analyze the Faroese situation in the context of Principles I and VIII. Are The Faroes a colonial territory? Furthermore, how were the islands integrated in the Danish Realm? *A priori* one can respond negatively to the first question, but a reasonable answer can only be provided, once the Faroese contextual sense of Principle VIII is assessed.

Norway claimed The Faroes as far back as the early eleventh century and The Faroes fell at this point under Norwegian jurisdiction. After 1452, Denmark and Norway formed a union, the Regal Monarchy Union, which was governed under a joint Monarch. After the Napoleonic wars, by the Treaty of Kiel, Article 4,[56] Sweden gained Norway. Though,

---

55   Principle V: "Once it has been established that such a *prima facie* case of geographical and ethnic or cultural distinctness of a territory exists, other elements may then be brought in consideration. These elements may *inter alia* be of administrative, political or juridical, economic or historical nature. If they effect the relationship between the metropolitan and the territory concerned in a manner which arbitrarily places the latter in a position or status of subordination, they support the presumption that there is an obligation to transmit information under Article 73 (e) of the Charter."

56   Article 4: "*Sa Majesté le Roi de Dannemarc, tant pour Elle que pour Ses Successeurs au Trone et au Royaume de Dannemarc, renonce irrévocablement et à perpétuité, en faveur de Sa Majesté le Roi de Suède et de Ses Successeurs au Trone et au Royaume de Suède, à tous Ses droits et titres sur le Royaume de Norvège, savoir les Evêchés et Baillages (:Stift:) ci-après spécifiés, ceux de Christiansand, de Bergenhuus, d'Aggerhuus et de Trondheim avec le Nordland et le Finmarken jusqu'aux frontières de l'Empire de Russie.*"

as Article 4 reveals, the Norwegian over-seas dependant territories the Faroe Islands, Iceland and Greenland were not ceded to Sweden and became thereafter Danish territories. This provision confirms *inter alia* that the Faroe Islands never ceased to be Norwegian territory during the Regal Monarchy Union, in spite of the Danish dominance. Following the Norwegian/Danish territorial dispute about the sovereignty of East Greenland, the Permanent Court of International Justice (5 April 1933) referred to the Kiel Convention when determining the Danish sovereignty in East Greenland. By the reasoning of the East Greenland Case of the PCIJ, Norway never ceased independently to exist as an independent state during the Regal Monarchy Union and neither did its over-seas dependent territories.

Under these circumstances, The Faroes were arbitrarily integrated into the Danish Realm pursuant to a post-war treaty. Of course, in the beginning of the nineteenth century, when a voluntary conception of international law prevailed, annexation and post-war territorial agreements were not prohibited under international law. Consistent with Article 64[57] of the Vienna Convention on the Law of Treaties, the appearance of a *jus cogens* norm does not have retroactive effect. A similar distribution of a territory, as established by the Treaty of Kiel would be inconceivable under contemporary public international law, but this does not change the legality of the Faroese integration into the Danish Realm in 1814.

Historically, it is, however, interesting to bear in mind that the Faroese people have never given their consent to be integrated into the Danish Realm. The islanders have only once expressed their will in a referendum on this question, on 14 September 1946! Furthermore, during the drafting of the Danish Constitution in the years before its implementation in 1849, the Faroese people were only represented by the former Danish Prefect in The Faroes, F.C. Pløyen. The Constitution was applied in the following year to The Faroes by an ordinary act of legislation, without any consent of the Faroese people or their Assembly (which had been dissolved by the Danish King in 1816, to be reconstituted as a consultative body in 1852). These circumstances can arguably be conceived as a determinant factor in deciding whether a territory qualifies to fall under the obligations of Chapter XI of the UN Charter, or when assessing whether the Faroe Islands are a colonial territory and if the insular people consented jointly and equally to being integrated into the Danish Realm in accordance with Resolution 1541 (XV).

Responding to the fourth and fifth principles, it should be noted in terms of geography that Tórshavn, the capital city of The Faroes, is 1300 kilometers away from Copenhagen. Furthermore, the Faroese people are, in terms of culture, separate from the Danish people,

---

Ces Evêchés, Baillages et Provinces, embrassant la totalité du Royaume de Norvège, avec tous les habitants, villes, ports, forteresses, villages et isles sur toutes les cutes de ce Royaume, ainsi que les dépendances, — la Groënlande, les isles de Ferroë et Islande non comprises, — de même que les prérogatives, droits et émolumens, appartiendront désormais en toute propriété et souveraineté à Sa Majesté le Roi de Suède, et formeront un Royaume réuni à celui de Suède". (Emphasis added).

57   Article 64: "If a new peremptory norm of general international law emerges, any existing treaty which is in conflict with that norm becomes void and terminates."

fulfilling Principle IV in Resolution 1541 (XV). The distinctiveness of the Faroese people is unquestionable. The Faroese people are of Norwegian descent and can be considered as an "independent" people. This is so both according to the Germanic objective[58] perception of a people that prevailed during the positivism of the late half of the nineteenth century; and also according to the French doctrine[59] of criteria for defining a people. The latter not only demanded the presence of the objective elements, but also demanded a collective will or a "common soul"[60] of a people.

Thus, Denmark is historically, morally and in accordance with international law bound to register The Faroes as a non-self-governing territory. The historical and legal arguments have already been examined.

In what concerns other moral reasons, it is interesting to see that on 16 December 1965, Denmark voted in favor of General Assembly Resolution 2070 (XX) "*Question of Gibraltar*". Under Principle 1, the General Assembly invited "the Governments of Spain and of the United Kingdom... to begin without delay ... [appropriate] talks...[towards] the implementation of the Declaration on the Granting of Independence of Colonial Countries and Peoples." This Resolution was approved with a broad majority[61] and the Danish affirmative vote is worth noting. In many ways, the Faroese integration into the Danish Realm is similar to that of Gibraltar, which became a British territory by the post-war Treaty of Utrecht in 1713. This Treaty has had the same constitutional importance for Gibraltar as the Treaty of Kiel has had for The Faroes. Gibraltar is today not a colony in the etymological sense, but was registered by the United Kingdom as a non-self-governing territory in 1946. It could therefore be argued that the Danish Government ought to maintain the same position *vis-à-vis* Faroese self-determination, as it does with regard to Gibraltar.

A Danish refusal to describe The Faroes under the obligations of Chapter XI of the UN Charter can only be explained away if Denmark in its conduct at the General Assembly, in the words of Professor Arangio-Ruiz, "did not mean it."[62]

---

58   The objective doctrine emphasizes the criteria to define a people are: a distinct culture, history, tradition, language, religion and race.

59   For a thorough analysis of these criteria, see: Renan E., *Qu'est ce qu'une nation ?*, *Textes choisis et présentés par Joel Roman*, Paris, Presses Pocket, 1992, 316 pp.

60   Renan E., *op. cit.*, "*une ame, un esprit, une famiille spirituelle, résultant, dans le passé, de souvenirs, de sacrifices, de gloires, souvent de deuils et de regrets communs; dans le présent, le désir de continuer de vivre ensemble. Ce qui constitue une nation, ce n'est pas de parler la meme langue ou d'appertenir au meme groupe ethnographique, c'est d'avoir fait ensemble de grandes choses dans le passé et de vouloir en faire encore dans l'avenir*", p. 52.

61   UNGA Resolution 2070 (XX), 91 affirmative votes, none negative and 11 abstentions.

62   Ruiz A., for an analysis of the UN Gen. Ass. as a soft-law legislator generator "The Normative Role of the General Assembly of the United Nations and the Declaration of Principles of Friendly Relations ", Revue Canadien du Droit International, 1972, vol. III, p. 432.

Conclusion

Some authors believe that it is too narrow to contend that international law is defined as that which the ICJ would apply in a given case.[63] International law has to be identified by reference to what the actors (most often states), often without benefit of pronouncement by the ICJ, believe normative in relations with each other.

Denmark has, I believe, when adopting Resolution 1541 (XV), actively and collectively participated in the emergence of these principles to customary international law. Combined with the collective enforcement and implementation of its principles against other UN Member States, this proves the existence in positive international law of the principles of the Resolution. Furthermore, The Faroes can be esteemed to fulfil the criteria set out in the Annex of Resolution 1541 (XV) and, therefore, be deemed as required to be registered as a non-self-governing territory. The failure of the Danish Parliament to adopt a resolution calling for the registration of The Faroes under Chapter XI could be viewed as an attempt to subvert normative public international law by contrary state practice.[64]

It is undeniable that Denmark by its conduct has taken part in establishing self-determination as an inalienable right for all peoples. Why should this reasoning not prevail for The Faroes? When Denmark held the EU Presidency in 1987, it addressed the representatives of most all of the world's governments at a meeting of the UN General Assembly:

> "The United Nations has a very important role to play in the regard of implementation of self-determination. Wherever the exercise of the right to self-determination is violated, it is only natural that the matter be dealt with in the world organization. The denial of this right anywhere is a concern of peoples every where."[65]

Based on such declarations and Danish votes in the General Assembly concerning the self-determination of all peoples it would appear that Denmark is duty bound to respect and advance the inalienable right of the Faroese people to self-determination by registering The Faroes under Chapter XI of the United Nations Charter.

---

63 Higgins R., *op.cit.*, p. 18.
64 See Ruiz A., *op. cit.*, p. 431.
65 UN Doc. 87/349, in 3 EPC Bul., 1987, no. 2, p. 130.

6 – The Quebec-Canada Case Compared to The Faroes and Greenland

Lauri Hannikainen

What Is the Legal Significance of the Advisory Opinion (Judgment) of the Canadian Supreme Court on Quebec's Claimed Right to Secede from the Canadian Confederation to The Faroes and Greenland?

Among the French-speaking majority population of Quebec there is substantial support for the view that Quebec should secede from Canada and form its own sovereign State. There came a time in the mid-1990's when the Canadian Government found it advisable to request an interpretation from the Supreme Court – how the alleged right of secession should be assessed in Canadian constitutional law and in international law. The Supreme Court was requested to give an advisory opinion. It is the practice of the Supreme Court to issue its advisory opinions in the form of judgments. As a legal pronouncement of the highest court of Canada these judgments/advisory opinions are treated as binding.

The first question posed to the Canadian Supreme Court by the Governor in Council in 1996 in the case *Reference re Secession of Quebec*[1] inquired about the competence of the leading organs of Quebec, under the Canadian Constitution, to effect the secession of Quebec from Canada unilaterally. The second question read as follows:

> "Does international law give the National Assembly, legislature or Government of Quebec the right to effect the secession of Quebec from Canada unilaterally?"

---

[1] Reference by the Governor in Council concerning certain questions relating to the secession of Quebec from Canada, as set out in Order in Council P.C. 1996-1997, dated the 30th day of September, 1996. The decision can be found in International Legal Materials, Vol. XXXVII, November 1998, pp. 1340-1377.

Sjúrður Skaale (ed.), The Right To National Self-Determination, *139-145.*
© *2004 Koninklijke Brill NV. Printed in the Netherlands.*

In the following, especially the Supreme Court's answer to this question is explained.[2]

The Supreme Court had to assess the status and content of the right of self-determination of peoples in international law, and especially the right of secession as a part of the right of self-determination – this means the external side of the right of self-determination. One would expect the Court to have given a definition of those peoples who have the international right of self-determination, but the Court did not do that, because it thought that it could give the answer without addressing this question. However, it expressed the opinion that a "people" may include only a portion of the population of an existing State. This means that there can be several "peoples" within a State.

The Court gave its advisory opinion on 20 August 1998. It is well-reasoned regarding the question of Quebec's claimed right of self-determination, a pertinent decision on the contents of international law. However, the Court did not have reasons to address in any detail some of those questions which are relevant in the assessment of the right of self-determination of The Faroes and Greenland. Yet, we learn quite a lot by reading the analysis of the Court.

The Right of Secession on the Basis of the Right of External Self-Determination

Before explaining the Canadian Supreme Court's position, I want to emphasize that after the massive decolonization process of the 1960's and 1970's the international community of States largely returned to its former position, i.e. to take a generally negative attitude towards attempts at secession from existing States. The international community prefers to keep the number of sovereign States limited, because with a smaller number of States the management of international order is presumably easier. However, this return to the pre-decolonization stand can hardly mean a complete return, since the right of self-determination of peoples is now one of the basic principles of international law and another basic principle, increasingly important, is respect for human rights. The right of self-determination is one fundamental human right.[3]

The Court states that contemporary international law does not grant component parts of sovereign States the legal right to secede unilaterally from their "parent" State. According to the Court, "international law places great importance on the territorial integrity of nation states and, by and large, leaves the creation of a new state to be determined by the domestic law of the existing state of which the seceding entity presently forms a part". On the other hand, international law does not deny in any explicit terms secession from an existing State against the consent of the Government of that State. Thus, if the population/people of a territory separate effectively their territory from the "parent" State, this seces-

---

2   The Supreme Court's answer to question 2 is on pp. 1368-1375.

3   See Antonio Cassese, Self-Determination of Peoples, A Legal Appraisal, 1995; Modern Law of Self-Determination, ed. by Christian Tomuschat, 1993; Lauri Hannikainen "Self-Determination and Autonomy in International Law" in Autonomy: Applications and Implications, ed. by Markku Suksi, 1998, pp. 79-96.

sion may win international recognition. In the words of the Court: "Secession of a province from Canada, if successful in the streets, might well lead to the creation of a new state."

The right of a people to self-determination is now so widely recognized that it has become a general principle of international law. According to the Supreme Court, the right of self-determination has established a few grounds which grant a given territory under the sovereignty of a given State the right to secede from that State without the consent of the Government of that State: 1) if that territory is under the colonial domination of that State; 2) if that territory is under the domination of a foreign power – in the words of the Court: "where a people is oppressed, as for example under foreign military occupation"; 3) if a definable group is denied meaningful access to government to pursue its political, economic, social and cultural development. "In all three situations, the people in question are entitled to a right of external self-determination because they have been denied the ability to exert internally their right to self-determination." The Court specifies that this denial means that internally their right of self-determination is "totally frustrated".

If a territory has the right of secession – the right of external self-determination – it has the right to decide on its future status. The options include creation of a new State as an independent entity, integration to some existing State, agreement on the creation of a federal State in which that territory is one of the constituent parts, or association with some existing State as a separate unit and with the right to change this status later.

Since the Supreme Court was specifically concerned with Quebec and Canada, it concentrated on the right of secession of a province which is an integral part of the territory of a democratic State and left other aspects of secession to a general assessment only. The Supreme Court considers that *territories and their peoples within the sovereignty of democratic States do not have any right of external self-determination and secession in international law.* Their claims can be settled in the framework of the democratic system. That may result in secession if there is consent to it by the leading organs of the State according to national law. The Canadian Constitution does not provide for a right of secession.

The Court could also refer to the history of Canada. The territory of the present-day Canada was a colony which emerged gradually towards independence. The representatives of different regions of Canada created a federal state as a result of several conferences in 1864-1867. The Constitution Act of 1867 included guarantees to protect the French language and culture, both directly, by making French the official language in Quebec and Canada as a whole, and indirectly, by allocating jurisdiction over education and property and civil rights to the provinces.[4] This legal situation is continuously in force. The French-speaking majority of Quebec are descendants of the French colonists.

---

4   This is in the Supreme Court's analysis on pp. 1354-1357.

Aspects Not Discussed by the Supreme Court

However, different cases have to be assessed according to their specific merits – the case of Quebec differs from those of The Faroes and Greenland. Quebec is an integral part of the territory of Canada, whereas The Faroes and Greenland are far away from Denmark.

When a territory's colonial status is assessed in international law and a claim for the right of self-determination is made, a fundamental requirement is the clear separateness of the territory concerned from the territory of the metropolitan State. Another important requirement is that the population of that territory is ethnically/linguistically different from the majority population of the metropolitan territory. Quebec clearly does not meet the first fundamental requirement. If Greenland and The Faroes claim that they have been/are colonies, they have to prove that they have not had the chance to exercise their right of self-determination.

When the above-mentioned requirements are applied to Greenland and the Faroes, it is clear that these two territories are clearly separate from the metropolitan territory of Denmark. They are far away from Denmark behind substantial sea areas, and they are distinct geographical territories surrounded by the sea. Especially the indigenous Inuits of Greenland are ethnically and linguistically completely different from the Danes. Denmark regarded Greenland historically as its colony whose "primitive" population had to be civilized. Also, The Faroes were regarded as not educated enough in constitutional matters. Greenland and The Faroes may arguably be seen as having been colonies which have not had the genuine chance to determine their own status according to the criteria of international law.

I am convinced that in other chapters of this work at least two of these questions relating to colonial status are addressed in depth. The geographical separateness is an undisputed fact.

The Supreme Court's View on Quebec's Peaceful Secession from Democratic Canada

The third (and last) question posed to the Canadian Supreme Court read as follows:

> "In the event of a conflict between domestic and international law on the right of the National Assembly, legislature or government of Quebec to effect the secession of Quebec from Canada unilaterally, which would take precedence in Canada?"

The Court came to the conclusion that there was no need to answer this question, since there is no conflict between Canadian law and international law: in a democratic Canada, the province of Quebec has no unilateral right of secession. However, the Court made a most interesting analysis on the procedure to be largely applied in Canada, if the apparent majority of the people of Quebec make a claim of secession.[5]

---

5   This analysis is at the concluding part of the decision of the Supreme Court, pp. 1375-
      1376.

The major rule of international law has been that secession from an existing State can be validly consented to by the Government of that State. The Court refers to the opinion of Antonio Cassese according to whom "no territorial change can be brought about by the central authorities of a State that is contrary to the will of the whole people of that State". The Court took this statement as its criterion when examining the Quebec question.

According to the Supreme Court, Quebec's secession could not be achieved unilaterally without principled negotiation with other participants in the Canadian Confederation within the existing constitutional framework. But:

> "The Constitution is not a straitjacket. Even a brief review of our constitutional history demonstrates periods of momentous and dramatic change. Our democratic institutions necessarily accommodate a continuous process of discussion and evolution, which is reflected in the constitutional right of each participant in the federation to initiate constitutional change. This right implies a reciprocal duty on the other participants to engage in discussions to address any legitimate initiative to change the constitutional order. While it is true that some attempts at constitutional amendment in recent years have faltered, a clear majority vote in Quebec on a clear question in favour of secession would confer democratic legitimacy on the secession initiative which all of the other participants of the Confederation would have to recognize.
>
> ...
>
> The negotiation process would require the reconciliation of various rights and obligations by negotiation between two legitimate majorities, namely, the majority population of Quebec, and that of Canada as a whole. A political majority at either level that does not act in accordance with the underlying constitutional principles we have mentioned puts at risk the legitimacy of the exercise of its rights, and the ultimate acceptance of the result by the international community."

The Supreme Court in its carefully drafted words makes it known that the Confederation and other provinces have to assess thoroughly the possible secession claim of Quebec without rejecting it out of hand, but that in the end it is the majority of the Confederation and its Government which decide about the realization of Quebec's secession.

The Supreme Court did not define what a "clear majority" vote in Quebec would require but confined itself to the statement that this will be for the political actors to determine. In my opinion, 60 percent or 2/3 of the votes cast is a clear majority if it includes over 50 percent of those entitled to participate in the vote.

Unilateral Danish Commitment?

In this respect it is notable that responsible Danish governmental officials have on many occasions recognized that if the people of The Faroes or Greenland clearly express their will to secede from Denmark, the Government will agree to the secession. In the Danish democratic discussion this view from the Government's side has, on several occasions, been clearly expressed.

Could these statements be taken as Denmark's unilateral commitment under international law? My reply is negative, because these statements have not been given to any other Government or intergovernmental organization. They are simply important statements by responsible authorities in the public discussion of the democratic Denmark. However, statements of such authorities can be taken as expressions of political consent and of moral commitment. The more there is evidence that in fact the Faroese and Greenlandic people were not offered fair conditions in a referendum to choose their status, the more importance the moral factor gets.

Expert Opinion by Professor James Crawford

When the Canadian Government decided to turn to the Supreme Court, it also requested an expert report from Professor James Crawford (University of Cambridge) on state practice in relation to unilateral secession. Professor Crawford can be regarded as one of the leading experts of international law. In his report entitled *State Practice and International Law in Relation to Unilateral Secession* in 1997 Crawford came to clear conclusions.[6] It has to be kept in mind, however, that Crawford was commissioned and paid by the Canadian Government.

Crawford concludes that in international practice, outside the colonial context, there is no recognition of a right of unilateral secession from a sovereign State based on majority vote of the population of a sub-division or territory, whether or not that population constitutes one or more "peoples" in the ordinary sense of the word. Even where there is a strong and sustained call for independence, it is a matter of the State concerned to decide how to respond. The Government is not required to grant independence; if it rejects calls for secession it can take all lawful means to oppose secession. Self-determination is achieved for peoples and groups within an independent State by participation in the governmental system.

According to Crawford, in practice unilateral secessions are recognized by external States only after the Government of the State concerned has given its consent to secession. Bangladesh forms a partial exception, but it has to be noted that Bangladesh was not admitted to membership of the United Nations until it was recognized as an independent State by Pakistan, nearly four years after Bangladesh's unilateral declaration of independence.

On the other hand, Crawford does not deny the possibility that in cases of dissolution of a State secession may take place even against the consent of the Government. "If it

---

6   <http:77canada.justice.ge.ca/en/news/nr/1997/factum/craw.html>.

becomes clear that the process of dissolution of a state as a whole is irreversible, the consent of the government of the predecessor state may cease to be required for the separation of its constituent parts." In such a case, the Government may lose its authority to represent the State. However, there is a strong presumption against the dissolution.

When one compares the views of the Canadian Supreme Court and of Crawford, one can note that the former gives somewhat more weight to the right of self-determination. Crawford may be excessively negative in his analysis. The Court does not exclude the possibility of unilateral secession in cases where internally a people's right of self-determination is "totally frustrated". However, in the case of democratic States, the Court and Crawford are unanimous.

One interesting question in Crawford's analysis is the right of secession in the process of dissolution of a State. What if both The Faroes and Greenland declared their determination to secede from Denmark? Am I a "devil's advocate" if I ask whether that could be understood as a manifestation for the dissolution of the present Kingdom of Denmark?

7 – A Phrase Loaded with Dynamite

Impressions from Walking the Corridors of the UN

Sjúrður Skaale

> States do not have friends. States have interests.

Winston Churchill

A great number of international conventions, resolutions and declarations talk of the right to national self-determination. Furthermore, the right to self-determination is one of the most discussed concepts in the theoretical literature on international relations.

Our quest has been to find out more about the issue by going straight to the horse's mouth. Walking the corridors of the UN buildings, chatting and meeting with officials and ambassadors, one gains the impression that it is all a question of taking a leap of faith – having secured the appropriate safety net first.

The UN is a club of states. A club of the mighty. If you are mighty enough, you may join. If someone claims to represent you already and considers you a mere subdivision, you may have your work cut out for you convincing the club that your might will suffice.

On this last point, Denmark claims to represent The Faroes and Greenland today. Therefore, one safety net to tie up is resolving whether the state of Denmark belongs to the more liberal or the more restrictive states when it comes to deciding whether to let a subdivision of potential might try its wings.

There have been some official Danish Government statements that have totally ruled out the possibility of Faroese or Greenland sovereignty, thus making it absolutely clear that the two countries do not have the Danish blessing to exercise the right to self-determination.[1] But during the last years of heavy debate on Faroese sovereignty, Danish Prime

---

[1]   In an official pronouncement on December 23, 1975, the Danish Prime Minister's Office, e.g., said it agreed fully with the following statement: "A home rule arrangement within the framework of the Danish "*rigsfællesskab*" excludes the possibility that the area

Sjúrður Skaale (ed.), The Right To National Self-Determination, *147-168.*
© *2004 Koninklijke Brill NV. Printed in the Netherlands.*

Ministers have often said that if and when the peoples of The Faroes and Greenland want independence, they are free to go. But at the same time they have made clear that their wish is to keep the two countries within the Danish Realm. Looking at history, there is no doubt that this is Denmark's clear political objective.

Returning to the club of states, what does the international community have to say on this? Does anyone really have the right to self-determination anymore? If that concept still exists as a valid point of law, then what does it mean to have this right? What, exactly, is this right to determine for oneself all about?

It is possible to find answers to these questions – both in theory and in the practice of the international community. However, the answers are not clear-cut. Indeed, they are so vague and leave so much room for interpretation that the Project Working Group which produced this volume could not determine, either based on conventional sources or on any unofficial hints, whether – or how – the right to national self-determination applies to the cases of The Faroes and Greenland.

Even though there are no accurate legal answers, the Group, nonetheless, thought that studying the attitude and practice of the UN when dealing with such issues would bring us closer to the substance of the matters discussed.

In order to get more reliable answers than theory alone can provide concerning self-determination, six members of the Project Working Group went to New York in October 2003.[2] In New York, we had meetings with – among others – the following people in the UN and Missions to the UN:

- Mr. Hans Corell, the Legal Counsel and Under Secretary General at the Office of Legal Affairs,
- Mr. Danilo Turk, Assistant Secretary General at the Department of Political Affairs,
- Ms. Elissavet Stamatopoulou-Robbins, Chief of the Secretariat of the Permanent Forum on Indigenous Peoples,
- Ms. Anna Theofilopoulou, Acting Chief of the Decolonization Unit of the Department of Political Affairs,
- Mr. Edward Mortimer, Leading Adviser to the Secretary General,
- Mr. Hjálmar Waag Hannesson, the Ambassador of Iceland to the UN,
- Mr. Christian Wenaweser, the Ambassador of Liechtenstein to the United Nations,
- Mr. Mark Ramsden, Adviser at the New Zealand Mission to the UN.

---

in question obtains the status of a sovereign state". (*Betænkning afgivet af Kommissionen om Hjemmestyre i Grønland,* 1978).

2   The following six members of the Project Working Group participated: Dr. Gudmundur Alfredsson, Professor of Law at the Wallenberg Institute; Dr. Ole Espersen, Professor of Law at the University of Copenhagen; Mr. Bogi Eliasen, Master of Political Science; Mr. Mininnguaq Kleist, Master of Political Philosophy; Mr. Kári á Rógvi, LL.M., Deputy Chair of the Faroese Constitutional Committee; Mr. Sjúrður Skaale, Master of Political science, Advisor to the North Atlantic Group in the Danish Parliament. Sjúrður Skaale has written the chapter that has been approved of by all the members of the Working Group who participated in the meetings in New York.

At the meetings other members of staff were also present and contributed.

We use the information gathered in various chapters of this volume, but the essential points will be summarized in this chapter.

None of the people we met will be quoted, and none of them are in any way responsible for anything that is said here. Rather, this chapter is based on the general impressions that the Group got from the talks in New York. Only the members of the Project Working Group are responsible for the text.

The right to self-determination and its relevance to the cases of The Faroes and Greenland is the central issue in this volume and was the main topic of discussion with the UN officials. A helpful starting-point might, therefore, be to explain in broad lines when and how the concept of self-determination has been used in practice, and to sum up the main interpretations of the concept that can be found in international law and legal theory.[3]

Self-Determination in Practice

Two of the first exponents of national self-determination were two men as different from each other as V.I. Lenin and Woodrow Wilson. The collapse of great empires was a fact of their time in power. Both saw great political possibilities in establishing the principle that each nation should have the right to constitute its own state and determine its own government, as self-determination is commonly defined.

Soviet Leader Lenin saw this as a great possibility for the establishment of new communist states. US President Woodrow Wilson, on the other hand, believed that the principle of self-determination could lead to stability and peace in Europe. Wilson put the principle powerfully on the international agenda when in 1918, spelling out the essential terms for peace after the First World War, he declared the following:

> "National aspirations must be respected; peoples may be dominated and governed only by their own consent. 'Self-Determination' is not a mere phrase. It is an imperative of action… What we are seeking is a peace that is a peace that we can all unite to guarantee and maintain and every item of it must be submitted to the common judgement whether it be right and fear, an act of justice, rather than a bargain between sovereigns."

The result of this principle was the fragmentation of the old Austro-Hungarian and Ottoman empires and Russia's new Baltic territories into a number of new states. Consequently, the

---

3   The facts and quotations in the parts titled "Self-Determination in Practice" and "Self-Determination in International Law and Legal Theory" are to a large extent based on information from these homepages www.un.org; www.osce.org; www.yale.edu; and from these books: Edward Mortimer (ed.): "People Nation & State", New York 1999; Sigvaldsson et al., "*Hvítabók*", Tórshavn 1999 (The Faroese Government's whitebook on the possibilities for Faroese national sovereignty).

period after the First World War is referred to as the first of three periods, when the principle of self-determination formed the basis for important international developments.

However, already back then, there were voices warning against the whole idea of letting peoples – and not existing states only – determine the borders of sovereign countries.

Indeed, Mr. Wilson's own Secretary of State, Mr. Robert Lansing, already in 1918 put forward this warning:

> "The more I think about the President's declaration as to the right of 'self-determination,' the more convinced I am of the danger of putting such ideas into the minds of certain races. It is bound to be the basis of impossible demands on the Peace Congress and create trouble in many lands.(…) The phrase is simply loaded with dynamite. It will raise hopes, which can never be realised. It will, I fear, cost thousands of lives."

Today, it is common knowledge that the self-determination principle, used in the creation of e.g. Czechoslovakia and Yugoslavia, did not lead to stable states. Even if big empires were broken up, too many and too large national minorities were still overruled. Wilson spoke of respecting national aspiration. This was indeed done. However, in respecting the aspirations of one people, the aspirations of other peoples were neglected. This dilemma is still one of the central problems related to the concept of self-determination.

The second period in time when self-determination was a leading principle in important events was the process of de-colonization during the first decades after the Second World War. The international law arrangements during this period were relatively clear: peoples had the right to self-determination – but only "peoples" understood as populations of entire colonial territories, not as ethno-nations. Furthermore, the geographical areas in question should be listed as non-self-governing territories according to Chapter XI of the UN Charter. As during these years there was, in addition to these clear provisions, also a strong advocacy from the international community in favour of decolonization, it resulted in an extensive and quite successful restructuring of the entire international community.

After this development, many commentators thought that the concept of self-determination was exhausted. But when the Berlin Wall came down, and the world saw the break-up of the Soviet Union, Yugoslavia and Czechoslovakia, the minority issue – and with that the concept of self-determination – forcefully re-appeared on the international agenda, now for the third time in the 20th century.

This time the international community did not act until very late, and the process revealed many of the major dilemmas connected to the right to self-determination: when a people is not understood as the population of a certain geographical area or territory, who then has the right to self-determination? What is the substance of that right? And how can ethnic minorities be protected?

In short, then: the concept of the right to self-determination was used when multinational empires broke up after the First World War, when colonies were decolonized after the Second World War, and when multinational socialist federations were dissolved after the Cold War. Some developments have been successful and some have not; and the extensive debate about the content of the explosive phrase "national self-determination" has still not clarified what the phrase means.

Self-Determination in International Law and Legal Theory

In the substantial theoretical writing on the issue and in international lawmaking, countless attempts have been made to clarify the many questions surrounding the concept of self-determination. The main questions are:

— What is a people or a nation?
— Which are the necessary preconditions for statehood?
— Who is the "self" in self-determination?
— What is it that this self has the right to determine?

Some of these complicated questions are dealt with elsewhere in this report, but it might be helpful to summarise briefly how they are answered in international law and theory.

There is no legal definition of a people, but in theory peoples are referred to as a societal community with clear cultural characteristics and identity that is domiciled in a certain geographical area. In addition to these objective criteria, the population in question must also identify itself as a separate people. Both Greenland and The Faroes, obviously, fulfil these criteria.[4]

The classic answer to the second question was given by the "Convention on Rights and Duties of States" on December 26, 1933. Article 1 of this Convention states:

"The state as a person of international law should possess the following qualifications: a) a permanent population; b) a defined territory; c) government; and d) capacity to enter into relations with the other states."

There is no doubt that The Faroes as well as Greenland fulfil the first three of these criteria, and, as is shown in Chapter 9 of this volume, both polities seem capable of fulfilling the fourth criteria as well.

---

4   The Faroese fulfilling the criteria for being a people is, for instance, debated in some articles in the Faroese Law Review: Geater and Crosby: "Self-Determination and Sub-Sovereign Statehood" 1 FLR (2001) 11; Alfredsson: "The Faroese People as a Subject of Public International Law" 1 FLR (2001) 45; Winther Poulsen *"Eru Føroyingar tjóð?"* 1 FLR (2001) 59. The article "The Origin of the Isolated Population of The Faroes Investigated Using Y Chromosomal Markers" in Human Genetics, Springer-Verlag 2004, concludes that "the admixture of Danish Y chromosomes into the Faroese population is small. The similarity of Faroese and Icelandic Y chromosomes is more apparent. It is possible that the male settlers of The Faroes originated from the same regions [Norway or Sweden with some contributions from the British Isles] and settled the archipelago at about the same time, as the male settlers of Iceland".

The question, who is the "self" in self-determination, is far more difficult to answer. After the First World War, this was obviously quite arbitrarily decided. After the Second World War, what formed the basis for the decolonization process was a lot clearer. In June 1946, all the Member States of the newly established United Nations were asked to inform the UN, which non-self-governing territories were under their domain. A list of 74 such territories was subsequently approved by the General Assembly. In addition to providing the UN with information about these territories, the "mother states" were under certain duties according to Chapter XI of the UN Charter. These included: to develop self-government, to take due account of the political aspirations of the peoples, and to assist them in the progressive development of their free political institutions, according to the particular circumstances of each territory and its peoples, and their varying stages of advancement.

In 1960, the UN decided that the colonies should have the right to choose between three options in order to achieve a full measure of self-government:
–   The establishment of an independent state,
–   The establishment of a free association arrangement with an independent state, or,
–   To choose integration into an independent state.

As the term "peoples" in this context was treated straightforwardly as the people within a certain territory, it was not very difficult to determine who had this right. Furthermore, as sovereignty was the clear political aspiration of most of these colonies, the road was clear for turning the vast majority of the 74 non-self-Governing territories into sovereign states.

Through clever Danish manoeuvring, however, Greenland was removed from the list of colonies in 1953, and The Faroes were never registered on the list in the first place. Therefore, these countries cannot refer – at least not as a matter of course – to these UN resolutions concerning the rights of non-self-governing territories.

However, there are other international covenants seemingly applicable to The Faroes and Greenland. The most important of these is perhaps the document referred to as "The Helsinki Final Act." That Act was endorsed in August 1995 by 35 states from Europe and North America – one of them being Denmark – participating in the Conference for Security and Co-operation in Europe.

Principle VIII of the Act refers to: "Equal rights and self-determination of peoples." The Act further states the following:

> "The participating States will respect the equal rights of peoples and their right to self-determination, acting at all times in conformity with the purposes and principles of the Charter of the United Nations and with the relevant norms of international law, including those relating to territorial integrity of States."
> "By virtue of the principle of equal rights and self-determination of peoples, all peoples always have the right freely to determine, when and as they wish their own internal and external political status, without external interference, and to pursue as they wish their political, economic, social, and cultural development."

> "The participating States reaffirm the universal significance of respect for and effective exercise of equal rights and self-determination of peoples for the development of friendly relations among themselves as among all States; they also recall the importance of the elimination of any form of violation of this principle."

The Helsinki Final Act was submitted to the Secretary General of the United Nations with a view to its circulation to all the members of the organization as an official document of the United Nations.

This clearly indicates that as late as in 1975 the right to self-determination was still an important guiding principle for international relations, and that the "self" having this right were not only colonies formally registered with the UN, but all "peoples." According to the Helsinki Final Act, both The Faroes and Greenland therefore seem to have the right to self-determination.

Finally, we turn to the last of the above-mentioned questions: what exactly is a people, according to international law, entitled to if it has the right to self-determination?

As far as the formally listed colonies are concerned, international law gives an answer that at least seems to be quite clear: it is the right to choose between the three aforementioned options, independence, integration or free association.

As far as other entities are concerned, what seems to be generally accepted today is that only in the following cases does a people have the right to establish its own state:

— If it is under foreign military occupation.
— If it is oppressed and its human rights are violated.

Peoples that do not live under any of these conditions may have the right to so-called *internal self-determination* – meaning the right to organize their own local affairs. They do not have, however, the right to *external* self-determination – meaning the right to establish their own state.

The Greenland people and the Faroese people are neither on the list of colonies, nor occupied or violently oppressed. Still, the two polities – or at least a great part of their political establishments – do persistently claim to have the right to external self-determination. How does the UN look upon this?

Analysis Based on Talks with Leading UN Officials and Missions to the UN

The Attitude of the General Secretary

From the talks with leading officials in the UN, one thing is absolutely clear: the right to self-determination is still a phrase that is loaded with dynamite – and maybe even more so today than it has ever been. It is not on the agenda of the UN today, and the states that have minorities and stateless peoples within their borders are so hostile to it, no-one dares to put it on the agenda.

A clear sign of a general shift away from UN advocacy of the self-determination principle could be seen in the 1992 report *"An Agenda for Peace"*, in which the former Secretary
General of the UN, Boutros Boutros-Ghali, made the following statement: *"The United
Nations has not closed its door. Yet if every ethnic, religious or linguistic group claimed statehood, there
would be no limit to fragmentation, and peace, security and well-being for all would become ever more
difficult to achieve"*.

The current Secretay General, Kofi Annan, is also clearly sceptical to the idea of
breaking up existing states. His views are well expressed in the speech he made to the
Council of World Affairs in Jakarta on February 16 in 2000. Even if he spoke about a specific case – Indonesia's relations to East Timor – he also made clear his general views on the
subject of self-determination:

> "It may well feel to some of you as if Indonesia's very existence is under attack from
> covert forces which believe the country is too large, and want to break it up. But,
> in fact, your case is not unique at all. Separatism is a challenge facing many coun-
> tries. Each case involves different realities and conditions; each requires a different
> approach. But, most of them do have one thing in common: although they may have
> security implications, they are, in essence, not security problems. They are political
> problems and, as such, they require political solutions. (…)
>
> We cannot say that separatism is always wrong. After all, many Member States of the
> United Nations today owe their existence to separatist movements in the past. But,
> please do not think that that means the United Nations is predisposed in favour of
> separatism, or that its purpose is to break up large States into smaller ones.
>
> On the contrary, the purpose of the United Nations is to enable peoples to live
> together without conflict. (…)
>
> The truth is that many separatist movements are wrong. Breaking up large States
> into smaller ones is often a wasteful and unimaginative way of resolving political
> differences. But those who oppose separatism have got to show that their solution is
> less wasteful and more imaginative. Minorities have to be convinced that the State
> really belongs to them, as well as to the majority, and that both will be the losers if
> it breaks up. Conflict is almost certain to result if the State's response to separatism
> causes widespread suffering in the region, or among the ethnic group concerned.
> The effect then is to make more people feel that the State is not their State, and so
> to provide separatism with new recruits."
>
> Like other political problems, separatism can be resolved successfully only through
> patient and painstaking confidence-building and dialogue. By showing that staying
> together is the best solution for all concerned. (…)
>
> Now that the right of the Timorese people to their own State has been clearly rec-
> ognized, their own leaders – showing great magnanimity and statesmanship – have
> been the first to recognize how important it will be for that State to have good rela-
> tions with Indonesia.

> An independent East Timor is, therefore, not a threat to Indonesia's security. Rather, it can enhance the stability and prospects of your region. By the very fact of its history and location, East Timor is connected with Portugal, Europe and the Iberian world, with Australia and the South Pacific. These countries and regions are crucial in assisting East Timor's transition to independence. And all of them, I believe, understand that East Timor has a far better chance to prosper as an independent State if Indonesia, too, is prosperous and successful."

Even if East Timor is a special and not very representative case, this sums up the attitude of the UN. Arrangements of autonomy for peoples within existing states are seen as ideal solutions, while "Separatist Movements" are looked upon with scepticism – the only exception being if they are the result of severe and long lasting violations of human rights.

The reason for this is obvious: the UN is an organization made up of states and financed by states. Only in extreme cases can the organization, therefore, express attitudes that are contrary to the interests of states. There are, indeed, several states that are not interested in having the right to self-determination put back on the international agenda. The UN, like every other international/intergovernmental organization, is a constitutional animal, and its rules are written by the Member States and for the Member States. Neither the Security Council nor any other UN office can act independently of the Member States.

There have been periods when the UN, because it has been the wish of a great majority of its Member States, has promoted decolonization and the principle of self-determination – but this is not the case today. The general rule at the beginning of the new millennium is the following: as long as there is no agreement between a non-sovereign entity desiring independence and the state in question, the UN will not get involved in any way. Until an agreement is reached, the issue is seen as an internal matter of the Member State and, therefore, something that the UN can neither get involved in nor express any opinion about. A state is seen as a "black box" and whatever happens within that black box is not an issue for the UN, except, again, if serious and deeply troubling violations of human rights persist.

The UN is Incapable of Deciding on Questions relating to Self-Determination

According to international law and legal theory, "peoples" that fulfil certain criteria, have the right to self-determination. Being a "people" is the most important prerequisite there is.

But, although the UN Charter says "We the Peoples," and although there are several definitions of a people, there does not exist an authoritative definition of the concept. There is no doubt that the people of the Faroe Islands and the people of Greenland possess all the criteria that have been set up for being "a people," and using common sense, nobody would doubt this fact. But the lack of a clear-cut definition makes it impossible for the UN to decide whether the Faroese and the Greenlanders should enjoy the status of being proper "peoples" or not. This is up to the Member State representing Greenland and The Faroes – Denmark – to decide.

Exactly the same goes for the self-determination concept. There is no doubt the original idea of this whole concept was that sovereignty should be vested in peoples as well as states, and that stateless peoples should have the right to determine their constitutional status; including the right to establish a new state. This has, indeed, been considered a right in certain periods in history, but today the UN has no authoritative and practicable definition saying what self-determination really means. Because of the lack of clear definitions, the UN does not try to assess who has the right to self-determination or not. The issue is left to the state in question to decide.

An example of how careful the UN is could be seen when on 26 July 2000 a letter signed by a leading official in the Department of Foreign Affairs in the Faroese Government was sent to the UN. The Faroese Government informed the UN that it had initiated negotiations with the Danish Government in order to conclude a treaty, which established The Faroes as a sovereign state, and complained that the Danish Government had not after three rounds of negotiations shown sincere readiness to conclude such a treaty with The Faroes. Therefore, the letter said, the Faroese Government was considering the option of requesting a third party to participate as an observer at the negotiations. Furthermore, the Faroese Government asked the UN "to inform the Office of the Prime Minister of the Faroe Islands (…) regarding all relevant procedures applicable when the United Nations and/or its agencies participate as a third party at international negotiations." The reaction from the UN was the only possible reaction of an intergovernmental organization that does not have any mandate in the area: the Legal Council contacted the Danish Mission to the UN, asking what the status was of The Faroes. The Mission gave the following information on 24 August 2000:

> "The Faroe Islands are part of the Kingdom of Denmark, but have a far reaching internal self-government with competences with respect to regulating their internal affairs. The Hjemmestyret ('the Home Rule Government') had no competence to appear at 'a level of international law', unless this is authorized by the government of Denmark pursuant to the 1948 Law on the Local Government of the Faroe Islands and within the cope of the Danish Constitution. (…) The home government has no authorization from the government to appear 'at the international law level' in this matter."

Based on this information, the Legal Council gave the Faroese Government this answer:

> "Please be advised that in accordance with its Charter, which is the constituent instrument of the Organisation, the United Nations, as an intergovernmental organisation established by Member States, may participate as an observer at negotiations only if it is so directed by one of its competent organs, for example the General Assembly or the Security Council. The competent organ can act on such a matter

only if it is put on the agenda of that organ. This can be done only at the request of a Member State. The same requirement must be observed by all subsidiary bodies of the United Nations."

This was no unusual exchange of letters. Every year the different departments of the UN are being contacted by peoples – also severely oppressed peoples – who, pointing to international treaty law as well as customary law, claim to have the right to self-determination, and ask the UN how they can exercise this right. In each case the answer is the same: the UN cannot get involved in any way. As the UN neither can say what a people is nor what self-determination means, there is little guidance in international law. Unless there is extreme violence and there are severe violations of human rights, any such conflict is considered an internal affair of a Member State with which the UN has nothing to do – unless the issue is raised by another Member State.

From the point of stateless peoples this leaves us with this rather sad conclusion: What today decides whether a people has the right to self-determination is, simply, the will of the metropolitan power. The cold reality seems to be in accordance the so-called "realistic theory" about how international relations work: Might is Right.

This attitude of the UN might even be considered by oppressed peoples as an encouragement to take up arms in order to draw attention from the international community. This is indeed what desperation has led stateless peoples to do on several occasions. But nobody says that the UN's rejection of such applications is wise. The problem is that the organization has no authority to do otherwise. Partly because of the fundamental respect for the sovereignty of the Member States, and partly because the numerous resolutions and rules about the peoples' right to self-determination remain quite empty as long as there are no clear-cut definitions of either "peoples" or "self-determination."

But, why has the international community, after so many years of debate, declarations, agreements and resolutions, not succeeded in defining what the peoples' right to self-determination is all about and when it can be applied?

One reason is the complexity of international relations. When peoples demand the right to self-determination, there are hardly two cases that are comparable. Therefore, it is extremely difficult to adopt a set of authoritative rules.

Another – and probably more important – reason is, that many states are not interested in undermining the sovereignty of states by guaranteeing stateless peoples such rights. These states – e.g. India, Indonesia, Russia, Argentina, Spain, Canada and Great Britain – are perfectly aware that once such rights are granted to peoples within their realm, their geographical and constitutional integrity might be threatened. And the room for interpretation of the relevant resolutions makes it easy for such states to refuse claims of self-determination.

There is also a real fear in the international community that small states could destabilize the world because they are too weak. They will, it is feared, create geopolitical chaos and a vacuum of power that can be abused by all kinds of criminals.

The prospect of having too many Member States of the UN is also something that some UN officials are doubtful about. Small states cannot afford to have many servants in the UN system, and as certain UN committee meetings cannot be opened unless a certain number of delegates are present, this has often caused problems. Sometimes it has simply not been possible to open meetings at the set time, because there have not been enough delegates present. This has caused a waste of time and irritation among delegates from some countries.

It obviously also becomes difficult to have active and efficient general assemblies if the number of Member States becomes too high. The solution, to some, is to find new and different procedures for the work of the UN. To others it is simply to lock the door for new members.

How afraid many countries are of the whole idea of self-determination became clear in 1993, when the General Assembly discussed a draft resolution put forward by Liechtenstein. The idea of the proposal was to study the realization of self-determination through the principle of autonomy.

The underlying intention was to give the international community a tool with which it, at an early state of a minority based conflict, could prevent it from developing into a major conflict or even a human catastrophe. According to the proposal, this should not be done by breaking up states. On the contrary, the aim was to explore the possibilities of autonomy to address issues of self-determination, and at the same time preserve the territorial integrity of existing states. Minorities should be given possibilities to take care of their own matters precisely in order to avoid separation. Secession should be an option only in extreme cases, where nothing else seemed possible.

This was an idea which appealed to common sense, and at the beginning there was great support for the proposed resolution. However, the fear of unwanted political consequences prevailed over the sympathy that many states felt for the idea. The aforementioned states put up the red flag, one by one the co-sponsors of Liechtenstein dropped off, and the result was that the proposal was withdrawn at the very same session when it was presented.

(The initiative of Liechtenstein was not totally in vain, though. The draft resolution and the ideas behind it are now a program that can be studied at Princeton University in New York).

Denmark Decides the Status and the Rights of Greenland and The Faroes

Seen from the UN, the world is divided into 191 states and 16 non-self-governing territories that where listed according to Chapter XI of the UN Charter after the Second World War. These are the only political entities there are. The 16 colonies are the only polities with a right to self-determination, except, again, from forcefully occupied, or severely oppressed peoples.

Greenland was taken off the list of colonies in 1953. As is shown elsewhere in this volume, this happened in a very questionable manner. However, even if it is being proved that the UN was seriously misinformed and manipulated by Denmark when Greenland was taken off the list, and even if the process prior to the inclusion of Greenland into the Danish Constitution did not follow democratic rules, this will not change the UN's view that Greenland is an integrated part of Denmark and does not have the status and the rights of a colony.

The fact of this whole matter is that the list of colonies was made in a quite arbitrary way. It was entirely up to the sovereign states themselves to list their colonies after the Second World War. Some listed many, some listed few. There might in certain cases have been informal pressure from other states (such pressure on Denmark was probably the reason Greenland was listed), but no state was forced to list any territory. And when in the fifties some states, sometimes in a dubious manner, included their colonies in their constitutions and took them off the list, the manner in which this was done was not very much monitored by the UN, and most de-listings have in fact never been challenged. In other words: there were states that did the same thing Denmark did, but the UN will not enter into specific cases making estimations of whether each such process has been democratically acceptable or not.

It is true that New Caledonia was put back on the list by a vote in the General Assembly, but this was a very special case. The vote was motivated by oppression of the people of New Caledonia and the view that the independence movement was the clear representative of the people.

The Faroes, as also is shown elsewhere in this volume, have always had their own legal and political system and have never been fully integrated into the Danish jurisdiction. The Faroese people have never at a referendum decided to become a part of Denmark – on the contrary, in 1946 they voted for independence from Denmark. There is indeed very strong historical and legal evidence against the Danish Governments' claim that The Faroes are an integrated part of the Danish Kingdom that has only been granted home rule through a Danish law (see Chapter 2).

But the UN cannot and will not undertake investigations and draw imperative conclusions of any kind about either Greenland or The Faroes. The UN is an intergovernmental organization established and financed by Member States and protecting the interests of these states. Greenland and The Faroes are seen as internal matters of the Member State – or the "black box" – called Denmark.

The question raised in Chapter 5 of this volume, whether Denmark is morally or politically obliged to list The Faroes as a non self-governing territory, is not a matter for the UN to decide.

As Chapter 9 shows, The Faroes and Greenland do have certain rights in the international community and their own international profile. The black box of Denmark is not entirely closed. Greenland is, for instance, a member of the UN's Permanent Forum on Indigenous Issues (see Chapter 4), and The Faroes are associated members of the International Maritime Organisation that is also under the umbrella of the UN.

This means that these countries are, at least in some areas, subjects of international law. Does this fact not influence any consideration of whether they have the right to self-determination?

Not to the UN. The stronger a polities' own and independent international profile, the stronger its political moral arguments. But to the central departments of the UN, this does not make either The Faroes or Greenland subjects that will in any way be treated or even looked upon seperately from Denmark. As they are neither states nor colonies, they do not exist as entities. You are not either a subject of international law or not a subject of international law. Being a subject in one international organization cannot automatically be used as a reason to put forward claims in other areas. And in order to become a subject to the UN, you need either to be a sovereign state or a formally listed colony.

Several Danish Prime Ministers have declared that whatever decision about the future status of The Faroes and Greenland is taken by the people of these countries, it will be respected by the Danish authorities. But neither this, nor the fact that Denmark in 2000 entered into negotiations about Faroese sovereignty, will change the UN's attitude. As the Danish declarations are given within the black box of Denmark and as the above-mentioned negotiations took place within this same black box, they are seen as internal matters only. There is a fundamental difference between an internal recognition of a right, and an external recognition, that is communicated to the UN.

It is Denmark that speaks on behalf of The Faroes and Greenland in the UN, and only Denmark has the right to inform the UN about the constitutional status of these two countries. The UN only relies upon the information submitted by Denmark, and this information – no matter whether it is given today or was supplied 50 years ago – will not be challenged.

As is shown in Chapter 8, the Danish Government as late as in 2001 declared to the UN that the people of The Faroes and the people of Greenland "consider themselves as being Danish". Although this is absolutely untrue, this is the way the UN must look upon the Faroese and the Greenlanders, because this is the information given to the organization by the Member State that represents these people.

Obviously any other Member State than Denmark also has the right to raise questions concerning The Faroes and Greenland. But this is not likely to happen. To put forward proposals or ask questions about what is considered another states' internal affairs is in the UN system seen as a serious provocation of the state in question. As Denmark is a very highly esteemed member of the UN, it is not realistic to expect any Member State to do this.

And even if some Member State should take it up, it is very unlikely there will be any support for views that are contrary to Danish interests. The high estimation of Denmark and the fact that many countries have the same kind of "problems" would most likely be the factors deciding the case. There was a time when e.g. newly independent African states "automatically" supported peoples who struggled for independence, but this is not so any more. Many newly independent states do themselves now have problems with peoples inside their borders who feel stateless, and these states are furthermore typical receivers of foreign aid. They are careful not to be provocative towards the donors. And one of the countries that donates the biggest percentage of its GNP to developing countries – is Denmark.

To illustrate how careful the UN is about not entering into the internal matters of its Member States, it can be mentioned that in recent years the organization has only twice become part of such conflicts.

In the case of East Timor the UN had never accepted Indonesian sovereignty over this country. And when the 1999 referendum, that was held with the help of the Security Council, ended in violence, the UN sent in peacekeepers that allowed the new state to be born. In the case of the island of Papa New Guinea, Buganville, the violent fight between the Buganvillian uprisers and Papua New Guinea had lasted for over a decade when the case was taken up by the UN – and it only happened when both parties to the conflict had asked the Security Council to do so.

It is a telling sign of the UN's attitude that the organization has not dealt with the crisis in Chechnia, and what happened in the former Yugoslavia also shows how careful the UN is when it comes to the breaking up of states. Even when there was a referendum with a clear result in Slovenia in 1990, a year and a half passed before the new country was recognized by the UN. The international community pressed for unity right up until the time when the human disaster was a reality, and when unity was definitely no longer a possibility.

And even if there is extreme ethnically based violence there is no right to the creation of a UN Member State – the best example being Kosovo, that has still not achieved UN membership.

Another thing is that although the UN Decolonization Unit still exists, although there are still 16 "colonies" whose "mother countries" give annual reports to the UN, and although New Caledonia was added to the list as late as in 1986, there is no doubt this whole system is coming to an end. It was set up in order to give the colonized peoples of the planet a free choise about their future status, but after all these decades they have had the opportunity to make up their minds. And, as also the discussion about the above-mentioned proposal of Liechtenstein showed, many strong states are vigorously opposed to the revitalization of a formal and authoritative UN policy on the right to self-determination.

It can therefore be said that the timing of events has been quite unfortunate for The Faroes and Greenland. The overruled referendum took place in The Faroes in 1946, but at this point in history there was not very much focus on self-determination. If the referendum had taken place in the sixties there would have been far more international interest and pressure. The same goes for the integration of Greenland into Denmark. It happened before too much international focus came on these issues. It would have been different in the sixties.

Now, of course, there is a strong international media, and people are very much aware of what goes on. This might be beneficial to those who want independence, but it is not entirely to their advantage, because while other states are more aware of things, they are also more afraid of things. They fear that what happens in Denmark might happen in their country as well. Therefore it might be difficult to get support. And in the discussions that have been held about self-determination in the UN, the ambassadors have stated very clearly that this has to do with decolonization only. When it comes to the right to internal self-determination or autonomy, states are willing to go a long way. But they clearly want this to be the only form of self-determination there is.

This fact, together with the general scepticism to the idea of granting too many small countries membership of the UN, clearly indicates that even though the UN has not yet closed its doors, the doorway will get narrower for each year that goes by. The doors are still open, but whether Greenland and The Faroes will be granted admittance, is for Denmark to decide.

No Clear Legal Right – But Good Political Arguments

What is the answer, then? Do The Faroes and/or Greenland have the right to self-determination or not? On the face of it the answer must be negative. Not being on the list of colonies, not being under military occupation and not being oppressed makes it, at least at first glance, a difficult case. But it is not quite that simple.

When it comes to entities that are not on the list of colonies there are some covenants, such as, the Helsinki Final Act, that support the view that The Faroes and Greenland indeed have this right. Furthermore it is clear that political acts and political practice of states create and reinforce legal concepts. And looking at arrangements that other states have made with their non-sovereign overseas teorritories, it is possible to find support for the view that The Faroes and Greenland are not only entitled to internal, but also external self-determination.

The many free association arrangements that, for instance, The United States and New Zealand have made with their former overseas territories definitely give the Faroese and the Greenlanders good arguments. These examples show that there are many possibilities of constitutional arrangements and they undermine the "all or nothing" attitude that has many times been expressed by Danish authorities. Indeed Denmark itself made such an arrangement with Iceland in 1918. This is obviously also a very strong argument for the two polities we are dealing with.

But the most important thing to Greenland and The Faroes is the very fact that in international relations there are very few rules that are imperative. International covenants and resolutions are not laws but guidelines. And when in the international community a question like whether a polity has the right to self-determination or is suitable for statehood is considered, what decides it is mostly the circumstances of the polity itself – not international covenants on the subject.

The position of the UN is that this is the best way of dealing with such matters. As there are never two cases that are identical, it is not possible to submit international relations totally to the rule of law. You cannot start with theory saying this is it, these are the rules and then examine how the concrete case fits to the rules. Every single case is influenced by geopolitics, history, the economical and administrative strength of the polity in case etc. Therefore, you must start by looking at the concrete cases themselves. Focus should first and foremost be on the players, not on the rules.

And although international rules do not totally shut out the possibility of a Faroese and/or Greenland right to self-determination, in our case looking at the players gives a far brighter perspective than looking at the rules only. Comparing the different criteria for statehood outlined by UN officials to the situation of The Faroes and Greenland, the picture looks quite promising.

As history shows, geography is extremely important when a new state is to be established. Granting the right to self-determination to a people whose geographical area is not clearly defined, might cause serious problems. Being islands, both Greenland and The Faroes have national borders that are as clear as they possibly can be.

The second most important precondition for a successful transition to statehood is that there is no big national minority whose wishes are being overruled. Also according to this parameter, The Faroes are certainly suited for statehood, indeed, even more so than most members of the UN. The Faroes, if they achieved UN membership, would be one of the very few one-nation states there are in the organization.

As for Greenland, the situation is more complicated. There is not only a big Danish minority (10-15%) in Greenland, this minority also holds many of the most important positions in Greenland society. The administration as well as the industry are quite dominated by Danes.

A third condition pointed out by UN officials is a stable political environment. There is no doubt the political environment in the North Atlantic is one of the most stable there are.

Recognition by other states is obviously also crucial for a new state. This condition is not there now for obvious reasons – but there is little doubt the two states would be recognized by their neighbors once an agreement with Denmark was a reality. Actually, Icelandic politicians have many times openly supported the Faroese struggle for independence and said they look forward to the day when The Faroes are a state.

Historically, as is documented elsewhere in this volume, The Faroes as well as Greenland have strong arguments for claiming the right to self-determination as these polities' integration into Denmark happened in a very questionable manner.

Geopolitically, both The Faroes and, particularly, Greenland were extremely important during the Cold War and Greenland is still today an area of major military importance. This obviously makes independence for especially Greenland and to a lesser degree for The Faroes a delicate international issue that puts pressure on the two countries' governments to be a trusting partner and to withstand and act according to the responsibility this geopolitical importance brings with it. But if these requirements are met, this can hardly be considered an obstacle to Faroese or Greenlandic sovereignty. Indeed, three former Danish ministers have said that giving NATO and the USA access to Greenland and The Faroes has indirectly given a great economic advantage to Denmark.[5] This indicates that the geopo-

---

5   These Ministers were: Foreign Minster, Jens Otto Krag; Foreign Minister, Uffe Elleman Jensen and Minister of Defence, Hans Engell. Jens Otto Krag: *Føroyar í kalda krígnum*, 1999. In a 1958 conversation between Mr. Krag

litical importance might even become an economic advantage to a sovereign Greenland state.

When it comes to economic and administrative strength and ability, there are again differences between the two countries. The Faroes are now very close to being economically self-sustained, while Greenland still receives a great part of its GNB from Denmark. The Faroese administration is run by Faroese civil servants, while there are many Danish civil servants in the Greenland administration.

The social situation might also be considered of importance to the workability of a newborn microstate, and also here there is a difference between the socially very well off Faroese society and the socially quite plagued Greenland society.

Another source for deciding whether it is reasonable to talk about a Greenland and Faroese right to self-determination are the processes that have led to the establishment of new states in recent years.

---

and the Ambassador Mr. Satterthwaite about the construction of a Loran C station in The Faroes, this was reported to the file: "After Foreign Minister Krag had read the Embassy's note on the Loran Station in The Faroes (…) he said that Denmark was always pleased to be able to help the United States and contribute substantially to fulfilling its NATO obligations by making available Greenland and The Faroes. He said this made the defence budget look better and have more meaning, and he was pleased to see that this fact was recognized by our Government and Ambassador Peterson".

Hans Engell: *På slotsholmen*, 1997: "The military efforts in the North Atlantic to a considerable extent are legitimizing towards our NATO-partners – not least the USA – a reletively low Danish military budget"

Hans Engell, *Sosialurin* (newspaper) 17 July 2003: "There has always been a hidden agenda. Denmark has, through the block grant to The Faroes and Greenland, ensured the stability in the North Atlantic Sea – and to the Americans it has had great importance for security in the area. (…) During all the years of the Cold War and in the eighties there is no doubt that The Faroes were of great importance to NATO. Greenland for sure was more important, but The Faroes were very important too. During all these years it was very difficult for Denmark to meet the demands that NATO put forward to the member countries. And it counted a lot, especially seen from an American point of view, that we undertook some tasks in the North Atlantic"(…) "Today the strategical importance of the North Atlantic is not the same, but there is no doubt this importance has saved Denmark from defence spending" (…) "Through The Faroes and Greenland, Denmark gave a contribution that counted more than if we had 2000 soldiers more or less".

Uffe Elleman Jensen, *Din egen dag er kort*, 1996: "The Faroes and Greenland were good cards to have in the hand when the NATO ministers gathered in the eighties. When one should mitigate the sourness over Danish footnotes, or when the other ministers asked how we were doing in increasing our military budget to the 3% of the GNP that the former Prime Minister, Mr. Anker Jørgensen, had promised in NATO, it could give some breathing space when I told them how important it was having stable conditions in the North Atlantic and in the Arctic, and how great amounts of money Denmark spent on securing this through our economical aid to The Faroes and Greenland."

The 10 last states to obtain UN membership were Lichtenstein, 1990; Micronesia, 1991; Marshall Islands, 1991; San Marino, 1992; Andorra, 1993; Palau, 1994; Kiribati, 1999; Tonga, 1999; Tuvalu, 2000; Timor-Leste, 2002.

As state activity creates international legal concepts, comparing these countries to The Faroes and Greenland is highly relevant to the discussion about the status and rights of these two countries.

The Working Group has not had the time to undertake such an investigation, but what is clear, though, is that many of the newborn states have populations that are smaller than the populations of The Faroes and Greenland, and many are less developed, less industrialized and have a weaker administration.

The above-mentioned facts and the comparable cases might become of great importance if and when the international community or some international court one day is to decide whether The Faroes and/or Greenland are entitled to national self-determination or not.

Another thing of importance are statements made by Faroese and Greenland authorities themselves. What is said and stated in an official form by leading politicians can have decisive influence if an international judge one day is to decide whether these countries are integrated parts of Denmark or not.

What is clear, then, is that The Faroes, and, to a slightly lesser degree, Greenland are suited for statehood. But neither The Faroes, nor Greenland can break away from Denmark unilateraly. Such an act would not be approved by the international community, and therefore not be successful. The establishment of a Faroese and/or a Greenland state can only succeed if it is the result of an agreement made with Denmark.

But if one of these countries succeeded in making such an agreement with Denmark, and the two parties came before the UN declaring that they wanted a new state to be established, there is no doubt this wish would be accepted by the UN. As was the case when Czechoslovakia was divided and two new states came into being, nobody will question such an agreement that is made in an orderly and peaceful manner – even if we, measured in populations, are talking about two very small states. The attitude of the UN to the granting of membership to microstates might change in some years, but today there is no doubt the answer would be positive.

Although at the moment there is no UN advocacy for self-determination and the cause of The Faroes and Greenland therefore seems weak, these countries do have strong arguments that, if they are put forward in relevant forums, can put pressure on Denmark to give up its claim that The Faroes and Greenland are integrated parts of the Danish Kingdom. No state wants to be labelled colonial – especially not a state that is so highly regarded and is such an unremitting spokesman for tolerance and democracy as Denmark. And refusing the right of self-determination to The Faroes and Greenland in spite of the above-mentioned facts might, in a political climate like the one in Scandinavia, be interpreted as being a colonial attitude. The Danish information submitted to the UN about the Faroese and Greenlandic people considering themselves as being Danish (see Chapter 8), is obviously also something that might damage the reputation of Denmark.

But what of course is more important than anything is a clear and continuous majority in the two countries themselves that stands firm on the claim for national self-determination and persistently puts forward arguments for its cause. Such a majority might even
solve the issue without the need of turning to the international community. A small majority that might change into a minority any time is definately not a solid ground for trying to
put international pressure on Denmark.

The Faroes and Greenland are Suited for Statehood

If The Faroes and/or Greenland one day should achieve membership of the UN – do two
such small countries have anything to do in this organization? Would they afford it? Would
they have any influence? And would they at all benefit from it?

In order to answer these questions, the Working Group visited the Missions of
Liechtenstein and Iceland to the UN. Although there are many differences between The
Faroes, Greenland and these two countries, there are also important similarities. Iceland
is a neighbour of Greenland and The Faroes. Iceland has been under Danish rule, its economy to a large extent is based on fishery. Although its population is about six times as big
as that of The Faroes or Greenland, it is still very small. Liechtenstein is first and foremost comparable because of its size. With less than 35.000 inhabitants the population of
Liechtenstein is, in relative terms, considerably smaller than the populations of The Faroes
and Greenland. Like The Faroes and Greenland, neither Iceland nor Liechtenstein are part
of the European Union.

Liechtenstein has been able to protect its national sovereignty because it has friendly
neighbors. This has enabled the country to stay a state in spite of being very small and
having no army. Even if the international relations and development of Liechtenstein
are closely related to those of Switzerland, the country has its own international profile.
Liechtenstein has embassies in 8 important international organizations and bilateral embassies in Switzerland, Austria and Germany.

Liechtenstein obtained membership of the UN in 1990. The reason for the application was that the authorities thought it right to represent the people of Liechtenstein in the
international community, show the nation's face and express its points of view in important
matters. The Mission of Liechtenstein to the UN is mostly engaged in humanitarian issues.
The country acknowledges that it does not have direct influence on the decisions that are
made in the UN, but sees it as a duty to tell the world what the country stands for.

The Mission in New York does not try to cover every issue that is on the agenda of
the UN, but carefully chooses certain subjects of interest and then attends all meetings that
are important to these subjects. This way Liechtenstein has avoided being criticized for not
attending meetings. On the contrary, the Mission can proudly state that in 14 years of UN
membership it has never missed a vote on the issues it has chosen to engage in.

As the economy of Liechtenstein is based mainly on banking and partly tourism, there
are few issues on the agenda that have direct influence on the country's economy. On the
other hand membership is not expensive either. Liechtenstein pays 8 million US dollars

a year to be a member of the UN. This is considered very little compared to the moral and political value of having the nation's voice heard in the international community. Five people work at Liechtenstein's Mission to the UN.

For a long time Iceland was the smallest state in the UN and arguably also the poorest. Iceland was by many considered too small to administer real statehood. Now there is a long list of states that are far smaller – and Iceland has become one of the economically best off Member States. This has given Iceland the position of a role model for the many microstates.

Iceland has had real and important influence on international laws, that are important to Iceland. The main achievement was the Law of the Sea Convention, where the country's Mission played a crucial role. The Convention gives each country the complete right to decide its own fishery policy, and as fishery is extremely important to the Icelandic economy, it is essential to the country that this convention is kept the way it is. A lot of the Mission's energy now goes into protecting this Convention, because recently there have been states that want it reopened. So-called "environmental states" like, for instance, New Zealand and Australia want fishery to be controlled by international law the way whaling is controlled today. There are indications that Iceland and the countries which share its views will lose this fight in the end, as still more states join the "environmental camp". Among Scandinavian countries only Norway supports the views of Iceland.

Therefore the message from the Icelandic Mission is clear: it would be welcomed warm-heartedly if two more Nordic countries, whose economy is based on fishery, became members of the UN. And it would be in the interest of both The Faroes and Greenland to be able to protect their interests in the UN – also because Denmark, that now speaks and votes on behalf of The Faroes and Greenland, does not work in favor of national management of the resources of the ocean, neither when it comes to whaling, nor fishery.

Pollution of the sea is also an issue that has direct impact on Iceland, and the Mission engages in a lot of work that aimes at preventing polution.

As Iceland engages in many issues, it has happened that the Mission has been lightly criticized for not attending meetings it has been supposed to attend. All in all eight people work at Iceland's Mission to the UN.

States like Liechtenstein and Iceland are not left to themselves in the UN machinery. They work closely together with different groups of other states. The Missions of Liechtenstein and Iceland are both in the group of countries in the European Economic Area (Iceland, Norway and Liechtenstein), and the Forum of Small States. (This group is not very united, though, as the UN definition of a small state is a state with less than 10 million inhabitants – meaning there are more than 80 states in this Forum).

To Iceland the far most important group is the Nordic Group that consists of all the Scandinavian countries. They cooperate very closely and have formal meetings every week. The Icelanders rely a lot on this group in order to get information about the issues that are being discussed. Other groups where Iceland is active are the group of Baltic States and the group of NATO countries.

To Liechtenstein the most important cooperation is through the bilateral ties with its neighbors Switzerland and Austria. In addition to this, and the EEA Group and the Forum of Small States, the Mission of Liechtenstein is part of a group consisting of the countries in the European Union, and a group consisting of Japan, USA, Norway, Iceland, Liechtenstein, San Marino and South Korea that tries to be a counter-group to the European Union in the UN.

Liechtenstein and Iceland are considerably more active than some other of the very small Member States in the UN. Some of these states do not in reality do very much in New York at all. Once they have obtained their representation, it seems as their goal is achieved. To these states the membership is more a question of national pride and identity than the possibility of having influence on world affairs.

But the examples of Liechtenstein and Iceland confirm that it certainly is possible to be a well-functioning member of the UN even if you are a small state. In some aspects it might even be an advantage. Because of the easy contact and often personal relations to the government ministers back home, ambassadors and officials of small states in New York can manoeuvre far more freely than their counterparts in the huge bureaucracies of big states.

Small states can influence important issues, and they certainly can use their seat in the UN to express their opinions on important matters and take their part of the responsibility for world affairs.

It is no easy task for a very small state to be a responsible member of the UN, but no hindrance is so tough it cannot be overcome. It would indeed be possible for The Faroes and Greenland to handle a UN membership of a more than merely symbolic character.

8 – The Faroes and Greenland in UN Documents

Bogi Eliasen

The aim of this chapter is to investigate to what extent The Faroes and Greenland have been discussed in the UN and what information the UN has about The Faroes and Greenland, as well as a general consideration of minority issues in the UN.

Additionally, there is a brief discussion of the 2000 report from the Council of Europe on Denmark, which heavily criticises Denmark for not considering the Greenland and Faroese people who live in geographical Denmark as minorities. The research is based on web searches, treaty language and specific inquiries regarding Greenland and The Faroes.

The position of The Faroes and Greenland in the UN context is not the same. Greenland was originally on the list of non-self-governing territories, but was taken off the list when the Territory of Greenland was formally integrated under the Danish Constitution in 1953. Greenland is categorized differently, as the inhabitants are seen as "indigenous people" and are thus protected under ILO Convention 169 (see Chapter 4 of this volume). Greenland has also participated in Danish UN delegations, while The Faroes have not.

It is important to examine the archives of key international organizations to see what material there is about Greenland and The Faroes, both what may derive from the polities themselves and what information has been provided by Denmark. The UN is the only international organization with a structure for self-determination, and under the Economic and Social Council Denmark has been obliged to provide information on self-determination.

Denmark has made a statement in the UN referring to customary law (Fourth Periodic Report) under the heading *Greenland and Danish Foreign Policy*: "International treaties concluded by the Danish Government and customary international law bind the Home Rule Authority to the same extent as they do the Government of Denmark, in order to ensure that Denmark and Greenland comply with their international obligations."[1]

This clearly indicates that customary law obligates Denmark, and thus the statements about The Faroes and Greenland and the special status of these countries can be seen in a

---

[1]   4th Periodic Report under the Committee on Economic, Social and Cultural Rights, "Implementation of the International Convenant on Economic, Social and Cultural Rights", p. 14, section 25, 28 April 2003.

Sjúrður Skaale (ed.), The Right To National Self-Determination, *169-178.*
© *2004 Koninklijke Brill NV. Printed in the Netherlands.*

UN context to have more value than the paper they are written on. But as examples show later in the text, Denmark cannot internally fulfil international obligations in policy areas that are taken over by The Faroes or Greenland in those respective territories.

Denmark claims that the Danish Realm is a unitary state. But the membership of the EU is divided, as only Denmark is a member. With that membership, Denmark has effectively vested sovereignty in EU supranational parts. Furthermore, the parliaments of Greenland and The Faroes have legislative power, and Denmark cannot implement international obligations in policy areas that are taken over by Greenland or The Faroes. The effect of this is that Denmark very often enters international treaties with territorial reservations for The Faroes and Greenland, thus underscoring that Denmark is not a unitary state with one undisputed legislative power, but a structure with some federative elements of divided power, as I conclude Chapter 10 of this volume.

In this context it is important to bear in mind that neither Greenland nor The Faroes have Denmark as their closest neighbouring country, nor do they have a border with Denmark. In geographic terms, both countries are *terra firme,* as they are separate from Denmark.

The Periodic Reports under the Economic and Social Council

The different councils of the UN regularly demand information on specific issues from the member countries. Most of the information used here was submitted by Denmark to the Economic and Social Council. The information is mainly from the third report from 1997.

The report starts with an introduction to its status in the Danish Realm. The last chapters are the subjects or questions answered in a Greenlandic context.

There is no information on or about the Faroe Islands, as the polity did not participate in producing the report. In a UN committee's examination of the report, Denmark is heavily criticized for not having information on The Faroes, but Denmark's response is that the polity has Home Rule and thus must pass on the information itself. However, the rest of the report concerns only Denmark proper without reference to The Faroes or Greenland.

It is stated that Greenland is a "geographically separate and well-defined part of the Danish Realm," which has a distinct language and culture.[2] It is also said that Denmark sees the right of self-determination as being applicable to indigenous peoples. But according to the report, Greenland has used its right to self-determination to gain Home Rule and by Danish ratification of ILO Convention 169.[3]

On Self-Governance and Self-Determination

There are several documents in the UN that mention the authority of Greenland and The Faroes and talk about the right to self-determination.

---

2   3rd Periodic Report 1997:3/1.
3   3rd Periodic Report 1997:3/4 & 5.

In the presentation of the third report of the Economic, Social and Cultural Rights Committee, the Danish delegation said that a commission of Danish and Greenlandic politicians was established in order to "realize the right to self-determination of that region. In addition, a large majority of the population of Greenland had approved the self-rule in a referendum and it had become effective".[4]

The UN asked Denmark if the Home Rules have a *sui generis* legal status comparable to other autonomies.[5] There is also a question about the decision-making procedures followed in formulating foreign policy and future Danish relations with Greenland and The Faroes. Is there a plan for strengthening links among the three territories or to hold a referendum on this or similar issues, the Committee wants to know.[6]

The Danish answer is repeated in this way by the Committee:

"The Home Rule Act vested decision-making power for international affairs in the Danish national authorities. In practice however, there was a constant dialogue between the Greenlandic and Danish Governments. Hence, a delegation on which Danes and Greenlanders were represented on an equal footing conducted negotiations with Greenland's neighbours for the demarcation of fishing zones. The Danish Minister of Foreign Affairs served only as an adviser in similar negotiations conducted by the Faroe Islands. There were no plans for a referendum on the full independence of the two territories. The intention was, rather, to improve the existing system within the framework of extremely amicable relations. In that regard, he stressed that, in the Commission on Human Rights, Greenland and Denmark cooperated closely on the matter of rights of indigenous peoples."[7]

This information is not true. The so-called *Independence Government* in The Faroes came into power in 1998 with the clear aim of establishing a sovereign Faroese state. In the autumn of 1999, just a few months after this hearing, the proposals for the future of The Faroes as an independent state were presented. At the time of this hearing the political debate on The Faroes was totally dominated by the issues of both independence and a referendum.

At the following meeting, the UN requested additional information on the right to self-government and the debate on self-government taking place in The Faroes.[8] The information given by Danish officials is quoted in these words:

---

4   Denmark Presents Report on Economic, Social and Cultural Rights Committee, 3.5.99, p. 2.

5   Committee on Economic, Social and Cultural Rights, Summary Record of the First Part (Public) of the 13th Meeting, 17.5.99, p. 2, section 3.

6   *Ibid.,* p. 2., section 4.

7   *Ibid.,* p. 3, section 9.

8   Summary Record of the 11th Meeting, 1.7.99, on 3rd Periodic Report from Denmark, p. 5, section 24.

"With regard to the right to self-determination, he [The Danish Government representative] said that its application was the topic of ongoing debate. He considered that self-determination was a continuous process and that the right could be exercised in varying degrees and in different forms, i.e. through the choice of more far-reaching autonomy. The Faroe Islands had therefore created a committee to study the possibility of expanding its autonomy, particularly at the international level. However, that was a matter for discussion by all the parliaments concerned."[9]

The words "The Faroe Islands had therefore created a committee to study the possibility of expanding its autonomy..." are, again, a clear twisting of the truth.

The Faroese Government had created a committee with the clear purpose of investigating the possibilities for Faroese national sovereignty. The report, finished in July 1999, was called: "The white book. The base for a treaty that establishes The Faroes as a sovereign state in co-operation with Denmark."[10]

The question of Faroese and Greenlandic self-determination has been discussed in the UN. Denmark does not deny the right of self-determination for The Faroes or Greenland, but clearly gave the UN inaccurate information when, as late as May 1999, it claimed that there were no plans for referenda on independence and that the Faroese Government was studying the possibilities of expanding autonomy.

In an answer to the questions to the third report, it is stated that "...the Faroese [Government] is the supreme authority in the educational system."[11] This shows that policy areas taken over by The Faroes and Greenland are not under Danish control.

In May 1999, the Committee on Economic, Social and Cultural Rights also asked the Danish government representatives about the consultation and decision-making procedures in formulating foreign policy as well as whether the Home Rules were comparable to other autonomies or had a *sui generis* status.[12] But the question does not seem to have been answered.

A representative of Greenland, Mr. Møller Lyberth, participated in some meetings on the Economic, Social and Cultural Rights. He underscored that political parties had raised the question of independence and that the question of Greenlandic self-determination had not been settled once and for all.

The Committee made many remarks about missing information, especially about The Faroes, but also Greenland. Denmark was criticized for not having Faroese and Greenlandic representatives in their delegations. Denmark replied on several occasions that in regard to

---

9   *Ibid.*, p. 5, section 26.

10   The Faroese title is: "*Hvítabók. Støðið undir einum sáttmála, ið skipar Føroyar sum eitt fullveldis-ríki í samstarvi við Danmark*". The Faroese Government, 1999.

11   Reply to the List of Issues: Denmark 10/07/96.

12   Committee on Economic, Social and Cultural Rights, Summary of the First Part (Public) of the 13th Meeting, 17.05.99.

policy areas under Faroese and/or Greenlandic responsibility, the Home Rules themselves have to provide the information to the UN.

There are several questions about the Thule Case in, for instance, the Committee on the Elimination of Racial Discrimination, 1221ˢᵗ Meeting, 18.03.97, as they do not see that Denmark is adequately addressing the problem.

The Minority Question in the UN and the Council of Europe

Denmark has declared to the Council of Europe that only the German minority in Southern Jutland is a minority according to the Framework Convention for the Protection of National Minorities.

In September 2000, the Council of Europe Advisory Committee on the Framework Convention for the Protection of National Minorities heavily criticized the fact that the Faroese and Greenlandic people that live in metropolitan Denmark are not considered minorities and do not enjoy the protection of the above-mentioned Framework Convention.[13]

Denmark replied that this was due to the territorial Home Rule arrangements, which offered Greenlanders and Faroese cultural protection, and to the fact that Denmark, according to the UN Covenant on Civil and Political Rights, defined the Faroese people as a "people" and the Greenlandic people as an "indigenous people".[14]

The Advisory Committee rejected the Danish view, partly because not all Faroese or Greenlandic people are living in The Faroes or in Greenland, and partly because having the status of a "people" or the status of an "indigenous people" does not exclude citizens from protection by the Framework Convention for the Protection of National Minorities.

The Danish argumentation is described by the Advisory Committee in these words:

> "If the reasoning of the Danish Government is to be followed, the result is that the Greenlanders and Faroese persons enjoy an effective protection of their identity (language, education, culture etc.) within the respective home rule areas, but no such protection outside these areas, notably in mainland Denmark".[15]

The minority issue has also been discussed in the UN. On May 22, 2001, the United Nations stated in a press release: "Committee on Rights of Children Starts Review of Report on Denmark". According to the six-page press release, the 12 representatives from

---

13　Advisory Committee on the Framework Convention for the Protection of National Minorities, Opinion on Denmark, adopted 22 September 2000.

14　"*Comments of the Government of Denmark on the Opinion of the Advisory Committee on the Report on the Implementation of the Framework Convention for the Protection of National Minorities in Denmark*", 7 June 2001.

15　Advisory Committee on the Framework Convention for the Protection of National Minorities, Opinion on Denmark, adopted 22 September 2000.

8 ministries of the Danish Government were asked many questions about Greenland and The Faroes.

An expert of the Committee, according to the press release, put forward, for instance, this direct question:

"While Germans living in the country were considered a national minority in Denmark, people from Greenland and the Faroe Islands were not considered as national minorities. What was the position of the Government on this?"[16]

The answer given by the Danish government delegation is quoted thus in the press release:

"The people of Greenland and the Faroe Islands had never considered themselves as minorities; they considered themselves as being Danish, the delegation said. Any international treaties signed by Denmark were extended to those territories although they were self-governing entities within the Danish State."[17]

This information, submitted to the UN by a Danish government delegation, can only be said to be blatantly untrue or expressed in total ignorance. Nobody with even the slightest knowledge of Greenland and/or The Faroes would claim that the Faroese and Greenlanders consider themselves as Danish, as they both have a distinct national identity.

The information provided by the Danish delegation can at the very least be considered peculiar given the fact that the year 2000 saw four rounds of negotiations between Denmark and The Faroes on Faroese independence, in which the Faroese claimed the right of self-determination as a distinct people.

In general, Danish information provided in this area lacks coherence. Several times over, Denmark states that it cannot fulfil international obligations in policy areas under the power of the Home Rules. As stated with respect to the Convention on the Elimination of Racial Discrimination, Denmark says about the situation in The Faroes and Greenland: "Greenland and Faroes have not been covered under the Danish act, as it comes under the Home Rule competence and it is their prerogative to decide how to implement the Convention."[18]

In another answer, however, it is stated that any treaties signed by Denmark were extended to those territories although they were self-governing entities within the Danish State,[19] as mentioned above.

---

16   Committee on Rights of Children Starts Review of Report on Denmark. United Nations Press Release, CRC, 27th session, 22 May 2001.

17   *Ibid.*

18   Committee on the Elimination of Racial Discrimination, 1221st Meeting, 13.08.97, p. 2, section 7.

19   Committee on Rights of Children Starts Review of Report on Denmark, 22.05.2001.

In a meeting under the Human Rights Committee, Committee member Mr. Ando pointed out that:

"...according to indigenous rights in Greenland, environmental protection was exclusively under Greenlandic Home Rule jurisdiction, while state security and defence were under the Danish central Government. He points out the potential conflict and asked if there were any conflict resolving mechanisms and if there had been any conflicts. Also he wanted to know about any disparity between indigenous practice and human rights standards in Denmark."[20]

The Committee also sees the non-transfer of administration of justice to Greenland as incompatible with Article 1 of the Covenant.[21]

The Case of Terrorism

As part of the UN's international struggle against terrorism the organization in 2001 asked Denmark to provide a progress report on the implementation of Security Council Resolution 1373 in Greenland and the Faroe Islands. Denmark responded with these words:

"The amendments of the Criminal Code do not apply for the Faroe Islands, but the amendments may enter into force by a Royal decree. Before coming into force of the amendments, the Faroe Home Rule must have the amendments presented for an opinion. It is the intention of the Ministry of Justice in the nearby future together with the Faroe Home Rule to take a thorough look at the criminal rules applying to the Faroe Islands in order to make sure that there are no loopholes as far as terrorism is concerned in the Faroese regulation.

Greenland has it own criminal code and therefore the amendments will not be put into force in Greenland. However, an existing Commission on Greenland's Judical System has the task to carry out a fundamental revision of the judical system in Greenland and to draft a revised version of the special Criminal Code and the special Administration of Justice Act applying in Greenland. The Commission is expected to hold its last meeting in the second half of 2002. The report is expected to be submitted in 2003. When the revised version of the special Criminal Code is available, the Ministry of Justice will examine it in order to ensure that all the obligations of UNSCR 1373 (2201) are fulfilled."[22]

---

20   Human Rights Committee, 1534th Meeting, 23.10.96, p. 9, section 70.

21   *Ibid.*, p. 9, section 67.

22   Denmark: Supplementary Report dated 8 July 2002 submitted pursuant to Paragraph 6 of Security Council Resolution 1373 (2001).

This answer from Denmark shows that the Kingdom of Denmark is not a unitary state. Both Greenland and The Faroes are considered distinct territories and jurisdictions, and Denmark does not have the legitimate right to unilaterally fulfil international obligations in those territories.

Financial Aspects

The Committee on Economic, Social and Cultural Rights in 1999 asked whether "... *the current financial arrangements facilitated the establishment of constructive dialogue with the indigenous people of Greenland on the question of their right to self-determination*", to which Denmark answered that they in no way use subsidies as a negotiating tool with Greenland.[23]

Denmark transfers a block subsidy to both Greenland and The Faroes. Whether or not this has been used as a negotiating tool in relations with Greenland is unclear. But it was a continuous argument used in the negotiations between Denmark and The Faroes in the year 2000 on Faroese independence.

International Treaties and The Faroes and Greenland

The Faroes and Greenland have exceptions from many international treaties. Some examples are listed here:

International Cocoa Agreement 1993. Geneva, 16 July 1993. The instrument of approval was accompanied by the following declaration: "This approval shall not apply to the Faroe Islands and Greenland."

Protocol to Prevent, Suppress and Punish Trafficking in Persons, Especially Women and Children, Supplementing the United Nations Convention against Transantional Organized Crime. New York, 15 November 2000. This was concluded with territorial exclusion of The Faroe Islands and Greenland.

Convention on Access to Information, Public Participation in Decision-Making and Access to Justice in Enviromental Matters. Århus, 25 June 1998. The Danish declaration to the treaty states:

> "Both the Faroe Islands and Greenland are self-governing under Home Rule Acts, which implies inter alia that environmental affairs in general and the areas covered by the Protocol are governed by the right to self-determination. In both the Faroe and the Greenland Home Rule Governments there is a great political interest in promoting the fundamental ideas of principles embodied in the Convention to the extent possible. However, as the Convention is prepared with a view to European countries with relatively large populations and corresponding administrative and social structures, it is not a matter of course that the Convention is in all respects

---

23   Committee on Economic, Social and Cultural Rights, Summary Record of the First Part (Public) of the 13th Meeting, 17.05.99, p. 5, section 24 and p. 6, section 27.

suitable for the scarcely populated and far less diverse societies of the Faroe Islands and of Greenland. Thus, full implementation of the Convention in these areas may imply needless and inadequate bureaucratization. The authorities of the Faroe Islands and of Greenland will analyse this question thoroughly. Signing by Denmark of the Protocol, therefore does not necessarily mean that Danish ratification will in due course include the Faroe Islands and Greenland."

Agreement between the Government of the Kingdom of Denmark together with the Home Government of the Faroe Islands, on the one hand, and the Government of the United Kingdom of Great Britain and Northern Ireland, on the other hand, relating to Maritime Delimitation in the Area between the Faroe Islands and the United Kingdom. 18 May 1999. "Done in duplicate at Tórshavn this eighteenth day of May 1999 in the Danish, the Faroese and the English languages, all three texts being equally authoritative."[24] Clearly, this agreement underscores the position of The Faroes as a distinct polity.

Polities in the UN

Since the creation of the UN, there has been an ongoing debate on how many members the UN could have and how many entities the international system would be able to manage. Upon its creation, the UN had 51 Member States; today the number is 191, almost four times the original number of members. One of the questions is whether there is a limit to how many members the UN as well as the international system in general can cope with.

However, the UN itself has a scheme of 257 entities. These include the 191 Member States, and 11 different groupings of autonomies and separate entities being:

1. Non-Self-Governing Territories
2. Self-Governing Territories
3. Territories
4. Crown Dependencies
5. Possessions
6. Self-Governing in Free Association
7. Overseas Departments
8. Special Administrative Regions
9. Commonwealth in Political Union
10. Commonwealth Associated with
11. Territorial Collectivity

Of these, several are uninhabited, but the list indicates that the UN is working with the overseas element, as all the entities, except Hong Kong and Macao have water between

---

24   The Agreement was signed in Tórshavn, the Capital of The Faroes; it clearly shows that The Faroes are not an integrated part of Denmark, but rather a distinct polity in the Kingdom of Denmark.

them and the metropolitan state. Thus, the first phase of working with autonomy and self-determination should concentrate on these entities, as they have clear natural boundaries and are seen as distinct in the international context. The list of entities can be seen on UN webpage: http://www.un.org/Depts/Cartographic/english/geoname.pdf.

Conclusion

The way The Faroes and Greenland have been categorized has changed over time. Several of the newer texts state that the Faroe Islands and Greenland have the right to self-determination.

But as late as 1999, information was given that there were no talks about independence in The Faroes. And in 2001 there is an example of a big Danish government delegation claiming that the Greenland and Faroese people do not have a distinct national identity, as they consider themselves to be Danish.

In several documents, Denmark states that a certain policy area is under Faroese or Greenland authority and thus their responsibility. This special status means that Denmark cannot fulfil internal international obligations in transferred policy areas. In such cases, Denmark can only fulfil its obligations in Denmark, not in the territorial areas of The Faroes and Greenland. This supports the view that the Kingdom of Denmark is not, in function, a unitary state.

In both the UN and the Council of Europe, Denmark has been criticized for not seeing Faroese and Greenlanders as minorities, both as part of the Danish state, but also as minority populations in territorial Denmark.

The list of entities shows that the UN informally operates with an overseas definition. In effect, The Faroes and Greenland are distinct polities on their own with effective participation on the international level and, one could say, belonging to the class of potential sovereign states, though Denmark sometimes seems to mislead itself and others on this issue.

9 – Non-Sovereign Polities and Their Access to the International Community

Bogi Eliasen

Introduction

At first glance, the title of this chapter may seem inconsistent, as the international community is often described as the interaction between sovereign states and the organizations established by them. My submission, however, is that the international community is changing and this leaves room for autonomous non-sovereign polities like Greenland and the Faroe Islands. The change is arguably from an international to a global community.

This chapter is divided into five parts, followed by two Annexes. The purpose of the first part is to identify the international profile of Greenland and The Faroes. The second part describes the opportunities for non-sovereign polities in international organizations. The third part compares the status and practice of other overseas dependencies in Western state structures. The fourth part examines the status vis-à-vis the EU of non-sovereign entities associated to EU Member States. Finally, the fifth part compares The Faroes and Greenland to other non-sovereign polities and their relations to the principle state. Annex 1 offers an overview of non-sovereign polities; Annex 2 lists the acronyms and full names of all the international organizations contacted during the research.

I myself lived for the first 20 years of my life in the Faroe Islands, a non-sovereign polity, situated overseas, far away from the metropolitan state of Denmark, with its own language, culture, flag, autonomous Constitutional Act, and yet officially without international recognition. At the same time, Denmark was entering an ever-closer union in Europe, with The Faroes remaining outside and Greenland even withdrawing from the EU. My university education in political science in Denmark provided no adequate explanation for this development of the association between Denmark and its associate countries, know as the Danish Realm. I proceeded on the assumption that "international law is what states make," as stated by Malanczuk:

Sjúrður Skaale (ed.), The Right To National Self-Determination, *179-204.*
© *2004 Koninklijke Brill NV. Printed in the Netherlands.*

"The main evidence of customary law is to be found in the actual practice of states, and a rough idea of a state's practice can be gathered from published material – from newspapers reports of action taken by states, and from statements made by government spokesmen to Parliament, to the press, at international conferences and meetings of international organizations; and also from a state's laws and judicial decisions, because the legislature and the judiciary form part of a state just as much as the executive does." (Malanczuk 1997:39)

The International Profile of The Faroes and Greenland

The main purpose of this chapter is to investigate which rights and possibilities the Faroese and Greenland People have in the context of the international community. In this first part, I try to identify the current profile of these two polities. My research has revealed at least ten different patterns of international relations concerning Greenland and the Faroe Islands:

— Denmark represents the entire Realm. Examples include NATO and the UN, though no longer the UN organizations.

— Denmark represents the Realm, but will hear The Faroes and Greenland. Examples of this include a number of international treaties with territorial reservations.

— Denmark represents the Danish Realm, but is bound by concessions concerning Greenland and The Faroes. Examples include the Universal Postal Union (UPU) and the International Civil Aviation Organisation (ICAO).

— Denmark represents the Realm, but delegates from Greenland and The Faroes serve informally on the relevant delegation. The International Whaling Commission (IWC) is an example.

— Denmark holds membership on behalf of the Realm with official representation on the delegation. The prime example is the Nordic Council, which grants seats to the autonomous areas.

— Denmark is a member on behalf of The Faroes and Greenland – the DFG system and, at the same time, Denmark proper is represented through its EU membership. Examples include NAFO, NEAFC and NASCO. In real terms, Greenland and The Faroes run the delegations, only at crucial occasions do Danish officials attend.

— The Faroes and Greenland are independent members, and Denmark is an observer. This is the case regarding NAMMCO.

— Denmark is the member on behalf of the Danish Realm, but Greenland and The Faroes have by treaty an observer status, giving them the opportunity for active participation. An example of this is ICES.

— The Faroes is an associated member of a UN organization. This recent innovation is the IMO, associate membership in the name of "Faroe Islands, Denmark." In connection with this membership, Denmark has informed the UN that The Faroes have a wide measure of home rule which includes the responsibility for safety at sea, and thus wish to become a member of the IMO.

—   Greenland participates in the Permanent Forum on Indigenous Peoples under the UN;[1] and the Inter-polar Circular Conference.[2]

In addition, Denmark holds memberships not including The Faroes and Greenland by territorial exception of The Faroes and Greenland. Thus, Denmark as an EU Member State is part of the EU's membership of various international organizations. This means that Greenland and The Faroes hold their own negotiations with the EU, and even have different treaties, as Greenland, for instance, has status as one of the "Overseas Countries and Territories". Both The Faroes and Greenland do mostly handle international negotiations on fishery by themselves. Potentially, policy areas not transferred to The Faroes and Greenland may be transferred to the EU, leaving The Faroes and Greenland without democratic influence.

International treaties of special importance for Greenland or The Faroes have to be submitted to Home Rule Governments before ratification. This includes both treaties concerning matters of great importance and policy areas transferred to Greenland and The Faroes. According to the Home Rule Compacts and Danish Government practice, such treaties have to be ratified by Home Rule parliaments prior to ratification by the Danish Parliament.[3]

By contrast, participation in other organizations, like NATO, has been viewed as a policy area of exclusive concern to the Danish Government on behalf of the entire Realm, excluding participation by the two associate countries.

In the field of non-governmental sports, the two countries have made great headway. Greenland national sports federations have achieved membership of five international federations recognized by the International Olympic Committee. The Faroese national federation has been recognized as independent of Denmark since 1939 and its national federations are members of nine international federations. Both countries participate in International Island Games, and Greenland in the Arctic Winter Games. Both countries are aspiring to Olympic recognition.

In conclusion, The Faroes and Greenland have a number ways of participating in the international community, which can be called a rather "confused" international profile.

International Organizations

There are various kinds of international organizations, mostly divided into intergovernmental (IGO) and non-governmental organizations (NGO). The latter include both private

---

1   http://www.un.org/esa/socdev/pfii/index.html.

2   http://www.inuit.org/.

3   Faroese Home Compact § 7, Greenland Compact § 13. *Statsministeriets vejledning af 16. januar 1991: 3.*

interest groups, such as Greenpeace and Amnesty International, with individual member-ship, and semi-official organizations like the Red Cross/Red Crescent, which monitors the Geneva Conventions, and the International Aviation and Travel Association, and the International Olympic Committee. Often, as the sports organizations illustrate, the non-governmental organizations divide along national lines.

The intergovernmental organizations include a subcategory of supranational organiza-tions that distinguish themselves by facilitating integration of the Member States using majority vote and independent sources of finance.

I find it important in describing the international profile of the Faroe Islands and Greenland to include the recognition – *de jure* or *de facto* – by IGOs and NGOs, including the sports associations, of the two countries.

As mentioned above, Danish EU membership does not include The Faroes and Greenland. The EU has a joint membership in a number of intergovernmental organiza-tions. This means that in some international organizations Denmark is included within the EU membership. However, as The Faroes and Greenland are not covered by the Danish membership of the EU, a new model was created. It has been called the "DFG system": Denmark on behalf of The Faroes and Greenland. This model is used in organizations where Denmark is included in the EU membership, and The Faroes and Greenland are included through Denmark.

It is important to emphasize that the DFG model is used in policy areas over which The Faroes and Greenland have the responsibility. Formally, Denmark has the final deci-sion in the DFG delegation. In practice, the Greenland and Faroese Governments make the decisions. Thus, the international profile of the Danish Realm is not that straightforward, allowing The Faroes and Greenland room to manoeuvre, enjoying *de facto*, though not formal, status as subjects of the international order.

The DFG system is constrained, first, where Danish interests take priority, and, sec-ondly, where Denmark itself may be constrained by its EU obligations.

A mainstream assumption would be that international treaties and membership entered into by Denmark would automatically include The Faroes and Greenland, if not specifically excluded. The problem, however, comes in the ratifying procedure. If it is in a policy area where The Faroes or Greenland enjoys responsibility, or which has great impact on them, Denmark cannot ratify the treaty without consent.

Access by Non-Sovereign Polities to International Organizations

As many scholars have pointed out, we live in a post-sovereign age. Wanting to investigate the status of autonomous polities, the only way for me to find answers was to undertake a basic empirical investigation, asking the relevant parties. I sent questions to 36 major European and international organizations and Western countries with non-sovereign, autonomous polities associated to their state structure and the autonomous countries themselves. The questions concerned the rights and possibilities for Greenland and the Faroe Islands in relation to the international community:

1.   Who can become a member?
2.   Who can become an observer?
3.   What is the process, when a newly independent state applies for membership?
4.   What is the process when an entity in the process of independence applies for membership?
5.   What is the process when a non-independent entity contacts the organization, e.g. for information on possible membership and/or status as observers?
6.   Does the institution have different kinds of membership?
7.   Can a non-independent entity use you as an advisory body?

If the specific organization had non-sovereign entities as members, associate members etc., I added this question, as in the case of, for instance, ICAO:
8.   The Cook Islands is a member of ICAO; is it likely that other non-independent entities could obtain similar status with ICAO?

In the letter attached to the questionnaire, I also asked for a definition of the term sovereign state, if that was a criterion for membership, gaining empirical insight into the working understanding of sovereignty. It proved valuable, as some of the organizations see the Cook Islands as a sovereign state, even if it has not proclaimed international legal sovereignty.

The Information Received

From the answers and other available information it becomes apparent that:
–   23 of the 36 organizations are open for interaction with non-sovereign polities.
–   Only four directly oppose this: the WEU, NATO, EU and IPU.
–   Seventeen actively interact with non-sovereign polities.

The UN, which allows observers, I have placed as neither for nor against, as it depends on the political will in the organization. In the UN, a state needs to sponsor a polity which expresses the wish to become an observer.[4] Membership depends on the political will among the members, as the Ukraine, Belarus, India, Philippines and Syria were founding members of the UN without being internationally recognized as legally sovereign. Something similar happened with the admission of former colonies and not least the sudden acceptance of first the European mainland microstates and then other microstates around the world.

The World Customs Organisation is an example of what I have labelled *functional membership*. For membership, the organization requires that the polity has the responsibility for the customs area and is thus a separate customs entity. The label *functional membership* is because the organization, in this case the WCO, does not focus on the international legal status or sovereignty; what is decisive for the WCO is if a specific polity has the responsi-

---

4   Answer from UN, 8.01.03.

bility over the area in which the organization operates. This may not be a *revolutionary* legal change as the memberships are in concordance with the metropolitan state and are most often associated memberships, but the innovation is that the non-sovereigns now work directly with the organization and thus take part in the expertise and standardization which occur there. This they do on their own and not through the metropolitan state, and this thus emphasizes their status as parties and subjects.[5]

A crucial limit has been broken, though, as the Cook Islands enjoy full membership, even if this polity has not yet proclaimed international legal sovereignty. Even if most of its foreign relations are vested in New Zealand, but through the Free Association Agreement, delegated from the Cook Islands to New Zealand, the Cook Islands are free to take their own decisions and hold different views.

Interpol also has non-sovereigns as sub-members, also for functional or practical reasons. For instance, in the case of the UK and Gibraltar, it would slow the process very much if direct contact could not be made with Gibraltar and everything had to go through the UK. Aruba has full membership in Interpol; as it has its own judiciary and executive authorities, Aruba could become a full member.[6]

Concerning Faroese associated membership of the International Maritime Organisation the logic is the following. The Faroese wanted an associated membership so that their authorities could take part in the international cooperation in this area, which is a Faroese area of responsibility. The Danish Government accepted, as The Faroes were lagging behind, not having ratified all the treaties to which Denmark was a party. Thus, we see a prime example of functional membership caused by functional sovereignty, the step in the stairway towards a global community, as it is no longer possible to distinguish categorically between domestic and international affairs.[7]

Functional Membership and Functional Sovereignty

A majority of the international organizations are open for non-sovereign polities that have autonomy (responsibility) in the specific area of responsibility of the organizations' concern. This is the case in e.g. Interpol, INTOSAI, OECD, ILO, FAO, WHO, ICAO, IMO, IWC, WMO, WTO, WtoO and WCO.

These organizations would either allow full or associate membership, but at the same time, they require acceptance from the metropolitan state. It might be jumping to conclusions to say that this verifies an international right for non-sovereign polities to become parties, but it is a model of frequent use and does exist in the global community today. It emphasizes that Greenland and The Faroes should not only be discussed inside the Danish constitutional context, as the international or global community is open to flexible practical solutions, as this research shows. It also emphasizes that non-sovereigns can gain a

---

5   Answer from WCO, 21.11.02.

6   Answer from Interpol, 24.9.02.

7   Schermers and Blokker 1995 §77.

position as some sort of a subject in the international environment, mostly for practical or functional reasons. Even if it seems to be possible for non-sovereigns to be a party to several international organizations, the non-sovereigns might not want too many memberships, as it is very expensive.

Thus, the research indicates that non-sovereign polities have access to international organizations, depending on three factors:

— Practice by the international organizations when contacted by non-sovereign polities.
— If the polity has responsibility (autonomy) over the policy area in question.
— If there is an acceptance from the metropolitan state.

With these criteria, the non-sovereign polities can obtain some kind of membership. Thus, the research shows a trend towards functional membership and, by implication, functional sovereignty, as the admission of The Faroes as an associate member of the International Maritime Organisation so clearly demonstrates.

Answers from Non-Sovereign Polities and Metropolitan States

I have narrowed this part of the research down to island non-sovereign polities attached to Western state structures, as the constitutional systems as well as the geographical circumstances are more open to comparison with the Danish Realm. I have examined 37 non-sovereign islands polities, associated to nine states.

In the process of identifying the international profile of non-sovereign polities I found it important to receive information from both the metropolitan state and the non-sovereign polity, as the status is not always seen in a similar way from both sides.

Questions Sent to Metropolitan States - In This Case, The United Kingdom

1. The constitutional status of the British entities.
2. International profile of the British entities, that means membership/observer status of or direct relations with international organizations and/or other states/entities.
3. The British entities' participation in British delegations in international organizations.
4. The status of the British entities in relation to the EU.
5. How the British entities are governed.
6. If they receive financial grants from the UK.
7. Whether international treaties/memberships of the UK are automatically valid for the non-sovereign British entities.

1.   The constitutional status of the Falkland Islands.
2.   International profile of The Falklands, that means membership/observer status at, or
     direct relations with, international organizations and or other states/entities.
3.   The Falkland's participation in British delegations in international organizations.
4.   The status of The Falklands in relation to the EU.
5.   How The Falklands is governed.
6.   If the Falklands Islands receives financial grants from the UK.

The United States of America[8]

Dependent areas: American Samoa, Guam, Northern Mariana Islands, Puerto Rico and
the US Virgin Islands. Also, Baker Island, Howland Island, Jarvis Island, Johnston Atoll,
Kingman Reef, Midway Islands, Navassa Island, Palmyra Atoll and the Wake Island.[9]

The United States of America is a federation, which, moreover, has several, island
entities attached to the state structure. All of them that are populated have their own constitution. The entities vary from commonwealths, such as Puerto Rico and the Northern
Mariana Islands, to non-self-governing islands, which are not incorporated under the
Federal Constitution, and to the Free Association with Micronesia, Marshal Islands, and
Palau that have chosen to be internationally legally sovereign. The federal states have their
own constitutions, so that the overseas polities have to have their own constitutions. The
polities are not included in the US's membership of NAFTA.[10]

The Northern Mariana Islands and Puerto Rico[11] have a commonwealth arrangement
with the US, while American Samoa, Guam and the US Virgin Islands are unincorporated
insular territories. The polities are not members of NAFTA as they are a separate customs area. They are permitted international membership in e.g. SPC, IOC, OECS and the
Caribbean Community and Common Market.[12]

The Netherlands

The Kingdom of the Netherlands consists of The Netherlands, Aruba and The Netherlands
Antilles. The three polities each have their own constitutions, and an overlaying Charter
constitutes the co-operation between The Netherlands and Aruba and The Netherlands

---

8   Only island polities with a permanent population are included. This means that entities
     only populated by military or meteorological personnel or the like are excluded.
9   http://www.doi.gov/oia/facts2000.html#fdi.
10   Answer from the Office of Insular Affairs, USA, 18.10 2002.
11   The USA states officially that Puerto Rico is in a commonwealth relation with the USA,
     but it looks very much like a Free Association. The Spanish name is *Estado Libre Asociado de*
     Puerto Rico.
12   Answer from the Office of Insular Affairs, USA, 18.10.2002.

Antilles. Both The Netherlands Antilles and Aruba are OCT areas in relation to the EU, and are thus not included in the Dutch membership.[13]

The Netherlands is comparable to the Danish Realm as it is a kingdom, has comparable constitutions and consists of a metropolitan state on the European continent and has two overseas countries in the realm.

Aruba and The Netherlands Antilles may have full membership in international organizations, but have to keep the Foreign Ministry of The Netherlands informed of the ongoing activities. They have memberships in e.g. UPU, ECLAC and the Association of Caribbean States.[14] Aruba is a full member of Interpol.

France

Territorial collectivity: Corsica. Overseas departments: French Guyana, Guadeloupe, Martinique, and Reunion. Overseas territorial collectivities: Mayotte, Saint Pierre and Miquelon. Dependent areas: French Polynesia, New Caledonia, Tromelin Island, Wallis and Futuna. There are further uninhabited dependent areas.[15]

France is by its own definition a unitary state, and the overseas territories are seen as an integrated part of France. France did not agree to have the overseas entities placed on the UN list of colonies and has so far succeeded in this. Only New Caledonia is on the UN decolonization list and has only been included on the list since 1986. Articles 72 to 75 in the French Constitution create the possibility of different relationships with the overseas polities. France might be characterized as the most centralized state in this research, even bearing in mind that the Constitution gives room for autonomy. As seen on the list, the French territories are put into four different categories, but all are seen as an integrated part of France. None of the polities has its own constitution or statute. The polities' relationship to the EU is in two groups: Mayotte, New Caledonia, French Polynesia, St. Pierre et Miquelon and French Southern and Antarctic Lands are OCT and are thus not included in France's EU membership, while the remaining French territories are DOM (dominions)[16] and are seen as an integrated (integral) part of the EU territory. Corsica is an exception though: it is not a DOM, but is included in the French memberships.

New Zealand

Free Association: Cook, Niue, Tokelau. The Cook Islands and Niue are in free association with New Zealand, and have as polities under the UN the right to external self-determi-

---

13　Answer from the Dutch Ministry of Foreign Affairs, 25.10.2002.

14　Answer from the Dutch Ministry of Foreign Affairs, received September 2002.

15　http://www.cia.gov/cia/publications/factbook/geos/fr.html or http://www.outremer.gouv.fr/outremer/front.

16　DOM for Dominions of France, Document of Overseas Countries and Territories, see note 14 above.

nation. Both polities have chosen so far not to claim international legal sovereignty, but have this vested in New Zealand. Both the Cook Islands and Niue have full membership in several international organizations. Some organizations under the UN even consider these entities as subjects under international law and they have the right to declare independence unilaterally. The Cook Islands has its own Constitution, while Niue has a Constitutional Act. Tokelau is in the process of establishing a free association relation with New Zealand and is in this context drafting a constitution.[17]

Spain

Autonomous island territories: Balearic Islands and Canary Islands. Every region is autonomous, but as the Spanish federalisation is built on an asymmetric system, where every autonomous part itself negotiates with the central government, not all Spanish states or autonomies have a similar status. Spain also holds sovereignty over enclaves on the coast of Morocco. The Canary Islands are not part of the EU customs union. All Spanish autonomic regions have statutes in relation to the area of responsibility they have.[18] The autonomy of both the Canaries and Balearic Islands is a part of the Spanish decentralization process.[19] With the exception of the customs part of the Canaries, the Spanish isles are part of the Spanish EU membership. Foreign affairs are under Spanish responsibility.

Portugal

Autonomous Regions: Azores, Madeira. Both the Azores and Madeira are far away from Portugal, but are inhabited by Portuguese immigrants. Both polities have statutes for autonomy and constitutions concerning their own areas of responsibility, authorized in the Portuguese Constitution.[20] Madeira and the Azores are included in Portugal's EU membership and are the only autonomous units in the Portuguese structure. Foreign affairs are under Portuguese responsibility.

Finland

The self-governing Aaland Islands refer to a Statute of Self-Governing, which in turn rests on the Guaranty Law of 1920, confirmed by the League Council Resolution of 1920 that both Sweden and Finland accepted. The Finnish Autonomy Act was approved in 1951 by both the Finnish and Aalandic Parliament, and the law can only be amended with mutual

---

17   Answer, 21.1.2003, Cook Islands; 5.2.2003, New Zealand.

18   http://www.la-moncloa.es/.

19   Olausson, 2002:11.

20   Portuguese Constitution §225-234 http://www.parlamento.pt/const_leg/crp_port/index.html.

consent of both the Parliament in Aaland and the Government of Finland.[21] The Aaland Islands do not have a constitution, but the Autonomy Act can only be changed in agreement between Aaland and Finland. Aaland is, with some exceptions, a member of the EU.[22] Aaland is, through Finland, a member of the Nordic Council. For other foreign relations, Finland has the responsibility, but has to inform, and treaties touching areas of Aalandic autonomy have to be accepted by the Aaland Government before they are valid there.[23] Finland has an obligation to inform Aaland of ongoing treaty negotiations.

Denmark

Denmark is not formally a unitary state, and both The Faroes and Greenland have a wide measure of autonomy through their Home Rule Acts. The Faroe Islands have their own Constitutional Act, whereas Greenland tends to regard the Home Rule Act as its constituting document. Both are however, formally covered by the Danish Constitution. Neither Greenland nor The Faroes are included in the Danish EU membership, and Greenland is an OCT area in relation to the EU.

The United Kingdom of Great Britain and Northern Ireland

Anguilla, Bermuda, Cayman Islands, Gibraltar, Jersey, Guernsey, Isle of Man, Montserrat, Pitcairn Islands, Saint Helena, Turks & Caicos Islands, British Virgin Islands, Falkland Islands, Wales, Northern Ireland, Scotland. The Hebrides, Shetland and Orkney are integrated parts of Scotland.

The United Kingdom consists of England, Scotland, Wales and Northern Ireland, where the sovereignty is vested in the Parliament in London. The devolution process has established home rule in Wales, Scotland and Northern Ireland, and these polities elect members for the British Parliament in London.

The overseas territories are former colonies, and ten of them are on the UN list of non-self-governing territories. That means that they are subjects under international law and have the right to external self-determination. One interesting difference is that most of the polities have their own constitution. The Channel Islands, Guernsey, Jersey and The Isle Man in the Irish Sea, are not integrated into the UK and are not members of the EU. They are not represented in the British Parliament, but several of them enjoy international membership.

---

21   Hannum: 1990:371.

22   Answer from the Finnish Ministry of Justice, 7.2.2003, http://www.lagtinget.aland.fi/.

23   Answer from the Finnish Ministry of Justice, 7.2.2003.

The Process

By looking more deeply into the sovereign statehood's relation to the non-sovereign entities under its umbrella, I have revealed different ways of how the situation is handled in different countries and the different status that the entities are given.

This puts the Faroese – Greenlandic - Danish construction into an international and comparative context. Of course, in this chapter, it is neither possible nor desirable to try to make a complete comparison of municipal laws between the different states, but the work shows differences in constructions of the non-sovereign entities and gives an insight into how similar situations are handled elsewhere.

Non-Sovereign Polities' Answers: An Overview

The Cayman Islands is an overseas territory of the UK and an OCT in relation to the EU. It has its own Constitution and is self-governing. The UK represents the Cayman Islands internationally, but it has membership of CARICOM and participates in regional UN meetings, and can participate in the UK delegations. The Islands do not receive any financial grants.[24]

The Falkland Islands is an overseas territory of the UK and an OCT in relation to the EU. It has had a constitution from 1997 and has its own currency. The Falkland Islands is economically and also in general independent, with the exception of defence that is taken care of by the UK. The highest executive power is vested in the Queen, through the appointed Governor.[25]

Jersey is a crown dependency of the UK and is responsible for its own domestic affairs, while defence and international affairs are under UK responsibility, but handled in consent between the parties. Jersey has no separate international memberships, but takes part in UK delegations and speaks on its own. Jersey does not fall under UK legislation and has its own Parliament. It is not part of the EU and does not receive any grants from either the UK or the EU.[26]

St. Helena is an overseas territory of the UK. The overseas territories of the UK are what before were called Dependent Territories in the British Empire, and that have not chosen independence. St. Helena has had a constitution from 1988 and foreign relations are mainly under British care, and the UK may become a party to treaties on behalf of St. Helena. St. Helena receives grants from the UK.[27]

---

24   Answer 31.12.2002 from the Cayman Islands Government.
25   Answer 28.01.03 from the Falkland Islands Government.
26   Answer 15.01.03 from Jersey's International Relations and Policy Officer.
27   Answer received 21.2.03 from the FCO on behalf of the Chief Secretary.

Turks & Caicos Islands is an overseas territory of the UK and an OCT in relation to the EU. It has had its own Constitution from 1976 (1988). It is a member of CARICOM (CDB, the Caribbean Development Bank, and Interpol, according to the CIA), but generally, foreign relations are taken care of by the UK. Turks & Caicos Island does not participate in any UK delegation to international organizations. There is no direct financial grant from the UK to the islands.[28]

Of the French overseas territories I received answers from Saint Pierre et Miquelon and New Caledonia.
New Caledonia falls under the French Constitution and is represented in the French Parliament. The polity has trade and cultural exchange with other Pacific countries. It has its own currency which is fixed to the Euro. France takes care of all international relations. New Caledonia receives grants from France.[29] (According to the CIA country profile, New Caledonia has membership in ESCAP (associate), FZ, ICFTU, SPC, WFTU and WMO).

The Cook Islands is in a free association relationship with New Zealand. It has it own constitution. New Zealand has no legal power with respect to The Cook Islands. It has full membership in several international organizations and is treated as a state in the concerns of the treaty by the UN. It participates on its own in international conferences, not as part of the New Zealand delegations, and has diplomatic relations with several states. Cook Islanders are New Zealand citizens by birth, with full rights in New Zealand, while New Zealanders need a visa and working permit in the Cook Islands. New Zealand, among others, gives grants to the islands.[30]

The Autonomous Entities in Practice

The USA has many different models, and as most of the areas are unincorporated they assumingly have the right to claim independence, have own constitutions and can have international memberships. Some of the bigger overseas territories also have a different direct parliamentary access to the US Congress, as they can elect one member who has a congressional member's rights and privileges, except the right to vote on the floor.

The Netherlands is different as its two non-sovereign polities have their own constitutions and the realm is combined by a charter between the three parties. Aruba and The Netherlands Antilles have the right of self-determination and are members of international organizations.

---

28   Answer 17.01.03 from the Turks & Caicos Islands representative in the UK.
29   Answer 20.01.03 from the New Caledonian Government.
30   Answer 21.01.03 from the Ministry of Foreign Affairs of the Cook Islands.

France has an opening in the Constitution for changes of the overseas entities' status, but is very centralized on this matter.

The United Kingdom is very asymmetric with 10 overseas entities which are on the UN decolonization list, one small overseas and three unincorporated entities in the English Channel and the Irish Sea. Most of the overseas entities have their own written constitutions, despite the fact that the UK does not have one itself. They are not included in the British EU membership either. The UK is an interesting case for this work, as the overseas aspect can be seen in the dependent territories; the ancient distinct status is reflected in Jersey, Guernsey and the Isle of Man; and the incorporated constitutional status exists in the case of Wales, Scotland and Northern Ireland.

New Zealand is very liberal; the Cook Islands and Niue have their own Constitutions and can have international memberships on their own. Tokelau is in the process of acquiring the same status.

Under **Spain**, the Canaries are not part of the EU customs union; the Canaries and Balearic Islands have autonomy like the other autonomous regions in Spain.

Under **Portugal,** the Azores and Madeira have autonomy, but do not act internationally.

Thus, we can observe a great diversity of different constellations. The possibilities of having own constitutions, limited parliamentary access, a charter to connect distinct constitutions in commonwealth and the Channel Isles' and Isle of Man's ancient status show great differences in constructions and constitutional bindings. Many non-sovereign polities are also allowed to participate in international organizations.

We can see ancient status giving the right as a subject, as in the case of Guernsey, Jersey and The Isle of Man.

The most liberal metropolitan state is by far New Zealand, which seems determined to progress the Cook Islands, Niue and Tokelau, without hesitating because of territorial greed.

All in all, the information shows, that non-sovereign island polities should not be discussed inside the metropolitan context only. Globalization has made many non-sovereign island polities into some kind of a subject which operates in the global community. In areas within their competences they can operate internationally where this gives practical or functional benefits.

There are two crucial points. First of all, New Zealand shines as an example of a very progressive metropolitan state giving room to the non-sovereign polities, finding very liberal solutions. Holland, that can be compared with Denmark in size and with two overseas polities, is also liberal and allows international memberships, while it has to be said that Denmark is fairly similar to France as a regressive type of metropolitan state. This leads us to the second point: that the non-sovereign polities should not only be discussed in an internal constitutional context; the international community has opened its doors for them.

The EU and the Island Polities

A deeper look into the colonies of the EU Member States and the island polities in Europe shows that traditionally these entities decide by themselves whether or not they join when their metropolitan state does.[31]

The island polities or island regions with EU affiliation are: Aaland, Azores, Balearic, Canary, Faroe, Greenland (is also an OCT), Guernsey, Isle of Man, Jersey, Madeira, Sardinia, Sicily and Svalbard, and to some extent Helgoland. All but Svalbard and Helgoland have special legislation.[32] I would also consider Gibraltar as a separate polity in this context, but technically it is not an island. In the cases of the Balearic and Canary Islands, the autonomy originates from the regionalization of Spain; and for Sardinia and Sicily, they where given the status through the regionalization of Italy and these entities do not enjoy fully developed autonomy.[33] Only the Balearic Islands were not given the right to decide whether or not to join the EU with the metropolitan state. The rest of the island polities where given the choice.

Of the remaining islands, the Aaland, Azores, Madeira and the Canaries have chosen to join the EU with their metropolitan state, although their accessions are with exceptions. The Balearic Islands are not part of the customs union and Helgoland is not part of the taxation union.[34] Helgoland is a special case, as the entity has no special status in Germany, neither to the federal state Schleswig-Holstein nor to the German state, only to the EU.

Greenland, the Faroe Islands, Guernsey, Jersey and the Isle of Man remain outside the EU, but a special status is given by the EU to these distinct islands polities, based on the objective criterion: being an island.

The OCTs and DOMs[35]

In addition to the island regions, the EU has distinct groupings of former colonies belonging to member countries and being outside the European continent.[36]

---

31   Olausson, 12:2002.

32   Olausson,:7:2002.

33   Olausson,:7:2002.

34   Olausson,:6:2002.

35   See http://europa.eu.int/scadplus/leg/en/lvb/r12300.htm.

36   Understood as outside the European part of the world.

The Overseas Countries and Territories (OCTs)

Greenland; New Caledonia; French Polynesia; French Southern and Antarctic Territories; Wallis and Futuna Islands; Mayotte; St. Pierre et Miquelon; Aruba; Netherlands Antilles; Anguilla; Cayman Islands; Falklands Islands; South Georgia & Sandwich Islands; Montserrat; Pitcairn; St. Helena, Ascension, Tristan da Cunha; British Antarctic Territory; British Indian Ocean Territory; Turks and Caicos Islands; British Virgin Islands.

The French overseas departments Guadeloupe, Martinique, French Guyana, Reunion, New Caledonia and Trommelin Islands (plus the uninhabited ones) are considered as *DOMs* and are part of the EU territory.

Islands Inside the European Continent

These are the islands inside the European continental border, that all except one have enjoyed self-determination on whether to join the EU with their metropolitan state or not. These are divided into the ones that joined and the ones that chose to stay outside. Members of the EU are: Aaland, Azores, Madeira, Baleares and the Canaries. Not members of the EU are: Greenland (is an OCT), Faroes Islands, Guernsey, Jersey and Isle of Man.

Islands Outside the European Continent

These are former colonies of European Member States which are outside the European continent. The OCTs are not members of, but have mainly an association arrangement with, the EU, while some of the French, the DOMs, are members of the EU.

The OCTs have formed an association with the EU, the aim is development of the OCT entities. Thus, the EU case is an example of advanced recursive self-determination, as the sub- polities of states joining this supranational organization and confederation are given the choice to enter or not. What might be odd is that in several cases these polities, according to the metropolitan state, do not enjoy the right to self-determination.

Denmark can hand over sovereignty – or powers – to the EU, but only for territorial Denmark, as the membership does not include Greenland and The Faroes. This means that the constitutional unity is broken, by Danish acts, and, therefore, it makes no logical sense to claim that the Constitution makes it impossible to let The Faroes and Greenland act by themselves internationally. By dividing its core areas of sovereignty, Denmark has effectively shattered its constitutional unity.

In conclusion, within the EU context, the island polities have gained some kind of distinct status and even self-determination, as they have been allowed to decide whether to join the EU together with their metropolitan state.

Denmark, Greenland and the Faroe Islands Compared to Others

The empirical research into the access of non-sovereign island polities to international organizations and the relations between these polities and Western metropolitan states makes it possible to compare Denmark, Greenland and The Faroes to other polities and metropolitan states.

In general, international organizations are open to non-sovereign polities, as they may have interactions with many of the organizations, if they have autonomy on the specific area of responsibility the organization operates inside; if the metropolitan state accepts this; and if there is a political will in the specific organization.

The Western metropolitan states have different models and can be divided into three groups:

— The liberals:[37] New Zealand, USA, UK and Netherlands, where the non-sovereigns are unincorporated into the metropolitan state structure.
— The socialist-conservatives: France, Denmark and Finland, with the non-sovereigns as incorporated into the state structure.
— The new democracies: Spain and Portugal, with the non-sovereigns as incorporated into the state structure.

Group 1

In particular New Zealand is very liberal in its relations to the Cook Islands and also Niue that have independent international memberships, own constitutions and are not incorporated under the New Zealand Constitution, as well as having the unilateral right to self-determination.

The USA has an arrangement whereby the non-sovereign polities are not integrated into the USA or fall under the Constitution of the USA. The non-sovereign polities have their own constitutions, some international memberships, but are not part of USA membership of NAFTA.

The territories under the UK are not incorporated into the unwritten British Constitution and the territories do have their own constitutions. The polities can partly act internationally and the former colonies have the right to self-determination.

In the Dutch realm, Aruba and The Netherlands Antilles have their own constitutions, which are bound by an overlaying charter. The polities can, with certain limitations, act internationally, if The Netherlands is kept informed.

It can be said that most of the polities are or have been covered by UN decolonization, with the exception of Puerto Rico, Jersey, Guernsey and The Isle of Man, while there is doubt about the status of The Falkland Islands.

---

37 Liberals in this context refers to the fact that the metropolitan states see the overseas polities as individual and/or separate entities, while socialist refers to an organic approach, where the overseas polities are seen as an integral part of the state structure.

Group 2

Of the French overseas polities, is it only New Caledonia that is or has been on the UN decolonization list. Greenland has been on the list of non-self-governing territories, but was later integrated into Denmark.

France sees the French entities as an integrated part of France, although some of them have OCT relations to the EU. The Aaland Islands is built on an agreement between Finland and Aaland, requiring that all changes have to be bilateral with the consent of both parts.

Neither the Faroe Islands nor Greenland are members of the EU, but are officially seen as integrated parts of Denmark, by the Danish Government. None of the non-sovereign polities in this group has its own constitution, but all are incorporated into the constitution of the metropolitan state. Greenland is an OCT country to the EU.

Group 3

The Azores and Madeira have an autonomous status in the Portuguese state structure, with their own constitutions, which are specified in the Portuguese Constitution, but they do not act internationally. The Azores and Madeira are the only entities with autonomy in the Portuguese structure. The Balearic Islands and the Canaries have autonomy like the other Spanish regions have and have their own statutes of autonomy and are under the Spanish Constitution. The Canaries and the Balearic Islands do not act internationally.

Most of the polities in Group 1 are or have been linked to the decolonization process under the UN.

With the exception of Greenland and New Caledonia, none of the polities in Groups 2 and 3 have been under the UN decolonization structure, though it has to be mentioned that the position of The Aaland Islands to Finland is based on a decision made in the League of Nations on the Aaland Islands' right to self-determination. Thus, the Aaland Islands have been treated in the international system.

In Group 1 the non-sovereign island polities are not seen as an integrated part of the metropolitan state, as the non-sovereign island polities are seen in Groups 2 and 3, thus the metropolitan states in Groups 2 and 3 are more regressive in this field. One would presume that the non-sovereign island polities under Group 1 have more room to shape the arrangement with the metropolitan state, as they are not constrained by constitutional bindings like the polities in Groups 2 and 3.

By putting the Danish Realm and The Faroes and Greenland into an international context it seems like Denmark belongs to the more regressive group of Western metropolitan states with non-sovereign islands polities in their state structure, in line with France. As a consequence, The Faroes and Greenland do not have the same room as the non-sovereign polities in Group 1 have.

The Faroes and Greenland are not the most progressive non-sovereign polities and this might be because of the constitutional limits of the Danish perception of the constitutional status. They are not permitted to follow the international development, where non-sovereigns are allowed to participate in the international community, if they have responsibility over a specific area and the power to ratify and implement treaties in fields of responsibility where the polity has autonomy.

Recent Cases: Entering the International Maritime Organisation – Exiting the Nordic Council

In November 2003, the Faroese Executive, on behalf of a unanimous Parliament, applied for full membership of the Nordic Council. Till then, The Faroes, Greenland and Åland had formed part of the Danish and Finnish delegations.

The Danish Prime Minister, Fogh Rasmussen, said that a full membership of the Nordic Council for The Faroes and Greenland would be against the Danish Constitution, without explaining why and which clauses would be violated.[38]

Based on the previous conclusions, it is very hard to uphold the legal argument that a full Faroese and/or Greenlandic membership would be against the Danish Constitution, especially bearing in mind that the assumption of the Danish Realm as a unitary state is not valid, as Denmark is a member of the EU while The Faroes and Greenland are not. With the EU being a supranational institution in several areas, the EU division of the Danish Realm breaks the unitary state structure. Taking into account that no direct paragraph in the Danish Constitution prohibits full membership for The Faroes and Greenland, and stressing that the Danish Realm is not a unitary state, leads to the conclusion that there is no Danish constitutional obstacle for full Faroese and Greenlandic membership of the Nordic Council and the Nordic Council of Ministers.

It is also hard to see any logical constitutional frame, when The Faroes were not only permitted to, but even encouraged to apply for associated membership of the IMO.

Is the Nordic Council Open For the Autonomous Polities?

This might require an update or change in the Helsinki Agreement, but that has been done several times before. And, as the empirical investigation of this chapter concludes, in the end it is the political will, in both the organization and the metropolitan state, that determines the outcome. In this case, Denmark has chosen to say that it is not possible according to the Danish Constitution. And as all the members have to agree on changes, leaving Denmark with the right to veto, the Nordic Council is not open for non-sovereign polities as full members. But the outcome is determined by the political climate in Denmark and the organization, not by juridical obstacles.

As Denmark went against the proposal and there has to be a unanimous decision of the members, there was no real discussion on the outcome, but the understanding was, that the step would have been possible if Denmark had been in favor. So this is a prime example of political will for non-sovereigns access, here the non-sovereign has the neces-

---

38   http://www.statsministeriet.dk/Index/dokumenter.asp?o=2&n=o&h=2&d=1705&s=1.

sary autonomy, apparently has the political will in the organization, but not the acceptance of the metropolitan state, thus failing to achieve the desired access.

The International Maritime Organisation

The Faroese membership of the IMO shows that with political will a great deal is possible. Of course, The Faroes are limited, as it is an associated membership and not a full one, but it is on its own now, not through Denmark, and membership has created a direct contact between the IMO and The Faroes.

In the IMO case, Faroese membership was seen as practical, as it is a very important policy area for The Faroes, and because of the fact that Denmark cannot ratify treaties internally on the Faroese jurisdiction on policy areas under Faroese power.

These recent cases of the international profile of The Faroes can be said to fit the pattern of political will. In the case of the IMO, there was political will in both the organization and the metropolitan state; in addition, The Faroes had the responsibility of the policy area.

In the case of the Nordic Council, the metropolitan state did not have the political will and thus blocked the possibility of The Faroes becoming a full member of the Nordic Council. This is despite the fact that the Danish Prime Minister in his opening speech said that The Faroes and Greenland would be given more room to manoeuvre in foreign affairs.

Conclusion

In the first part of this chapter, I tried to describe the international profile of Greenland and the Faroe Islands, finding that they operate according to a number of different models and *de facto* subject status.

In the second part, I carried out empirical research on the relations between non-sovereign polities and the access to the international community. I found that they have access, but that the access depends on the will of the metropolitan state and the political will in the organization, although many of them have opened up for some kind of membership, if the polity has the responsibility of that area.

In the third part, I looked into the constellation of other Western states with overseas non-sovereign polities in their state structure. There is a clear tendency to give international room to the non-sovereign polities. In the fifth part, we saw that Denmark is among the more regressive states in this area.

In the fourth part, I looked at the island polities attached to European countries and their relations to the EU. Surprisingly, I found that most of them have voted on whether or not to join the EU, together with their metropolitan state. Therefore, they have been given the right to exercise self-determination on whether to join the EU or not, somewhat at odds with their respective metropolitan states claiming that the associates do not have the right to external self-determination.

Most of the international organizations are open for non-sovereign polities, as long as they have responsibility on a specific area and internally can ratify and implement the treaties of the organization. Moreover, the acceptance of the metropolitan state and the organizations' members are needed.

Finally, the Danish integration into the EU has, in my opinion, completely shattered the constitutional unity of the Danish Realm, leaving no constitutional excuse for increased autonomy to The Faroes and Greenland in foreign relations.

The news is that non-sovereigns can act on their own in the international or global community inside the areas in which they have autonomy, and even if it has to be with metropolitan state acceptance, in many cases, they do the interaction themselves, not through the metropolitan state, which in my opinion manifests a *de facto* status as a subject. The problem concerning the Danish Realm is that so far everything has to be done with the acceptance of the current Danish political will, maintaining a system of great power asymmetry and the danger of populism. A look into other metropolitan states and non-sovereign polities has revealed that it is possible to have systems that are more flexible and in line with the current international or global community, and thus room for functional memberships and functional sovereignty.

Annex I

Non-Sovereign Polities – An Overview

	Constitution	Int. profile	Metro delegation	EU/NAFTA member	Grants
Anguilla	Y(1982)	Y[1]		OCT	
Bermuda	Y(1968)	Y[2]		OCT	
Jersey	Unwritten	No	Yes	OCT	No
Guernsey	Unwritten	No		N	
Isle of Man	Unwritten	OECD/WTO		N	
Cayman	Y (1958)	Y[3]		N	
Falkland	Y (1997)	N[4]	Y[5]/UK	OCT	Defence
Gibraltar	Y (1969)	Y[6]		OCT	
Montserrat	Y(1969)	Y[7]		OCT	
Pitcairn	Y (1964)	Y[8]		OCT	
St.Helena	Y (1988)	UK	No	OCT	N
Turks & Caicos	Y (1988)	Caricom/ UK[9]	No	OCT	Y
Br.Virgin	Y (1977)	Y[10]		OCT	
Fr.Guyana	French	Y[11]			
Guadaloupe	French	[12]			
Reunion	French	[13]			
Mayotte	French	[14]			
S. Pierre et Miquelon	French	[15]			
French Polynesia	French	Y[16]			
New Caledonia	French	[17]			
Madeira	Y			Member	
Azores	Y[18]			Member	
Aruba	Y (1986)	[19]		OCT	
D.Antilles	Y(1954)	[20]		OCT	
Canaries	Spanish			Member	
Baleares	Spanish[21]			Member	
Åland		[22]		Member	
Cook	Y (1965)	[23]			
Niue	Y (1974)	[24]			
Tokelau	No	[25]			
A. Samoa	Y (1966)	[26]		N	
Guam	Organic act (1950)	[27]		N	
N. Mariana	Y (1978)	[28]		N	
Puerto Rico	Y (1952)	[29]		N	
US Virgin	Organic act (1954)	[30]		N	
Greenland	Danish	[31]		OCT	
Faroes	Danish	[32]		N	
Scotland				Member	
Northern Ireland				Member	
Wales				Member	
Hong Kong		[33]			
Macao		[34]			
Taiwan		[35]			

The references are mainly from the CIA's Country profile.

1   CARICOM (associate), CDB, Interpol (sub-bureau), OECS (associate), ECLAC (associate).
2   CARICOM (observer), CCC, ICFTU, Interpol (sub-bureau), IOC.
3   CARICOM (observer), CDB, Interpol (sub-bureau), IOC, UNESCO (associate).
4   Falkland is only a member in United Kingdom Overseas Territories, and OCT.
5   UN Committee on Decolonization and Commonwealths Parliamentary Association.
6   Interpol (sub-bureau).
7   CARICOM, CDB, ECLAC (associate), ICFTU, Interpol (sub-bureau), OECS, WCL.
8   SPC.
9   CARICOM (associate), CDB, Interpol (sub-bureau).
10   CARICOM (associate), CDB, ECLAC (associate), Interpol (sub-bureau), IOC, OECS (associate), UNESCO (associate).
11   FZ, WCL, WFTU.
12   FZ, WCL, WFTU.
13   FZ, InOC, WFTU.
14   FZ.
15   FZ, WFTU.
16   ESCAP (associate), FZ, ICFTU, SPC, WMO.
17   ESCAP (associate), FZ, ICFTU, SPC, WFTU, WMO.
18   Both Azores and Madeira have own constitutions on own affairs, and are also under the Portuguese Constitution.
19   CARICOM (observer), ECLAC (associate), Interpol, IOC, UNESCO (associate), WCL, WToO (associate).
20   CARICOM (observer), CCC, ECLAC (associate), Interpol, IOC, UNESCO (associate), UPU, WCL, WMO, WToO (associate).
21   Both the Baleares and the Canaries have statutes, as the other Spanish autonomous regions, on own affairs.
22   Nordic Council.
23   ACP, AsDB, ESCAP (associate), FAO, ICAO, ICFTU, IFAD, IFRCS (associate), IOC, OPCW, Sparteca, SPC, SPF, UNESCO, WHO, WMO.
24   ACP, ESCAP (associate), FAO, Sparteca, SPC, SPF, UNESCO, WHO, WMO.
25   SPC, UNESCO (associate), WHO (associate).
26   ESCAP (associate), Interpol (sub-bureau), IOC, SPC.
27   ESCAP (associate), Interpol (sub-bureau), IOC, SPC.
28   ESCAP (associate), Interpol (sub-bureau), SPC.
29   CARICOM (observer), ECLAC (associate), FAO (associate), ICFTU, Interpol (sub-bureau), IOC, WCL, WFTU, WHO (associate).
30   ECLAC (associate), Interpol (sub-bureau), IOC.
31   NC, NIB.
32   NC, NIB.
33   APEC, AsDB, BIS, CCC, ESCAP (associate), ICC, ICFTU, IHO, IMO (associate), Interpol (sub-bureau), IOC, ISO (correspondent), WCL, WMO, WToO (associate), WTO.
34   CCC, ESCAP (associate), IHO, IMO (associate), Interpol (sub-bureau), ISO (correspondent), UNESCO (associate), WMO, WToO (associate), WTO.
35   APEC, AsDB, BCIE, ICC, ICFTU, IFRCS, IOC, WCL, WTO.

Annex 2

International Organizations Contacted in the Empirical Research

Date of answer

EPO http://www.european-patent-office.org	European Patent Office	2.9.2002
WEU http://www.weu.int	Western European Union	28.8.2002
CoE http://coe.int	Council of Europe	4.7.2002
OSCE http://www.osce.org	Organisation for Security and Co-operation in Europe	21.8.02
EFTA http://www.efta.int	European Free Trade Association	8.7.2002
EBRD http://www.ebrd.com	European Bank for Reconstruction and Development	4.9.2002
CEPT http://www.cept.org	Central Conference of Postal and Telecommunications Administrations	30.10.2002
ECMT http://www1.oecd.org/cem/	European Conference of Ministers of Transport	23.9.2002
OECD http://www.oecd.org/	Organisation for Economic Co-operation and Development	16.9.2002
NATO http://www.nato.int	North Atlantic Treaty Organisation	14.10.2002
NAM http://www.nam.gov.za/	Non Aligned Movement	28.8.2002
IPU http://www.ipu.org	Inter Parliamentary Union	22.82002
INTOSAI http://www.intosai.org	International Organization of Supreme Audit Institutions	22.8.2002
ICPO/Interpol http://www.interpol.int	Internationa Criminal Police Organisation	24.9.2002
OIE http:// www.oie.int	Office International de Épizooties	No answer
CABI http://www.cabi.org/		21.8.2002
ICSTI http://www.icsti.su/	International Center for Scientific and Technical Information.	21.8.2002
ILO http://www.ilo.org	International Labour Organisation	23.10.2002
FAO http://www.fao.org	Food and Agricultural Organization of UN	Information from homepage
UNESCO http://www.unesco.org	UN Educational, Scientific and Cultural Organization	Information from homepage
ICAO http:www.icao.org	International Civil Aviation Organization	22.10.2002
WHO http://www.who.int	World Health Organization	Information from homepage
IMO http://www.imo.org	International Maritime Organisation	16.9.2002
ITU http://www.itu.int	International Telecommnication Union	25.9.2002
WMO http://www.wmo.ch/index-en.html	World Meteorological Organization	Information from homepage
WIPO http://www.wipo.int	World Intellectual Property Organization	29.10.2002
UNIDO http://www.unido.org	UN Industrial Development Organization	26.9.2002

IAEA http://www.iaea.org	International Atomic Energy Agency	25.9.2002
WTO http:www.wto.org	World Trade Organization	25.9.2002
WToO http://www.world-tourism.org	World Tourism Organization	26.9.2002
CTBTO http://www.ctbto.org	Preparatory Commission for the Comprehensive Nuclear-Test-Ban Treaty Organization	14.10.2002
OPCW http:www.opcw.org	Organisation for the Prohibition of Chemical Weapons	25.10.2002
WCO http://www.wcoomd.org	World Customs Organisation	21.11.2002
IWC http:// www.iwcoffice.org	International Whaling Commission	25.10.2002
UN http://www.un.org	United Nations	8.1.2003
EU http://www.eu.int	European Union	10.2.2003

Other international organizations with which the non-sovereign polities in the research have interaction.

ICES	International Council for the Exploration of the Sea
CITES	Convention on International Trade in Endangered Species of Wild Flora and Fauna
NAFO	North West Atlantic Fisheries Organization
NEAFC	North East Atlantic Fisheries Organization
NAMMCO	North Atlantic Marine Mammal Commission
NASCO	North Atlantic Salmon Conservation Organization
CARICOM	Caribbean Community and Common Market
ECLAC	Economic Commission for Latin America and the Caribbean
IOC	International Olympic Committee
ICES	International Council for the Exploration of the Sea
WCL	World Confederation of Labor
CDB	Caribbean Development Bank
ACP Group	African, Caribbean, and Pacific Group of States
AsDB	Asian Development Bank
ESCAP	Economic and Social Commission for Asia and the Pacific
IFAD	International Fund for Agricultural Development
SPARTECA	South Pacific Regional Trade and Economic Cooperation Agreement
SPC	South Pacific Commission
SPF	South Pacific Forum
FZ	Franc Zone
WFTU	World Federation of Trade Unions
ICFTU	International Confederation of Free Trade Unions
APEC	Asia-Pacific Economic Cooperation
BIS	Bank for International Settlements
CCC	Customs Cooperation Council
ICC	International Chamber of Commerce
InOC	Indian Ocean Commission
IFRCS	International Federation of Red Cross and Red Crescent Societies
UPU	Universal Postal Union
OECS	Organization of Eastern Caribbean States
BCIE	Central American Bank for Economic Integration

10 – The Danish Realm and Developments in the EU

Bogi Eliasen

Denmark, like the rest of the EU countries, has been in a process of integrating its defence, currency, judiciary and citizenship into the EU.

Although the Danish people voted "No", there is a strong political will to transfer these four fields of responsibility to the EU, but this will only happen through a referendum. As it is, Denmark has these areas as derogations in its relations with the EU. Currently, the areas defined as Kingdom Affairs, and the core of sovereignty in the Danish Realm, are: defence, the Supreme Court, citizenship and foreign relations; that is to say, largely the same policy areas.

The Faroes and Greenland are not members of the EU. The Faroes never entered the EU and Greenland withdrew from it. This means that Danish obligations in the EU do not cover The Faroes and Greenland.

Greenland and The Faroes are not part of the Danish EU process. They do not participate in referenda on EU questions and they have their own separate bilateral agreements with the EU.

The last referendum on the single currency was not held in Greenland or The Faroes, because these entities are outside the EU, so technically it was not a referendum concerning The Faroes or Greenland. It would, however, be difficult to deny the obvious functional impact on The Faroes and Greenland had the Danish people voted in favor, which emphasizes the problems of definition in this area.

This situation is, on the other hand, a clear manifestation of Greenland and The Faroes as distinct entities or polities. A state, claiming to be unitary, is comprised of three distinct entities, of which one is a member of the EU, while the other two are not.

Under the present construction, if Denmark is to be fully integrated into the EU, The Faroes and Greenland will be ruled from an institution to which they have democratically decided not to belong.

Sjúrður Skaale (ed.), The Right To National Self-Determination, *205-208.*
© *2004 Koninklijke Brill NV. Printed in the Netherlands.*

No Status Quo

Maintaining the status quo is therefore not possible. Taking over the areas of responsibility that Denmark transfers to the EU would be one option. The second would be to join the EU with or under Denmark, which should be possible given the fact of Greenland's former status within the EU. The third option would be to declare independence and join the EU as a sovereign state (the example of Malta provides a precedent). The fourth would be to continue as though everything is the same and be ruled from Brussels, without being a member.

1. Remaining outside the EU and taking over the areas of responsibility that Denmark transfers to the EU will still have implications with respect to foreign policy, e.g. the DFG system.
2. Entering as a part of Denmark might provide one of the Danish seats in the EU parliament, such as Greenland had it during its membership.
3. Joining the EU as a sovereign state.
4. False status quo, becoming an asymmetric condominium of the Danish Realm and the EU.

Under the construction of the Danish Realm today, Greenland and The Faroes have the final decision in areas of responsibility that are in the hands of their Governments. Denmark's transfer of power in such areas to the EU has little significance domestically for Greenland and The Faroes. But it would be much more complicated if Denmark were to transfer powers to the EU that are otherwise defined as Kingdom affairs. These affairs are what some would claim to be the core of sovereignty: defence, citizenship, the Supreme Court and foreign relations.

Even if there is, as it would seem at present, a political will to transfer areas of responsibility other than those mentioned in the Home Rule Acts, problems will still arise in the international functions of these areas, as they would still have to go through the Danish Foreign Affairs system.

Breaking the Danish Kingdom Structure

The Danish Kingdom or Realm is comprised of three entities, of which one is dominating and two are dominated. Denmark on behalf of itself and the dominated polities nevertheless has the power to administer certain common or Kingdom affairs. If Denmark transfers sovereignty in these matters to another institution/entity, this breaks the structure of the union. The situation becomes even more complicated if both of the dominated polities have chosen not to be a part of the EU. Therefore, at the point at which Denmark decides to transfer Kingdom affairs to the EU, powers over these areas should simultaneously be transferred to Greenland and/or The Faroes if they so wish. Alternatively, simultaneous referenda could be held in Denmark, Greenland and The Faroes, with the vote in Denmark concerning the transfer of sovereignty to the EU, and the referenda in The Faroes and Greenland concerning the taking of sovereignty in the same areas of responsibility.

There are nuances in this process, as the Home Rule Act divides areas of responsibility into different categories: areas that can be transferred unilaterally, if the one part wishes it, either Faroes/Greenland or Denmark (A); areas that must be negotiated (B) and areas that cannot be transferred, namely Kingdom affairs, which are technically all the areas not mentioned in categories A or B.

Areas A and B present no complications, because responsibility for them can be taken over by Greenland and The Faroes without difficulty. The complications arise in relation to Kingdom affairs. The former Danish Government, for example, was of the opinion that Kingdom affairs cannot be transferred to The Faroes. The present Danish Government does not appear to be quite so adamant, but this can change with the political majority and the most recent signals are that it will be possible to take over areas that are not mentioned on the list, but not the areas that are considered the core of sovereignty (see below). Negotiations are now underway between The Faroes and Denmark on a law which makes it possible to take over all areas apart from those defined as the "integrity of state."

In democratic terms it is difficult to defend the apparently existing option for Denmark to transfer sovereignty to an institution, of which both the other polities in the Realm have chosen not be to be a part.

The very possibility that Denmark will hold a referendum on these matters is enough to justify The Faroes and Greenland being given the opportunity to take over these areas of responsibility already now. Kingdom affairs are major areas, which for Greenland and The Faroes will require a great deal of preparation.

One other approach could be that the dominated polities are given the responsibility for Kingdom affairs (at least those that might be transferred to the EU), and the polities decide themselves whether they shall be administered from the EU, but with the option to recall these areas of responsibility unilaterally.

One solution might be to suggest that The Faroes and Greenland not only take over the areas of responsibility that Denmark transfers to the EU, but also the international functions with respect to the same areas. This may clash with the normal perception of sovereignty (absolute sovereignty), but would be in keeping with my empirical research regarding the access of non-sovereign polities to international organizations, and would thus be in line with what I claim to be functional sovereignty.

Comments on the core areas of sovereignty:

— Defence: Can be transferred to the EU and is combined with international cooperation through NATO. Some microstates do not have their own national defence, e.g. Iceland.

— Citizenship: Can be transferred to the EU. Citizens of some of the non-sovereign polities in the UK do not enjoy full citizenship in Great Britain.

— Judicial: Can be transferred to the EU and non-sovereign polities have this competence, e.g. Aruba, Scotland.

— Currency: Non-sovereign polities, e.g. The Falkland Islands and New Caledonia have their own currency.

It is no longer possible to make the classical distinction between foreign and domestic relations, as many areas of responsibility today are directly related to commitments made through membership of international organizations and through bi- and multilateral treaties with the equal competence of other countries, such that the so-called core of sovereignty is not that persistent around the world.

In conclusion, the following question can be raised: if Denmark can transfer areas of responsibility to the EU without providing Greenland and The Faroes with a democratic voice in the process, and with the obvious functional impact this would have on Greenland and The Faroes, does this not create a situation of modern colonial non-access?

It is therefore necessary for Greenland and The Faroes to have the right to take over the policy areas that Denmark transfers to the EU, and an appropriate approach would be simultaneous referenda in all three parts of the Danish Kingdom.

MARTINUS NIJHOFF PUBLISHERS — LEIDEN • BOSTON